## Praise for *Immigrant Soldier*

"In this debut historical novel, a young German Jew flees his homeland before World War II and is later drafted into the US Army, serving closely under the legendary Gen. George S. Patton. Lang-Slattery effectively mines family history to create a solid work of historical fiction from her uncle's real-life derring-do. . . . In the sunny glamour of the book's California passages, she effectively evokes the young immigrant's overflowing hope. . . . Overall, her uncle's fictionalized adventures never fail to interest, whether he's slipping behind the lines for Patton or simply attempting to romance the local girls. An often engaging tale of one man's involvement in the world's most horrific war."
—Kirkus Reviews

"Lang-Slattery grounds the memories and stories of Lang, who was her uncle, with a great deal of research, and she tells those stories in vivid prose and very lively dialogue to make a memorable WWII-era coming-of-age story."
— Joanna Urquhart, Historical Fiction Society

"Written by Herman's niece, *Immigrant Soldier, The Story of a Ritchie Boy*, has an appealing personal touch. Interwoven through the story is a wealth of well-researched and often little-known information about World War II. Time reading this book is time well-spent, and anyone—from teens to adults, history buffs or not—will enjoy it."
—Marion Coste,
Editor and award-winning children's book author of *Kolea*

"A captivating book, extremely well written. Thanks to the army's Camp Ritchie Military Intelligence Training Center for molding soldiers like Herman Lang and to the author for sharing his story with us."

"K. Lang-Slattery has uncovered small but significant details that not only add to the fascination of her novel but also bring material before the public never hitherto disclosed. Beyond that, her brief character sketches bring us, in miniature, samples of the "greatest generation." And her style keeps the reader glued to the page!"

"This work of historical fiction closely follows the story of Herman Lang's WWII experience. Lang witnesses the rise of anti-Jewish sentiment and laws as a young teenager in Germany, eventually gaining passage to England as he awaits a hard-won US visa. He succeeds, but is carried forward into the tides of war. . . . The plot follows Lang's service in the Third Army under General Patton as they battle eastward through France and Germany. Most of the characters are based on famous WWII personalities like Patton, with special focus on the G-2 Intelligence Service of the US Army. . . . Lang succeeds in his mission through accurate character assessment and intellectual guile. . . . The author, Captain Lang's niece, has relied heavily on facts, only fleshing out conversations and internal thoughts of characters. A useful map and a short biography of the real Herman Lang is provided. The result is engaging and informative."

# IMMIGRANT
# SOLDIER

## The Story of a Ritchie Boy

K. Lang-Slattery

2nd Anniversary Edition

ISBN 978-0-9906742-3-8 (paperback)
ISBN 978-0-9906742-4-5 (hardcover)

1. Germany - History - 1933 - 1946 - Fiction
2. The Ritchie Boys - History - Fiction
3. Nazis - Fiction
4. World War II - Fiction
5. US Military - Intelligence Training - World War II - Fiction
6. Allied Occupation - 1945 - 1946 - Fiction
7. Jewish Refugees - WWII - Fiction
8. Jews, German - Fiction
9. Holocaust, Jewish -1939-1945 - Fiction
10. General Patton - Fiction
11. US Third Army - WWII - Fiction

Library of Congress Number: 2017901882

Cover Design and Map Design by Cole Waidley
Book Design by Lorie DeWorken, Mind the Margins, LLC
Edited by Lorraine Fico-White, Magnifico Manuscripts, LLC

*Immigrant Soldier* is a work of historical fiction. Apart from the well-known actual people, events, and locales that are part of the narrative, the names, characters, places, and incidents, as well as all dialogue other than excerpts from public speeches, are products of the author's imagination. Any resemblance to current places or living persons is entirely coincidental.

# DEDICATION

This book is dedicated to all those who, through foresight, determination, and luck, were able to escape Nazi Germany before the trap was fully closed. Their lives were uprooted and changed forever. And, most especially, I dedicate it to those immigrant Ritchie Boys who returned to Europe and used their knowledge, experience, and training to help bring an end to the Nazi terror. Each day, fewer of them are here to share their stories. Finally, but not least, I dedicate this book to the memory of Herman Lang and his wife, Marge. They welcomed me into their home, shared their stories, and encouraged me to write this book.

"*Few will have the greatness to bend history itself,
but each of us can work to change a small portion of
events, and in the total of all those acts will be written the
history of this generation . . . It is from numberless diverse
acts of courage and belief that human history is shaped.*"

Robert F. Kennedy,
Day of Affirmation Address,
June 6, 1966

# TABLE OF CONTENTS

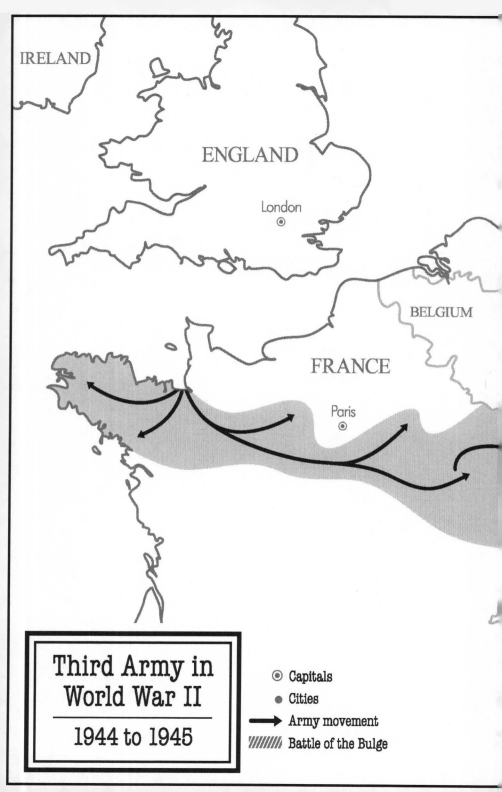

IRELAND

ENGLAND

London

BELGIUM

FRANCE

Paris

**Third Army in World War II**

1944 to 1945

◎ Capitals

● Cities

➔ Army movement

////// Battle of the Bulge

# CHAPTER 1

## KRISTALLNACHT

THE QUIET OF THE EARLY November morning was shattered by loud voices and the screech of brakes. Herman peered through the crack in the stable door. A prickle of fear shot up his neck at the sight of a covered truck, two police motorcycles, and a black sedan in front of the homes across the street. Two brown-shirted SA officers, the Swastika symbols on their armbands blazing, pounded on his cousin's front door.

Hatred rose in his throat. Nazi Storm Troopers—they were nothing more than thugs, bullies for Hitler and his political party. Two more men in ugly, brown uniforms beat at the door of the neighbor's home where Herman rented a room from the horse dealer and his wife.

The faces of the SA men contorted with anger and their words polluted the air. *"Achtung! Alles 'raus!* Attention! Everyone out! Get out, you stupid Jews. Wake up! *Schnell! Juden! Alles 'raus! Schnell!* Fast! Jews! Everyone out! Fast!"

The thud of Herman's heart was palpable. Pain seized his gut. The door of his landlord's home opened a crack. One of the SA men kicked it wide, and the loud smack of his boot against the wood sent a chill down Herman's spine. As the Nazis pushed into the house, he heard the confused sounds of loud voices and smashing furniture. An image of the horse-dealer's wife, beautiful Frau Mannheimer, exploded in his mind, her nightdress ripped, her golden hair gripped in the SA man's fist. He heard her high-pitched scream leak into the cold morning, and he lurched forward, outside the barn.

He was barely through the stable door when a policeman stepped from behind the black truck. His pistol glinted in the gray morning light, and the sight of the weapon shocked Herman like a jolt of electricity. His wild impulse to be a hero evaporated. He ducked behind the wide doors, angry and ashamed, listening to his heart pound. He pressed both hands against his abdomen and took several deep breaths.

He shook his head to clear it and again put his eye to the crack between the door and the jamb. The policeman must have heard something because he waved his pistol menacingly. He was poised in a half crouch, as if ready to run, and his gaze swept past the stable, down the street, and back again. Finally, he turned and moved toward the open door of the Mannheimers' home.

Herman inched farther back into the shadows and waited. Less than an hour ago, he had walked to his morning job, the feel of the street cobbles solid and familiar under his feet, his breath visible in the cold air. In the stable yard, blades of stubborn, frost-crusted grass pushed through the trampled earth. He had dipped his fingers into the water trough, breaking the thin film of ice that glistened in the dawn light. The black surface of the water mirrored a reflection of his gray eyes, strong chin, and the curl of dark hair that fell over his forehead. He pushed back the loose hair with his wet fingers and entered the barn.

The warm odor of straw and manure enveloped him. The powerful draft horses moved in their stalls. The soft stamp of their hooves and the bump of their flanks against the boards comforted him like a morning lullaby.

Herman had gone to the tack room to get the curry brush. His motorcycle, which he was allowed to park there, gleamed amid the coils of rope, harnesses, and bridles. He ran his fingers across the shiny black fender, up the rounded shape of the gas tank, and whispered, "Good morning, baby." For two years he had saved every *pfennig*, until finally six months ago, as a celebration of his eighteenth birthday, he had gathered his savings and bought the nearly new motorcycle from a local man bound for the army.

Riding gave him a sense of freedom he couldn't get from any other part of his life. On his days off work, Herman left the cobbled lanes of Suhl and escaped to the countryside, riding from early morning until the long afternoon shadows bled into dusk. At the crest of a hill he would hesitate, then with a twist of the throttle, speed forward. The sensation when he swooped down the hill lifted his spirits. Sometimes, if the road was straight and flat, he would let go of the handlebars and stretch his arms out on either side like a tightrope walker. The wind pushed against his hands, tugged at his jacket, and battered his face. For a moment, he could imagine he was fleeing this horrible new Germany. On his way home, as day faded into night, the single head-lamp dimly illuminated the road ahead. He felt like a man returning to prison.

Now he stood in the darkened barn and listened to the muffled sounds that came from outside—the thud of boots, the slam of doors, and shouts of "*Raus! Raus!*" Above everything, he heard the heartrending sound of a woman screaming, "*Nein, bitte . . . nien, tun Sie ihm nicht weh!* Don't hurt him!" He edged forward cautiously and looked outside again.

His cousin's wife, Hilda Meyer, normally neat and proper, stood in the street in her night clothes, her robe half on, half off, its belt dangling. Her hair stuck out at odd angles, uncombed and tangled from sleep. She moaned as her husband, still in his pajamas, grasped her shoulder, trying to steady her. He moved one hand to cradle her chin and leaned forward to talk softly into her ear. Cousin Fritz, usually funny and full of stories, was serious now. The words he whispered seemed to calm his wife. Herman could see the movement of shadows in the house doorway, and he knew that little Anna huddled there. An impatient SA man clutched his baton and stomped over. He yelled as he prodded Fritz in the ribs with his club. The controlled look on his cousin's face dissolved, and his eyes grew wide with fear. The storm trooper took no notice and shoved his victim toward the truck. The whack of the stick against Fritz's back as he scrambled up into the vehicle was muffled by distance, but the sight made Herman flinch as if he had been struck himself.

Two other SA men emerged from his landlord's door, the horse dealer between them. Herr Mannheimer was shoeless, the long tails of his unbuttoned shirt flapping in the chilly breeze. Blood streamed from a cut over his eye, dripped down his cheek and neck, and soaked into his shirt collar. He seemed dazed, only half conscious, as he clambered into the back of the truck where Fritz grabbed his neighbor to steady him.

The horse-dealer's wife was nowhere to be seen. Herman bit his lip and closed his eyes as he tried to imagine her hidden safely in the cupboard under the stairs, but the picture that surged into his head was of her body sprawled on the entryway floor, an SA man, his club raised, towering over her. He opened his eyes allowing the stark reality of the street to erase the image.

Herman saw the flash of Anna's nightdress as she darted out of the doorway, into the street, and clutched at her mother's thin flannel dressing gown. The little girl buried her face in her mother's stomach. Hilda's shoulders shook, and she released an audible moan as she encircled her daughter with her arms.

The sudden thought of his own mother, alone in their home in Meiningen, pushed Herman into action. He jerked away from the barn door and lurched into the tack room. With one kick of his boot, he flipped up the stand of his motorcycle, struggled to wheel the heavy machine into the stable, and with a last glance toward the wide doors facing the street, pushed it out the back to the paddock and a little-used dirt alleyway. With a practiced swing of his leg, he mounted and kicked the engine to life. The powerful machine took off with a surge of speed that lifted the front tire as it jumped over the first ruts. Icy wind blew his cap from his head, but he raced on. The frigid air stung his ears and drowned out the sounds that echoed in his head. He forced himself to think only of getting home—fast.

# CHAPTER 2

# SAFE IN MEININGEN

HERMAN SPED DOWN THE NARROW lane, only half aware of the passage of time. His mind swirled around a vortex of fears and questions. Were the storm troopers pounding on doors only in the little industrial town of Suhl? Was his hometown involved? How bad would it be? What should he do?

He knew it was finally time for him to make a move, but he had no idea how to escape. He was without a passport and no longer considered a citizen of the German nation. He had been declared a Jew, even though he had never worn a yarmulke, lit a Hanukkah candle, or set foot in a synagogue. He knew nothing of Jewish culture or religion, but all four of his grandparents had been Jews long ago, and now that was all that counted in the Third Reich.

The road twisted and turned under him as he sped toward home. He forgot his own safety until he felt the front tire slide in the gravel on a stretch of soft shoulder.

He struggled to steady the cycle and forced himself to slow down and think. He could simply veer off the road and disappear into the countryside. The peaceful farms beckoned to him. He could sleep in the stacked winter hay of a barn at night and hide among the tall forest trees during the day. Maybe he could escape to Switzerland, cross the Alps into Italy, and make his way to North Africa, where he would join the French Foreign Legion like the heroes of the books and movies he loved.

Herman shook his head to expel this wild plan, but he could not shake the worried thoughts from his mind. Italy was ruled by Hitler's Fascist allies. Besides, winter was coming. Freezing temperatures and mountain snow would leech success from an attempt to cross the Alps. And what about his mother? His daydreams came to an abrupt stop. He could not go anywhere without first making sure she was safe. After that, there would be time to try to get a passport and an exit permit, make a sensible plan, and figure out how to survive. Nazi law prohibited Jews from taking money with them if they fled. He tried to concentrate, but there was too much to think about. Could he actually join the Foreign Legion? How would he pay for passage to North Africa? Could he find work on a tramp steamer? One thing he knew for sure—it was past time to put aside his doubts and leave Germany.

As he neared Meiningen, the road circled the familiar castle-topped hill and approached the Werra River. The steel gray waters of the river slid slowly past the brewery, which used the waterpower to run its machinery. Herman felt his gut tighten. A knot of tension sat heavy in his belly. He slowed the rumbling machine to a workday pace, straightened his shoulders, and surveyed the street ahead for any sign of a police vehicle.He eased past a group of men who had arrived at the brewery gate for the morning shift and started across the wide bridge that spanned the river. His gaze was pulled to the Duke of Meiningen's palace where the familiar white walls gleamed through the bare trees of the royal park. Behind the palace, an ominous cloud of black smoke rose above the walls. Something burned in the old Jewish section where his grandmother had lived. Two laborers in coveralls paused on their way to work. They pointed toward the smoke, laughing and slapping each other on the back.

He rode slowly across the bridge into town and onto the busy main street that led to the downtown shopping district. Everything seemed normal. A meat delivery wagon maneuvered around a streetcar filled with office workers and shop girls and past the English Garden, where he had often played as a child. Herman gunned the motorcycle and made a right turn from the busy street through the double gates of his family home directly across from the garden. He skidded to a stop in the yard and looked around for anything out of the ordinary. All seemed quiet. He quickly hid his cycle up against the wall behind a hedge and ran up the porch stairs.

Relieved to find the big front doors already unlocked, he slipped noiselessly into the entry hall, then bolted up the wide stairs, two at a time, to his mother's apartment. In this grand home, where she had once raised three children and directed housemaids and a cook, she now lived, widowed and alone, in a small converted apartment squeezed into half of the second floor. At least she had the tower room overlooking the street. "It was enough," she said, "for one very small woman."

His mother, Clara, though less than five feet tall, had a solid spirit that had always given him comfort. She waited on the landing, her dressing gown loosely tied. Herman could see she had not been awake long. One swath of her hair still hung to below her waist, and the dark brown sheen of it caught the morning light. She had only managed to get the other portion of her hair half-braided, and it draped over her right shoulder and across her ample chest. She clasped the loose end of the braid with one hand and reached out with the other to touch her son. "I saw you through the window," she said, her look steady and calming. "I'm glad you came home."

Herman, taller than his mother by five inches, enveloped her in his arms. "You're safe," he whispered.

"Certainly I am." She wrapped her free arm around him protectively. "Come inside. We don't want to linger on the landing this morning."

Herman entered the apartment, closed the door, looked around at the familiar furniture and pictures, and turned to his mother. "Mutti, something terrible is happening. I left in such a hurry, I didn't think about anything except getting here to make sure you're safe."

His mother carefully turned the bolt on the door. "Of course I am safe." She slowly finished the braiding of her loose hair as she talked. "I've been listening to the radio and the news is bad. It's you . . . the men . . . who are in danger."

Herman grasped his mother's hands. "I saw Fritz and Herr Mannheimer being taken. They dragged Fritz directly from bed and into the street. He was still in his pajamas. I saw them beat him." He sank into a chair. "Herr Mannheimer was worse. His face was covered in blood." He brushed away tears that threatened to roll down his cheeks. "I should have helped. Oh, Mutti, I didn't know what to do."

He slumped in the armchair and lowered his head, his hands over his eyes. His mother grasped his shoulder and with her other hand, firmly lifted his face to meet her gaze. "No," she said. "There was nothing you could do. You were right to come here." She turned away and stood by the window but did not pull open the heavy drapes. "Fritz will be all right." Her voice was firm. "And the horse dealer, too."

"But Hilda. And Frau Mannheimer." Herman's voice broke as he said their names.

She turned back toward her son, and her hand brushed his cheek. "Hush. The women and children are probably safe. It's the men . . ." Her next words were barely a whisper. "Together we will make it through."

They huddled all morning in the gloomy apartment, listened to the radio, and talked in low tones until midday, when their friends downstairs slipped a newspaper under the door. The front page story proclaimed that the erupting violence against Jews and destruction of Jewish property all over Germany was spontaneous, justified anger over the murder of a man named Ernst vom Rath, a Third Secretary of the German embassy in Paris.

Herman sat wrapped in a blanket in his father's old chair. The same news droned endlessly on the radio. His head felt dull and a muscle in his temple twitched. He reached over and switched the sound off. "Why, Mutti? It doesn't make any sense." His voice broke and he closed his lips to keep his fear inside.

His mother shook her head. "Nobody cares about this man or his killer. It's an excuse."

"The boy they've arrested is my age," Herman said. "It sounds like he's half-crazy because of the deportation of his family to Poland."

"He's Jewish. That's all the excuse they need." Clara walked over to where Herman sat and touched his shoulder gently. "You must stay out of trouble," she said.

Suddenly, the strident ring of the telephone intensified the tension. Herman's mother strode quickly to where it sat on a hall table but hesitated with her hand on the earpiece as it rang a second and third time. "You must never answer it," she whispered. "No one can know you are here."

Slowly she raised the instrument to her ear and spoke into the receiver. "This is Clara." She motioned to Herman to come over and stand with his head close to hers, so they could listen together. She mouthed the words, "Cousin Renata." He could hear the faint sound of the old lady's sobbing through the earpiece.

"They took him away . . . my strong Morris, but his heart is weak. He could do nothing to resist."

Clara's voice was low next to Herman's ear as she tried to calm her cousin. "Don't worry, Renata. All will be well. In a day or two he will return."

Herman felt his mother's tremor of doubt.

The voice in the phone rose, the edge of hysteria clear. "What will he do without even his trousers? Only his nightshirt. Barefoot. He will be cold . . . and his heart medicine still beside his bed. I'm terrified. I must go to the police station with his coat and shoes, but all I do is stand here and cry."

"Be calm. Steady yourself." His mother tried to make her cousin slow down but she could not hear beyond her own voice.

"And the synagogue! In ruins. Still smoking. I can see it from my window."

"Stop! Listen now!"

Finally, Renata's voice was quiet.

"Make a bundle of the coat and shoes and Morris's medicines. Pull yourself together and go to the station. Doing something will calm your nerves."

"Yes. Yes, you're right." There was a deep, shuddering sob on the phone line. "I'll try . . . I must try."

"Call me back this afternoon . . . or any time."

"Clara, what of Herman?"

His mother laid her finger to her lips and shook her head. "No word from him," she said into the phone. "But he is resourceful. I know he will be safe."

"Yes. Herman is a strong boy. I must go now . . . I'll call again."

The radio news announced that Jewish men were being pulled from their homes and arrested everywhere in Germany. Repeatedly, Clara tried to telephone Great-Uncle Martin who still lived in the old Jewish section of town, but his phone went unanswered. As the day progressed, the news worsened. Jewish shops were being vandalized and looted. Synagogues across the country burned to the ground while firemen stood by and watched. It was a full-fledged Nazi pogrom.

Herman reminded his mother that the Meiningen police didn't know he was at home, and if no one had seen his early morning arrival, it would be assumed he had been picked up where he had been living. In Suhl, maybe they hadn't noticed he wasn't among the arrested, or they simply didn't care. The family home in Meiningen wasn't in the Jewish section of town and nowhere near the synagogue. The police had pounded on the door at other times, including several visits in 1936 and 1937—days when they confiscated silver and other valuables—but this day, as Herman huddled in his mother's small rooms and wondered at the evil in his homeland, the police didn't knock.

Late that night, Herman returned to where he had abandoned his motorcycle. He lifted the kickstand and straddled the heavy bike, then started the engine as quietly as possible. Slowly, hoping the sounds blended with the noises of late-night buses on the nearby main street, he rode to the back garden, a narrow space between the house and a high brick wall. He pulled a flashlight out of his pocket and turned it on. Its thin beam of light revealed what he looked for—an old, windowless toolshed leaning against the garden wall, overhung by the branches of a fir tree. The dilapidated shed was small, and the roof probably leaked, but in the winter to come no one would need the garden supplies stored there.

Herman parked the cycle near the shed, turned off the engine, and entered, flashlight in hand. He brushed away tendrils of spider webs, stacked a few buckets and a half-filled bag of manure in the far corner, and shoved two hoes, a shovel, and a rake behind a pile of broken terracotta pots. There would be barely enough room. Outside, he straddled the cycle, then with difficulty, maneuvered it backward through the door, carefully turning and cramping the front wheel to make it fit. He positioned the cumbersome motorcycle so it faced the shed door. He knew the effort might save his life. If he ever needed to get away fast, he would be able to get it out and started in a matter of minutes.

In a last gesture, he rubbed his hand across the bulbous gas tank and gave it an affectionate pat. He closed the shed door and turned away. The darkness enveloped him. He walked up the front stairs of his home and into hiding.

CHAPTER 3

# BECOMING A JEW

WHILE HERMAN CONTINUED TO HIDE in his mother's small suite of rooms, German newspaper reports referred to the violence against Jews as Kristallnacht, or "Night of Broken Glass." He had been lucky. His mother talked to relatives and friends, and they confirmed that most Jewish men over the age of eighteen had been arbitrarily arrested and thrown into prison.

Herman worried about Uncle Martin and wanted to search for him, but his mother begged him to stay inside.

"Martin is a smart old man," she said. "He will contact us if he returns safely."

Her reasoning did not reassure Herman. "Uncle is old. He may be wandering confused somewhere." He knew the argument would do little good, but he wanted desperately to get out and relieve the confined boredom in his mother's house. He wanted to do something, even if it made no sense.

Clara was firm, though her ideas were as wild as Herman's. "Maybe Martin has gone to relatives in Frankfurt or perhaps he has fled to France where he has friends." She rubbed her eyes. "It's you, Hermanle, who worries me the most. You must stay hidden for a while longer. The police are still making arrests and even Cousin Renata's dear Morris isn't home yet. Meanwhile we must think about getting you out of Germany. I'll write to your father's cousins in Chicago." She turned and walked to the window and pulled aside the drapes slightly, letting in a thin shaft of pale winter daylight. "Mae and Walter helped your brother, Friedel. I can beg their help again. Or perhaps their older brother, Herbert, will sponsor you. Your brother is doing what he can from California, but it's slow work getting a US visa. We must ask everyone we can for help."

She let the drapes fall, turned back to face Herman, and spoke in the calm voice he knew from his childhood. "I can't lose my son to these monsters. No one . . . nobody can know you're home. It must be a secret." She walked over and put her hand on his arm, her gaze steady and pleading. "I know it's hard for you to be cooped up, but you must stay safe for your mother."

As the weeks went by, Clara continued her normal activities. She dusted, prepared simple meals, and listened to the radio. Each day she did her bit of grocery shopping at the remaining Jewish grocery in the old district. She walked down the Bernhardstrasse, past the greengrocer and butcher shop she had patronized for years, but which now had a sign in the window that read, "No Jews will be served."

Sometimes friends would sidle up next to her as she crossed the main square. They would match her stride to walk apace for a few moments in imitation of a chance encounter. With them she shared whispered words. At Herman's suggestion, she spread the story that he had fled Suhl on his motorcycle and was constantly on the move and in hiding around the countryside. She whispered a tale of how he slept in haystacks and barns, contacting her when he could by telephone to let her know he was all right. She even wrote this fabricated story to her daughter in England in case the police were reading her mail. And she wrote the promised letter to her dead husband's cousins in America asking them to try to expedite the visa process from there. She hoped the American newspapers had reported stories of the recent pogrom and they would understand the urgency.

Most days, Herman spent endless hours huddled on the window seat by the curved windows of the tower room. From there he could read or listen to the radio and still watch the street below through the crack between the heavy drapes. He stared at the English garden across the street and remembered happier days. Light winter snow frosted the bare branches of the trees. The small lake, where he had chased ducks and caught frogs as a child, had turned black and bottomless with its slick coating of thin ice. He dreamed of the warmth of North Africa and studied the maps of France and Algeria in the old family atlas. Finally, he turned the pages to look at the map of the United States and located Chicago, where his father's elderly cousins lived, so far north it sat right next to the border with Canada. Slowly he traced his finger from there, across the page, to California where his brother had settled. It was such a long way.

One morning, he stood at the mirror in the tiny bathroom and pulled on the sparse beard that darkened his chin. He couldn't help but feel sorry for himself. The best years of his youth had been stolen by the Nazis. He was a fugitive in his mother's rooms when he should be out walking the streets with a girl on his arm. He peered at his reflection, rubbed his cheeks, and remembered the summer afternoon when he had enjoyed his one and only kiss.

Sophia, Frau Mannheimer's niece, had come for a visit, and he invited her for a ride on the back of his motorcycle. She tied a flowered scarf over her mass of red curls and wrapped her arms around his chest as they rode out of town and down the river road. He remembered the feel of her firm breasts pressing against his back and the tickle of her breath against his ear. When they reached the café at the overlook, giddy with the thrill of the ride, they had recklessly gone in for a coffee. They clutched each other's hands and walked confidently past the sign that said, "No Jews allowed."

They chose a table that overlooked a rocky gorge and the billow of mist that rose from a waterfall. Herman looked around. The café seemed friendly, and he ordered spiced cookies to go with their coffee. The air had been warm and bees buzzed around the potted flowers on the veranda. Sophia's dark blue eyes sparkled as she lifted crumbs of powdered sugar on the tip of her finger and licked them off with her tongue. Herman stared, mesmerized by the sugar dust that coated her rosy lips. As he watched, unable to move his eyes, a bee landed on her lower lip, enticed by the color and sweetness. Sophia's eyes widened and reflexively she swatted at the insect.

"Ow . . . ooow." The moan had been soft, and her eyes darted around the veranda. They must not attract attention or someone might ask for their papers. Her lip began to swell, and she covered it with her hand. Tears rolled down her cheeks.

Herman left some bills on the table, and they walked hand in hand out of the café. As they stood by the motorcycle, Herman lifted her hand away and saw the sting, angry and swollen, her lip distorted. The stinger was still there. Gently he pushed it out and away with the nail of his thumb. She rewarded him with a lopsided smile.

"Thank you," she whispered.

His heart filled with tenderness, and he leaned forward to kiss her softly, surprised when her lips yielded to his.

"Ooow." This time Sophia's whisper brushed against his cheek, and her warm fingers touched his hand. On the ride home, he could feel her tears on the back of his neck. But the next day she was gone—the summer was over.

Now as he studied his face in the mirror, he saw a darkhaired version of his blond, older brother. Often in the past, as a young boy, he had spied on Friedel, always in the company of pretty town girls who flocked around him and flirted shamelessly. His older brother would wink at him and tease, "Your turn will come, little brother."

But it hadn't. By the time Herman was fifteen, the Nazi laws had come instead. Suddenly he, who knew nothing of

Judaism, had been branded a Jew and was subject to police curfew that barred him from the streets after dusk. The new laws declared it a crime for him to flirt with German girls or walk with them hand in hand down the main street as his brother had done. Once, when he was still in school, a group of girls had crossed to the other side of the street as he approached. They had huddled in a closed circle and whispered secrets when he passed. One of the prettiest had turned to stare at him, a hostile glare her only sign of recognition, though she had sat two desks in front of him for the entire term.

He hadn't known any Jewish girls until he had been sent to live with Cousin Fritz in Suhl. The beautiful, married Frau Mannheimer danced in his nighttime dreams, but in his daydreams, he imagined real girls like Sophia, who would let him kiss their lips.

Herman walked into the living room and to his mother who sat on the sofa. The click of her knitting needles matched the rhythm of the string section of the symphony playing on the radio. He stood in front of her and demanded her attention. "Look, Mutti. I'm getting a beard." He grasped her hand and made her touch his cheek. "See how it grows. But I'm imprisoned in the house like a toddler on my mother's apron strings."

Clara sighed. "I know you hate being inside, Hermanle. Surely it will end soon. It must." She brightened and patted his cheek. "This stubble is a good thing. Let it grow. When it's time for you to reappear, a beard will confirm that you have been living on the run in the countryside and hiding in haystacks like I've been telling everyone."

Finally better news arrived from family members. News came that Herr Mannheimer and Fritz Meyer were safely home in Suhl. They prepared to emigrate as soon as possible with their families. If they had to abandon most of their possessions they did not care, as long as they found safety in any country that would take them. But no word came from Herman's beloved Great-Uncle Martin. He had simply disappeared. Fritz had seen him among a group of prisoners at Dachau, but he glimpsed the old man only once and had not been able to talk to him.

Clara's letter-writing campaign took on new intensity. She wrote again to her husband's cousins in Chicago, then to her own cousin who had fled to Shanghai, and to a school friend who lived in Switzerland. The only ones to answer were Cousin Mae and her brother Herbert from Chicago. Mae pled with them to move quickly; the situation was getting more and more difficult with so many trying to flee Germany. Herbert promised to help—he had already filled out an affidavit of support for Herman with the US State Department. Now the boy had only to find a safe place to wait for his American visa. Already, several times a week, Clara mailed a letter to Friedel and his American wife in California. She entreated them to try to hurry up the process of sponsorship that would allow Herman to get a US visa and join them.

His application for visas had been started months ago, but so many desperate people had applied that the United States quota system was clogged. With endless red tape, countless forms, and thousands of German Jews standing in line for the coveted visas, the wait, already lasting as much as two years, grew longer all the time.

Clara's oldest brother, Bruno, who had lived in England since before the First World War, now seemed the last hope. Though he was a British citizen, his English wife was a serious problem. Nelda hated everything German and denied her husband's Jewish background. Because of his wife's attitude, Clara had hesitated to ask her brother for help again. He had helped Edith, Herman's sister, when she first arrived in England and that had brought months of strife to his marriage. Now Clara felt she had no other choice, and in early December, she wrote to her brother and his wife. Herman's safety depended on their answer.

Within a few weeks, word came from Uncle Bruno. He urged Herman to get a transit visa for Britain and come as soon as possible. News of Kristallnacht had shocked England, and the country was energized to help. The first train of the Kindertransport project left Germany for England on December 1, but Herman was too old by two years to qualify. Bruno and Nelda promised they would take their young nephew in for however long it took to get his US immigration papers processed.

It was time for Herman to come out of hiding. He needed to make a formal appearance with the local police in order to get exit papers and a passport, which would require reams of detailed paperwork, exorbitant processing fees, and a clearance that verified he was not a criminal and owed no outstanding fines.

The evening after the arrival of the letter from Uncle Bruno, Herman and his mother sat at the table and discussed what to do. "We must make a show of your return to town," Clara insisted, "and we need help to get the paperwork processed as quickly as possible. Before something else happens."

Herman ran his fingers over his roughly bearded chin. "What about the chief of police, Captain Mueller? His son was Friedel's best friend, wasn't he?"

Clara brightened. "Yes! A good idea. Those two boys were always getting into trouble together."

Herman could see the hope grow in her expression as she spoke.

"Surely Herr Mueller remembers how close his son was to your brother. He ought to remember how Friedel once saved Hansy from drowning. I'll certainly never forget it! Your brother came in that night, soaking wet and full of the story of how he had rescued his friend from the mill stream near the old city gate. In his telling, the stream was a raging river full of ice floes." She laughed at the thought. "Friedel was puffed up with his own importance for days afterward."

The next morning, Clara went in person to the chief of police. After a two-hour wait in the vestibule, she was finally ushered into the chief's office. He did not ask her to sit down. She stood before his desk, her hands clasped in front of her and spoke. "Sir, thank you for seeing me. I have an issue to discuss regarding my son."

"Yes . . . yes. I have been told. What is it you want?"

He still had not looked up at her, but she continued in as firm a voice as she could manage. "Chief Mueller, I was a good friend to your wife when we were young. When you and my Hugo were both fighting in the Great War, she and I spent many afternoons together knitting baby clothes. And my oldest son, Friedel, surely you remember him? He was such a good swimmer, remember? And a good friend to your boy, Hansy. Our families have known each other—"

He raised his head and with cold eyes looked at her. "Get to the point, Frau Lang. I do not have much time to spare for a Jewess."

Clara swallowed hard and wiped her damp palms down the sides of her skirt. "Forgive me, sir. I have come to ask for help for my younger son, Herman. He has been on the run since early November. Since that bad night for us Jews, he has been afraid to come home." She hesitated and gulped, her words stuck in her throat. The icy stare of the chief of police did not encourage her, but she had to continue for Herman's sake. "Sir, my son wants to come home. He wants to begin the paperwork to emigrate as soon as possible. He is ready to leave Germany and join his brother who lives now in the United States."

Herr Mueller grunted. Clara took this as an encouraging sign. At least he was listening.

"Please, sir. Can we hope he will not be arrested when he returns? He has done nothing wrong." The chief of police did not speak, but Clara could see him glance at the framed photo of his wife and son displayed to one side of his desk. She must be very careful how she phrased her request for help. "Please, sir, will you see him and make sure he gets all the forms he needs for permission to emigrate? Sir, our sons are precious to us. I know you feel this, too. I no longer have a husband to protect my son. I must entreat you myself. Please remember what Friedel—"

Herr Mueller stood and looked at her with naked contempt. "Quiet! You do not need to beg. Because of the debt I owe your older boy for my son's safety, I will do what I can." He looked down at his desk, scrawled some words on a paper, which he folded in half, and held out for Clara. "Get this to your son. Tell him to come into my office in two days' time. He should come very early, before the regular day starts. Six in the morning on Thursday. I will meet him then . . . or not at all."

Clara moved forward and took the note from his fingers. "Thank you, sir. Thank you. He will be here."

But Herr Mueller had turned away and begun to shuffle papers in the filing cabinet behind his desk. Quietly, she backed out of the office and walked as fast as she could into the cold and stony winter street. As soon as she was around the corner and out of sight of the police station, she stood in a doorway and unfolded the note. The words of the police chief's scrawl were barely legible. "Safe passage, Herman Lang, 5 Dec. to 7 Dec. 1938." And his signature.

As Herman walked to the Meiningen police station in the gray light of dawn two days later, he patted his pocket for the reassuring feel of his identity papers and the folded note from Herr Mueller. His stomach churned with nervousness. He was confident that he looked like someone who had spent several weeks as a fugitive in the country-side. His hair was shaggy, the brown waves curled around his ears and over his collar, his beard remained untrimmed, and his scuffed work boots, the only shoes he had, were still stained with traces of horse manure. He wore the same patched work pants and heavy woolen sweater he had hast-ily pulled on that last morning in Suhl. As he left the house, he grabbed his father's oversized, loden-green hunting jack-et that he had found stashed away in a back cupboard. He put it on over his sweater, with the thought that it would remind the police chief of the days when the two men had been in the same lodge. Now Herman feared this touch had been too bold.

Two black uniformed SS men chatted in the entryway of the police station and looked up as he walked down the hall. They stared at him as he passed and a chill surged up Herman's neck. He dipped his chin, an abbreviated greeting he hoped would satisfy these officers. Surely if they looked him in the eye, they would see his hatred and fear ready to spill out. With relief, he heard them return to their conver-sation as he walked past and down the hall.

Herr Mueller had been friendly in the past, but now he was a member of the Nazi party, and Herman didn't know what to expect when he walked into the man's office. Based on his mother's experience, the reception would not be a warm one. A portrait of Hitler was prominently displayed on the wall over the police chief's desk, and the Nazi pin on his lapel shone in the light of the desk lamp. The man's body shifted upward as if he was about to rise to greet Herman, but he seemed to think better of it and simply waved his hand toward the straight-backed chair placed in front of his desk. Herman sat on the edge of the hard seat, his hands on his knees to steady himself.

"Good morning, sir. I appreciate your—"

The policeman raised his hand, and Herman stopped talking midsentence.

The interview was brief. "Both your mother and my wife have pled your case to me. But I can only help you if you look as if you've been in prison for the last weeks and have recently been released." He did not smile. "Your hair is the most obvious problem. All prisoners had their heads shaved. You have too much hair. You must get it cut. Very, very short." He nodded as if this idea had only now come to him. "Yes, I think shaving your head will make you look like the other Jewish men in town. That's the best thing."

Herman's scalp prickled, and he gripped his knees hard to prevent his hand from going to his head. He was suddenly very aware of the long lock of hair that fell down over his forehead. "Yes, sir," was all he dared say.

"Do it today." Mueller pushed a folder across the desk toward Herman. "Here is the paperwork you need to start the process of getting permission to leave Germany. Fill out everything carefully and as fast as you can. Call me when you need it signed and stamped." He stood up and Herman rose, too. For the first time the man looked Herman in the eye. "Good luck to you. Don't waste time. Get your head shaved and leave Germany as soon as you can." He added in a softer tone, "And your mother must apply for papers, too.

Make her do it. I have talked with my wife, and it seems they were confidants in the past. I did not know."

Herman extended his hand but the policeman didn't take it. "Thank you, sir." Herman faltered and lowered his hand to his side. "I'll do as you say." He turned and walked out of the office. The SS men were no longer in sight, and he exhaled a long breath of relief as soon as he was outside the police station.

On his way home, Herman avoided the main street and walked as fast as he could without running. Safe inside his mother's apartment, he blurted out the police chief's conditions and his final warning.

Clara quickly understood the situation but refused to talk of any plans for herself. "We must get you out first. I am only a widow woman. I will be safe, waiting quietly in my own home." She turned away and rummaged in her sewing basket for her scissors. "Put a towel around your shoulders and sit down." She pulled a straight-backed chair near the light of the window and turned up the radio. The choral voices and orchestra of Beethoven's *Ninth Symphony* filled the room and seemed to calm his mother.

Herman sat in the hard chair but turned to look at her. "We must make plans for you, too."

"Sit still and be quiet." His mother's stern voice made it clear she was not in the mood for nonsense. She lifted the sharp scissors and began to cut.

He watched the brown waves of hair drift to the floor. His best feature, the one he felt made him sexy, lay scattered on the linoleum. But what difference did it make now? He allowed the sounds of the symphony to sweep his thoughts away.

Clara had kept her husband Hugo's shaving kit and found it in a back corner of the bathroom cupboard. Slowly, carefully, she began to shave Herman's head.

"Mutti, don't make it too neat. They wouldn't have been gentle in prison. And not too close. Remember, it's supposed to have been done several weeks ago."

Clara bit her lip and worked faster. When she nicked him, she did not apologize, but only wiped the blood away and kissed him gently on the wound. "I so miss the music of Mendelssohn," she said, her words soft against the freshly bare skin of his head. "They won't play him on the radio any more. His family was like ours. His Jewish parents refused to circumcise their son, or so your father told me when he would not allow the same for your brother and you." She rubbed his head, brushed strands of hair from his shoulders, and handed him the razor. "Now you can shave your beard," she said. Then she went to the closet where she kept the broom and silently swept up the pile of brown curls.

Within hours, Herman, who had always been vain about his hair, walked the streets of his hometown with a raggedly bald head. No friends came up to greet him, but he felt the weight of eyes on his back and the whispers. He walked down the narrow streets to the old section where, from his childhood visits to his grandmother, he remembered a small Jewish-owned haberdasher. The store remained, but the display window was broken and had been boarded up, the rough wood smeared with the word "Jude" in ugly black capital letters three feet tall. Next to the graffiti there was a small sign that said, "Open."

As he pushed on the door and entered the dim shop, a bell rang. A thin man behind the counter looked up at the sound of the bell and stopped sorting through a box of gentlemen's gloves and scarves. "Ah, young man, I see we have the same barber." He ran his hand over the top of his head, and the stubble of gray hairs that remained stood up like an old worn hairbrush. "What can I do for you?"

Herman surveyed the dark store with its nearly empty shelves. "I need a hat, please. To cover this barber's work." He walked up to the counter, leaned forward and added in a low voice as if he were sharing a secret. "Besides, I'm planning a trip to England. I want a hat that will look stylish in London."

The old man nodded and moved to the shelves behind him. "Yes, a trip to London is the best thing right now. I have the perfect hat for such a journey. A fine, black fedora—very sophisticated and stylish." He twirled the hat on his fist, buffed the brim with his shirt sleeve, and held it out for Herman to try on.

The hat sank down over Herman's nearly bald head and settled pleasantly above his ears. He turned to see his image in the standing mirror nearby and cocked his head. Liking what he saw, he smiled at his reflection.

The old man pursed his lips and shook his head. "It seems a bit big." He came around to the front of the counter and twisted the hat on Herman's head. He flicked the brim with his fingers, and the hat tipped. "What's your hair like when it grows out? If it's thick or curly, this should fit fine later. If not, maybe one size smaller." He looked at the price tag. "Half price to you, in honor of your travel plans." His serious expression turned into a smile. "Son, it makes you look like a movie star. A good hat makes a man."

Herman turned to the mirror again. The fedora made him feel sophisticated and worldly. He touched the brim and savored its silky softness. "I'll take it. This hat will never come off except when I sleep."

The old man smiled and again rubbed his hand across his own short hair. "Hair will grow." His voice was low and Herman could barely hear his next words. "But the anger and shame lingers."


HERMAN FILLED OUT THE ENDLESS paperwork, everything in triplicate, and waited through the cold months of winter for his passport. While he waited, he traveled to Suhl to get his clothing, books, and other personal items. Herr Mannheimer and Fritz Meyer wrote him letters of recommendation and wished him luck on his journey.

The Meyers were packed to leave. Their US visas had finally arrived. "Maybe we'll see you soon in Chicago," Fritz said as they embraced in farewell.

Herr Mannheimer was desperately trying to get visas for himself and his wife to Argentina or Paraguay, where he hoped his knowledge of horses would be appreciated.

Germany, it seemed, was anxious to get rid of its Jews, and within two months, Herman's documents arrived in a thick brown envelope. Herman hated the big ugly "J" stamped on the cover of his passport to designate the carrier was Jewish, but most of all, he detested the false name of "Israel" that had been substituted for Ludwig, his true middle name, on the inside page. If the passport had been processed before January first, he could have avoided the insertion of the fake middle name on his official papers, an automatic code word recently mandated for all Jewish males by new Nazi laws. In spite of this, his exit permit and his British transit visa were stamped inside. He was cleared to leave.

Herman knew he had to sell his beloved motorcycle before he left. He sought out Otto Warner, who had once been his friend and who had always longed for a motorcycle. The young Nazi offered to buy Herman's beloved cycle for half its value, an offer he pointed out was probably the best any Jew could expect. Before he relinquished the machine, Herman polished it carefully until the metal gleamed, then gave each shining fender a final caress. That afternoon, he rode to his ex-classmate's home, parked the cycle in their street, and knocked at the front door.

Otto did not come down, though Herman had seen his form at an upstairs window. The housekeeper, an elderly lady who knew him well, opened the door a crack and handed him a sealed, blank envelope. Herman looked at the envelope, tore it open, and counted the money inside. The amount promised was there, but not a penny more, and there was no note. He shoved the bills into his pocket and handed the ignition key to the housekeeper who hovered at the partially open door. He walked down the porch stairs to the sidewalk. Near the shining motorcycle that was no longer his, he hesitated and let his hand stroke the gas tank one final time.

"Good-bye, baby," he said under his breath. Then he turned away and began the long walk across town to his home.

Herman and his mother agreed that on his last night at home they would set aside their sadness and celebrate his journey. Clara went to the market and spent a large sum on a quarter kilo of beef, which soon simmered on the stove and filled the rooms with its delicious aroma.

In his bedroom, Herman packed his small bag. It was difficult to decide what to take. He put two shirts in, took them out, put in a sweater instead, then took it out and put all the items on the bed in a row. He looked up at his mother who had come to stand in the doorway to the bedroom.

"You'll need your leather jacket," she said. "It can be cold in England, even in the summer."

"I know, I know. It's hard to decide when I know whatever I leave will be gone forever." Herman folded up a good sweater and his jacket, but they took up half the suitcase. "I'll wear these on the train." He moved the heavy clothing to one side and began folding the three shirts he would take. "Leave me alone, Mutti. I don't need you standing there. If I can't manage packing alone, how will I . . ." He left the thought unsaid, walked over to his mother, and took her hands. "I'll be okay. Stop worrying. I'm not your baby anymore." He dropped her hands and turned his back. "Go away and let me do this alone."

Clara lingered in the doorway a minute longer before she turned and walked down the hall to her alcove kitchen. As he finished packing, Herman heard the whack of her knife hitting the wooden block as she chopped vegetables, backed by the ever-present strains of classical music from her radio. Later, when he came into the living room, the pot roast waited on the table in a covered tureen. He lifted the lid, breathed in the rising steam, and sighed at the comfort of the warm fragrance of meat, gravy, carrots, and potatoes.

Clara rummaged through one of the cupboards. "I know it's here somewhere," she muttered. "Here it is!" She turned, a triumphant look lighting up her face. She handed a dusty bottle of wine to Herman. "Read the label," she said.

He remembered the bottle, a vintage Burgundy. "That's the wine Father was always saving for a special occasion. He'd never let you open it."

"It was a gift to your father from one of his theater friends." She wiped the grime from the bottle with the back of her apron. "He kept saving it and saving it for the appropriate occasion. And after he died, I saved it out of habit. But there will be no more happy occasions in this house." Clara set the bottle in the center of the table, lit two candles on either side, and handed the corkscrew opener to Herman. "Tonight is special enough for me. We'll open it and make a toast to . . . to . . ." She shook her head and spread her hands in bewilderment. Finally she looked up at her son. "To something good."

Slowly he twisted the opener into the bottle and pulled. The cork crumbled in his hand as it came out, smelling musty. Herman poured the deep red wine into two glasses and handed one to his mother. They held their glasses up. "To your safety," she whispered.

Herman struggled to think of the perfect words, but finally, because he could think of nothing he wanted more, he simply said, "Till we are together again." They touched their glasses, the gentle tap of the crystal making a clear bell-like sound. "Please, Mutti, make an application to the United States for a visa. It's the best place in the long run and you can be with your sons. It will take some time, but you can go to England first if it takes too long."

Clara looked around the small room. This was all that was left of her life. She took a sip of the wine at the same time as her son raised his glass to his lips and took a big gulp.

Herman had to force himself to swallow the stuff and not spit it out. His eyes smarted from the bitterly sour taste. He looked at his mother and saw her smile. Bubbles of laughter pushed up in his chest, and as the rumble erupted, his mother joined in until the small room was filled with the sound. They laughed while tears streamed down their cheeks.

"What a joke on us," Herman managed to choke out between spasms. "It's turned to vinegar." As quickly as it started, the laugher died in his throat. He reached across the table and touched his mother's shoulder. "Germany has gone sour, too. The Nazis will soon enough be causing trouble even for widow ladies. Promise me you'll apply for a US visa and a British transit visa right away. Please come to England soon. You can be with Edith or your brother while you wait for your US papers."

Clara looked seriously at her son. "I promise," she said. Her cheeks were wet with tears. "I promise."

"Till then, we must write," he said. "We must write only in English to practice for when you arrive."

She reached up and touched his cheek. "Yes, I promise. In English."

## CHAPTER 4

# INTERLUDE IN ENGLAND

ERMAN TOOK THE OVERNIGHT TRAIN across Germany toward Holland and the channel crossing. The train cars were dark and full of shadows. He sat, not even trying to sleep, his suitcase clutched in his lap. Every few minutes he patted his pocket to make sure his passport was safe. At the border, soldiers and guards inspected every car, from engine to caboose, and carefully checked all the passengers' documents.

In spite of the cold, perspiration slid from Herman's armpits to his ribs while the armed soldier flipped through his passport. A smirk spread across the man's face when he saw the large "J" on the cover. Now, when he returned it to Herman, he held the document by two limp fingers.

"Good riddance, Jew," he said. "Don't come back. England can have you."

After the rough and frigid crossing of the English Channel and a final train from Dover, Herman finally arrived in London's Paddington Station. He stepped from the train with his single suitcase and only a few marks left in his pocket. He was one of thousands of emigrants waiting in Britain for permission to travel on to a final goal. Some sought permission to go to Palestine, a British protectorate; others waited for visas to Brazil, Argentina, or Panama. For others, there was the slim hope of getting permission to stay in Great Britain or to immigrate to Australia.

Herman dreamed of America, but for now he would be living the life of a slightly unwelcome guest in his uncle's home. As he descended into the station, his eyes searched the crowds. For the umpteenth time, he studied the photo of Uncle Bruno his mother had given him. He clutched a letter from his uncle that said to wait by the newsstand nearest the Praed Street exit.

Herman walked over to the designated kiosk, its piles of newspapers and periodicals displayed across the counter and the back wall. The cavernous station echoed with a cacophony of voices, and he felt isolated even as the hurrying travelers surged around him. His nerves on edge, he set his suitcase down, straightened his fedora, and tried to look like he belonged.

Out of the crowd a face emerged, familiar and smiling like in the photo. Uncle Bruno strode toward him, his hand out and his face aglow with pleasure. "Herman Lang? Herman! You look like your father when he was young." His handshake was vigorous and warm. "Welcome!"

"Sir. Thank you for having me, sir."

"Of course. It was understood." He put his hand on Herman's shoulder and squeezed it gently. "No need to be formal. We're family. Now let's go home." He turned toward the street. "Follow me."

A black Bentley was waiting by the curb, a tall, thin man standing at attention next to it. When the chauffeur saw them approach, he rushed over, nodded his head in greeting, and said, "Allow me, sir" as he took Herman's luggage.

Bruno put his hand on the man's shoulder. "This is Charles," he said. "Charles, meet my nephew, Mr. Lang."

Charles smiled in greeting and actually clicked his heels together.

Bruno chuckled. "At ease, Charles. Mrs. Kohn isn't with us today."

Charles didn't smile, but he didn't click his heels together again either. He walked to the car, swung the suitcase into the boot, and moved to hold the back door open for the two of them. Bruno motioned Herman in first, then slid in himself, placing his hat on a hook and leaning his gold-handled cane casually against the back of the front seat. Unwilling to show any disrespect, Herman removed his hat and held it with both hands in his lap, embarrassed by his ragged haircut. Uncle Bruno didn't seem to notice.

The driver sat ramrod straight in the front, expertly navigating the crowded streets of London. Herman leaned back against the leather seat, tried to relax, and studied Uncle Bruno, an elegant man in spite of a solid paunch that pushed gently against the vest of his gray, three-piece suit. His dark hair and neatly trimmed goatee were peppered with silver and white. He seemed to be a classic English gentleman, yet Herman knew he had been born in Germany and had lived in Nuremberg until his early twenties. Now Bruno turned to his nephew and spoke in their native German. "Herman, *mein Junge*. I'm very glad to be able to offer you a place of safety during these uneasy times." He studied Herman, his gaze friendly and appraising. "I hope you will come and visit me at my offices at the factory. See our line of thermos bottles in all their variety."

"Yes, sir. I'd like that." Herman knew that he must make himself the most receptive and grateful of guests. "Mutti told me you make all kinds. Some even gold-plated or silver-etched."

Bruno's gray eyes held a gentleness that put Herman at ease. "Ah, but most are utilitarian. They are destined to carry the sweet, milky tea of workers to shops, docksides, and factories. In a nation of tea drinkers, the thermos business is a good one. We ship to the Far East, too—India, Hong Kong, even Japan. Tea drinkers all." He smiled a broad, warm smile. "It's too bad you can't come to the factory and work with me. I regret Nelda and I were never able to have children of our own, but now my sister has loaned me her son." He rubbed his temples as if to banish an unpleasant thought. "Unfortunately, the laws governing your stay here prohibit you from working. Also, you must report to the Hampstead police station once a month. The transit visa allows you to stay in England only as long as it takes to get your US visa approved. It's too bad. I would have liked to have you learn my business."

Bruno pulled a tobacco pouch and pipe from his inner coat pocket. He tamped a few pinches of fragrant tobacco shreds into the ivory bowl of the pipe and placed the stem between his teeth. A match flared, and he bent to the task of getting his pipe started. The smoke rose in puffs as the tobacco caught the flame, and he turned again to Herman. "Well, we will need to encourage your mother to come to England. But meanwhile, how will you keep busy? Do you like to read? I have a large library. All in English, though. Nelda will not abide books in German. Do you like to draw as your mother did? I was much older than she. I remember Clara only as a young girl and how much she loved music and drawing."

"Yes, sir. She still loves music, but she no longer has her piano." He felt a tightness in his chest, remembering his mother's tears as the burly workmen removed her beloved grand piano from their house and took it off in a truck, while the SS officer who had requisitioned it slapped his boot impatiently with his riding crop. Herman pushed the thought away. "She still has her violin," he said. "I love music, too. We used to listen to records together. And the radio, of course. Mutti's radio is always playing classical music. But I have no talent for drawing or for playing the piano. I think my brother inherited all the family talent."

"Ah, Friedel. I don't know him. He went to your father's relatives in Chicago, I think. But Edith, I like her, though her main talent is flirting and attracting boys, which led to a hasty marriage with a soldier." Bruno chuckled, then became serious. "She has her hands full now with her little one and a rough husband. We don't see much of Edith. I'm afraid she and Nelda are like sandpaper rubbing together."

Herman could imagine. "My sister can be headstrong," he said. "But her heart is gold, and my mother misses her dearly."

Uncle Bruno put his hand gently on Herman's knee. "But you, my boy, what is it you like besides music?"

"I love to read, sir. And I like movies. I'm anxious to improve my English. And I enjoy being active and outdoors." He thought for a moment before he continued. "I hope to help your wife in any way I can, sir."

"Ah . . ." Bruno said and turned to look out the car window. They had left the country road and now passed through a gateway flanked by tall stone pillars. The drive was lined with a row of trees, their bare branches reaching to the gray sky. Beyond, gentle hills were covered with a patchwork of dark earth, scattered remnants of snow, and clusters of early crocus, yellow and lavender against the white and brown. A few large, twisted oak trees stood majestically at the top of one hill.

"This is my estate," Uncle Bruno said proudly. "We call it The Wilderness." As the road made a turn, he gestured toward a small lake and in the distance, some fences. "Over there, that's my tennis court," he said with a note of pride. "In a few months the weather will be fine enough to use it again. I'm still able to play an acceptable game of tennis. Do you play, Herman?"

"No, sir. But I'd enjoy watching you."

"Good enough. You may find there is more to watch than an old man swinging a racket." Uncle Bruno's smile held a mischievous twinkle. "My neighbor and tennis partner has two daughters who use the court sometimes. They're a pleasure to watch, I assure you."

Herman looked out the window as the Bentley crunched to a stop in the gravel driveway at the front of a stately, two-story house with broad steps and a massive front door.

From the moment Herman walked into the marble-floored entrance hall, he knew who was in charge. Aunt Nelda stood stiffly at the bottom of the stairway leading to the second floor. She waited there as the two men handed their coats to the butler and walked across the wide hall.

"My dear, this is my nephew, Herman. Finally, safely arrived." Uncle Bruno had switched from German to very proper English.

Herman's aunt extended her hand and shook his fingers limply. Her smile was forced. "You are welcome here. Matilda will show you to your room. I look forward to talking to you at dinner."

"*Vielen dank.* Thank you." Herman's words were hesitant.

His aunt's faded blue eyes seemed to pierce him, taking in every travel-worn detail with no hint of a welcome. "We speak only English in this home." Her voice was stern and without humor. "You can meet my sister Gracie at dinner. She is having her nap now." Her lips clamped in a tight line, she motioned to the housekeeper who stood off to one side, then turned away from Herman without a backward glance and walked across the hall and into a sitting room beyond.

Herman didn't have a chance to say another word. When his aunt's straight back disappeared, he turned hesitantly toward the amply built housekeeper. She gave him a warm smile but said nothing, only motioned with her hand that he should follow. At the top of the stairs, they continued some distance down a wood-paneled hallway and turned into a cozy room with a fireplace, a single bed, and a table and chair under the window. The housekeeper pulled the heavy drapes aside. The window looked out to the back gardens and toward the garage where the chauffeur was already washing the city grime off the Bentley.

Herman turned to the housekeeper who lingered by the door. "Thank you. This is a very nice room." He made his best effort to speak clearly in English.

The housekeeper rewarded him with another smile. "You speak English, sir. I'm glad. I wasn't sure. Anything you need, you just ask." She patted down her starched apron and added, "Dinner is at seven, sir. It's best to be prompt if you want to please Mrs. Kohn." With that warning, she turned and left the room.

Herman closed the door and sighed. His mother had warned him that Uncle Bruno's wife had a reputation for being stern, argumentative, demanding, and bitter. She had only agreed to Herman's stay on the condition it was temporary. He knew that if his stay was to be bearable, he must win over Aunt Nelda.

It didn't take long at dinner to see that his aunt had a soft spot for her younger sister. Gracie was in her mid-thirties, a slightly pudgy woman with a short bob of brown hair. She wore a flowered dress, sensible shoes, and had the manners of a well-trained five-year-old. Herman knew from family stories that Gracie was mentally simple, but no one had said how much Nelda doted on her. It was obvious that all the thwarted maternal instincts of the older sister were lavished on Gracie. Nelda helped her fold the big linen napkin on her lap and buttered her roll. When the younger woman began to stir her soup to cool it down, Nelda gently stopped the motion of her sister's hand.

"Give it a minute, Gracie, dear," she said in a hushed tone.

Gracie smiled shyly at Herman and after her soup was finished, looked across the table at him. "I don't always get to eat dinner down here with Nelly and Bruno. This is special because you came to visit. I like using the fancy silver. When I eat early in the upstairs sitting room, I use the second silver."

"I'm very glad you were able to join us," Herman said. "It's a pleasure for me to finally meet you. Maybe sometime I can come up and eat early with you. I often get hungry before seven."

"That would be fun. We could both use the second silver. And maybe play a game after. Do you like cards?"

"Certainly. What do you like to play?"

"Go Fish!" Her joy in the game was obvious. "And I like puzzles, too."

"I love puzzles." Herman was glad this was totally true. It would not be difficult to be nice to Gracie.

She smiled her big smile, wiped her mouth carefully with her napkin, then turned to her older sister and beamed with pride. "See, Nelly. I know how to eat and talk with company."

"I know you do, Gracie." Nelda patted her sister's hand. "Maybe with Herman here we will have some extra fun. What do you think?"

"Yes! I'll do a puppet show. And you said soon it will be warm enough for walks in the park. Right, Nelly?"

"Yes, indeed." Nelda's voice was calm and reassuring. "If it doesn't rain tomorrow, maybe we can walk to the hill and look for early crocus."

"Oh, yes." Gracie gave a sigh of anticipated pleasure. She waved her hands over her plate and almost upset her water glass. Herman noticed her hands were soft and white, her nails cut very short. "Do you think those pretty yellow flowers will be up yet?" she asked.

"Daffodils," Nelda reminded her. "Probably not yet, sweetheart."

The housekeeper had taken away the soup plates and was serving the roast and potatoes. When the dinner plate was placed in front of Gracie, Nelda leaned toward her and whispered, "Would you like me to help you cut your meat?"

Gracie hesitated and looked up through her lashes at Herman. "No, I can do it myself." She very carefully picked up her knife and fork and slowly began to saw through the tender beef.

Herman was charmed by Gracie's innocence and her efforts to be independent. After dinner, while Nelda went upstairs to help her prepare for bed, he joined his uncle in the library.

Bruno swept his arm in an arc to indicate the expanse of shelves laden with volumes. "You are free to read any book that strikes your fancy," his uncle said. He turned to a side table, where two brandy snifters waited, a crystal decanter filled with amber liquid nearby. He poured an inch of brandy in each glass and handed one to Herman. He left the toast unspoken and took a sip of the liquor. Herman sank into the deep leather sofa and followed his example. Later, in his upstairs room, Herman pulled back the curtains and stared into the dark night. Loneliness descended. He felt trapped again, this time in a safe English house in the countryside with nothing to do but wait. He would simply have to make the best of it.

THE DAYS SETTLED INTO A ROUTINE. Herman usually spent the morning in the upstairs sitting room with the ladies. Most days, when the weather was cold and wet, he and Gracie played card games and worked on her huge collection of jigsaw puzzles. Aunt Nelda sat quietly to one side, knitting or reading. Occasionally she came over to the puzzle table, inspected the colorful chunks of cardboard, and with a swift gesture, selected a piece and deftly fitted it into the partially finished puzzle. On mornings when the English sunshine illuminated the air, the three of them put on their heavy shoes and explored the estate grounds. Gracie enjoyed finding flowers, which she gathered into a bouquet. She would bury her nose in the bunch of freshly picked flowers and inhale the smell of springtime.

During these walks, Aunt Nelda forced Herman into conversation in English. Most often she spoke about the history of Britain and the latest news or quizzed him about the books he was reading, but one afternoon she became more personal.

"What are your plans for the future, Herman?" she asked.

"America. And California."

Nelda looked stern and pounded the ground with her walking stick as she always did when he gave what she called lazy answers. "Full sentences, my boy. How will you improve your English if you don't use it properly?"

"Sorry, Aunt Nelda." He organized his thoughts. "I vant to go to America first," he started slowly. "I go to my brother in California, but after . . . I don't know."

"Herman, you're not a schoolboy anymore. A man needs to make plans for the future. Think. What do you want to do with your life?"

"I vant to be free to do anything. Maybe I have a girl-friend. I find a fun job in America and earn money. Not like in Germany. There . . . I could do nothing." He looked at Nelda for understanding. "It is a long time since I think about vhat is good for me. I never care to be a bookkeeper, but it is the only education I can have. I learn to type. I learn to keep books. But I don't like these things. I am a man for action. I vant to do something outdoors . . . something exciting." He thought of all his dreams of travel and exploring Africa and South America. But he knew they were the dreams of a boy, and Nelda wouldn't approve. "I have not been able to think of a free future, but now I can, Aunt Nelda. I think about it."

Nelda stopped walking and stood to face Herman. "Want. Not vant. Watch the way you pronounce the *W*. Saying it with a *V* sound will reveal your German back-ground. Maybe it's not such a good thing these days. And say each word separately and clearly. The past tense of learn is learned. You learned to type. You learned to keep books. You must use the past tense when it is appropriate. And use 'will' when you talk about the future." The corners of her mouth curved in the hint of a smile. "I do see improvement. You learn quickly."

She turned and took Gracie's hand. "Time for tea, darling. Cook has made your favorite biscuits for lunch today."

"Gingersnaps?" Gracie began to walk faster. Nelda was pulled along behind as the younger woman headed back to the house.


IN THE AFTERNOONS, GRACIE WAS encouraged to take a nap and during these quiet hours, Herman retreated to the library. He loved the tiers of shelves filled with books, both old classics and newer novels. A tall ladder on wheels slid from one end of the wall to the other, making even the top shelf accessible. All the books were in English, and he always read a page or two out loud to practice his pronunciation. Then, with an English/German dictionary by his side, he settled into the enjoyment of the story. In the evenings, he listened to the radio in his room and repeated after the announcer until he could duplicate the proper English tone and pronunciation.

At the end of the first month in England, Herman's aunt let him know he could call her "Aunt Nelly." It would be "less confusing for Gracie." And she paid him another compliment. "You are beginning to sound like an Englishman, except for those pesky *W*s, which you persist in pronouncing like *V*s."

# CHAPTER 5

# KISSING MOLLY

ONE SATURDAY AFTERNOON IN MID-APRIL, Uncle Bruno found Herman sprawled over the sofa in the library reading one of his favorite books in its original English. "I thought I'd find you here," he said and reached down to tip his nephew's book in order to read the title. "*King Solomon's Mines*, an absolutely wonderful African adventure! But come on. It's a glorious day, and there's nothing like England in the spring! I'm off to meet my neighbor at the tennis court." He grasped Herman's arm and pulled him to his feet. "You can watch us for a while and even have a few whacks at it if you want."

Herman sat on a wooden bench at the edge of the court, the warmth of the pale English sunshine on his back and neck loosened the tension of the winter's uncertainty. His head swiveled back and forth as he eagerly followed the tennis game. The thunk of the ball hitting the racquets punctuated the energetic back-and-forth play, and it was pleasant to hear the deep voices of the men as they bantered between sets. He decided he had been spending too much time with the ladies of the house.

Uncle Bruno came alive playing tennis, and Herman admired his energy and stamina. Though Bruno played a strong game, his friend Roger was even better and their volleys were vigorous. After their second set, Uncle Bruno walked over, wiped the sweat from his forehead with a small cotton towel, and rubbed his belly. "This is my winter paunch. It'll be gone after a summer of tennis."

Herman laughed. "You'll have to cut back on those big English lunches, too," he teased. "And all those nice, sweet puddings after dinner you like so much."

"A young chap like you shouldn't make fun of an old man." A smile accompanied Bruno's stern voice. "I've seen how many scones and little tea sandwiches you can pile on your plate. You'd do well to take up tennis, too. Want to give it a try?"

Herman shook his head. He yearned to play, but he didn't want to be a bother and, besides, he would probably be leaving soon—it was best he didn't get started. "No, thank you, sir. I do love watching, though. If you can teach me about the scoring, then I can understand the game better. I'd like that. And I can help pick up balls or anything else you want."

Herman spent several hours most weekends at the courts. He watched the two men play, learned the fine points of tennis, and ran after errant balls.

One Saturday, Roger's two daughters appeared like English goddesses—splendid and lithe in their white tennis skirts and court shoes. Betsy, only fourteen, had that day returned home from boarding school for a long weekend. Rosy cheeked and healthy, with two braids swinging, she flashed him a toothy grin when she was introduced. The older girl, tall and slender, was a golden vision who made Herman feel insignificant and unworldly. Waves of amber hair, caught back by a large tortoise shell clip, framed her delicate face, and her peachy arms were sprinkled with a few freckles. When she waved her hand in greeting, the tokens on her silver charm bracelet glittered in the sunlight. "We call her Margaret, like the little princess at Buckingham Palace," her father said, and she laughed.

"I'm no princess," she declared. Her eyes sparkled, and she held her hand out to shake. "I have a flat in London and take classes at the Art Institute. In the winter I seldom make it home, but when Betsy's back from school, I try to come more often." This caused the younger girl to grin again. "My friends in London call me Molly," the golden sister added, "and you should, too."

From that day on, Herman found an excuse to be at the tennis court every Saturday. When the girls were not there, he spent the weekend unmotivated and listless. When they were both home, the sisters often played doubles with their father and Bruno, but Herman liked it best when the two men grew tired and left the court to Betsy and Molly. When Betsy's boarding school closed for summer break, they began to come midweek to play tennis at The Wilderness with friends, and Bruno's court was always active. Herman deserted the library and his reading.

Every day, morning and afternoon, he walked nonchalantly toward the tennis court and pretended he was on his way somewhere else. If the girls were there, he lingered to watch them play. He was both in ecstasy and misery over Molly, who, besides being older by several years, was totally outside his reach socially. She was an upper-class English girl, the product of boarding school and a life of ease. In summer, when she had no classes to attend, she wandered around the garden with her sketch pad, attended parties, and played tennis. She seemed unapproachable to Herman because of his present situation. She was always friendly, though, and would often wave her manicured hand to beckon him over.

One afternoon, he saw her in the kitchen garden behind the courts. Alone for once, she cradled her drawing pad in her arms and stared pensively at the rows of runner beans and cabbages. He hurried over, hoping that Betsy wasn't crouched low where he couldn't see her and might suddenly bounce into view. His feet crunched on the gravel path as he approached. Molly looked over and a smile of pleasure lit up her face.

"Good morning, Molly," he said. He felt his own smile blossom in response to her obvious delight.

"Hi, Herman. What a lovely day it is." She looked toward the tennis courts, then back at him with a smile. "You've become a real fan of tennis, I've noticed. Why don't you play with us sometime?"

Herman shrugged. "I've never tried. I'd slow the play down." He added in a low voice, "Besides, watching you play is more fun."

She either didn't hear or chose to ignore this comment. "How are Nelda and sweet Gracie?"

Her radiant smile left him fumbling for words. "Aunt Nelda's fine. You know . . . I was a bit afraid of her at first, but now she teaches me English. And Gracie . . . she's very special."

"What a dear Gracie is. Mrs. Kohn's devoted to her ever since their parents passed away and Gracie came to stay. She's a bit like a mother hen guarding her chick, don't you think?"

Herman stood speechless. He tried to think of something sophisticated to say and finally blurted out, "Gracie has a new puzzle. It's a picture of daffodils and lilies. She loves flowers." He stopped. How stupid. "How is your drawing coming?" He hoped she would have a long answer.

"I've finished a portrait drawing class, but I find it difficult to get a likeness. I keep trying to draw Betsy. They come out pretty enough, but she always looks different somehow. Never quite herself."

"Oh, I'm sure they look just like her." So gauche. Now he had contradicted her.

Molly laughed softly. "Well, more like a cousin or distant relative, I'd say." She reached out and touched his chin and pushed his face gently back and forth. "Would you pose for me? I think I need a male face to practice on. Someone with more angles. Betsy's too round and soft."

Herman's chin tingled where she had touched him, while his whole face burned under her scrutiny. "Yes, of course!" It was difficult not to suggest they begin that very afternoon. "Whenever you want. I never go anywhere important—except to the constable's office in Hempstead once a month to get my papers stamped."

A few days later, he sat on a hard chair in the rose garden as she studied his face. She would look at her paper, then look up again, and let her eyes probe his face. Finally, to his great relief, she would concentrate on her pad. As she began to draw, her mouth pursed in concentration and she licked her lips. The flick of her tongue mesmerized Herman, and he couldn't take his eyes off her red lips as he waited for her to moisten them again. He slid his hands into his pockets to cover their trembling. Her conté crayon moved slowly, then fast, and again she pursed her lips. After another concentrated stare, she seemed to relax, her eyes softened, and she began to talk while her hand scurried across the paper. "What do you do with your days? It must be hard to always stay out here in the country."

"Sometimes I visit my sister in London. I enjoy the train ride in and back. But my visa says I must spend my nights here, so I can't stay more than a few hours." He hesitated, then spilled the full truth. "Besides, her husband can be nasty, and I don't like him much." Molly seemed to suck the air out of his lungs, but she never noticed how flustered he was. "What do you do in the city? Between art classes, I mean."

"I share a little apartment with a friend who studies sculpture. After class we go to the local pub for a sherry. The boys from the institute show up, and we have a few drinks and talk about art. The guys are worried about the possibility of war, so we girls try to get their minds off serious topics. I know what's happening in Germany is important, but . . ."

"It's good to forget all that sometimes," Herman said. "I read a lot and try to entertain Gracie. That keeps me from worrying."

OVER THE NEXT FEW MONTHS, Molly asked him to pose almost every week. She did profiles and full-face sketches, some with his hat on and one with his hair pulled down over his forehead. With each session, the portraits improved. While she worked, she shared tales of her days in the city. She told of parties and what she wore, of the plays she saw at the theater, and she described the movies she saw with her friends. She talked about her roommate and how they squabbled about whose turn it was to wash the dishes. She mentioned lots of different boys, some from classes and some she knew from her family. Once she mentioned a man she had been engaged to for a few months.

"That was two years ago." She shrugged, and her gaze drifted off to the rose bushes behind him. Herman heard a tremor in her voice as she continued. "I thought we would be happy. But it turned out badly. He was seeing another girl from the theater district. I couldn't marry someone who was . . . you know, unfaithful." She shook her head and smiled again, then her eyes lit up as she spoke. "That's when I decided to follow my dream and study art. Actually, it was a stroke of luck."

One warm afternoon, he watched the bees buzz around the roses and concentrated on keeping perfectly still while Molly's hand danced over her pad. But inside his head his thoughts revolved around the latest news from his mother. As promised, she wrote to him in English almost every week. Most letters were filled with the difficulties of life in Germany, her loneliness without family or friends, and her efforts to get her visas. But the letter he had received the day before was upbeat.

*Dear Hermanle,*                  *June 14, 1939*

*I have met a lovely new friend. He is a doctor. Dr. Wilhelm will no longer see me or any other Jewish patients. We all must go to Dr. Fiedler now. He is kind and concerned and runs a clinic that is very busy because of patients like me. He says that I suffer because "external factors have disrupted my homeostasis."*

*I think this is his scientific way of saying it is my nerves. I like his gentle manner, and the herbal tea he prescribed has eased my headaches. He called me this afternoon and invited me to come to a little concert at his home.*

*"Just friends," he said. "An evening of music to help you relax." He said it was doctor's orders, and he would walk me home afterward. How did he know how much I like music? When I told him, he encouraged me to bring my violin and join the ensemble. I hope they don't mind.*

*I am going to go. I need a pleasant time with friendly people.*

*Hugs from your Mutti.*

He knew his mother was lonely, but he wanted her to come to England, not make friends in Germany. His face must have shown his worry because Molly's gentle voice interrupted his thoughts.

"Herman. Look pleasant for me, please. I don't want to draw that scowl."

He looked up and tried to smile, but his heart was only half in it.

"What are you thinking about that makes you pensive?" Molly said. Her voice was soft, and her persistence made him want to tell her.

"Yesterday, I received a letter from my mother that worries me." He wasn't sure how to explain what was bothering him. "She has had to go to a doctor," he said.

"I hope it's not serious. Is she all right?" Molly's concern was real.

"Yes. Yes, I guess so. She says it was only nerves. But now she is seeing him again . . . seeing him socially." He looked up and hoped Molly might help him understand why he felt puzzled and worried.

She giggled, covered her mouth with her hand, then shook her head by way of an apology. "I'm not laughing at you, honestly not. But it is truly droll. You are unable to think of your mother as a woman who needs to be loved. To you she is only your mother. It's always this way. We like to forget that our mothers are also women."

Herman felt the warmth of surprise and embarrassment flood his face. "You're right, of course," he said. "I hope this new friend doesn't change her mind about coming to England soon." He tried to smile, though he was relieved that Molly's attention had returned to her drawing. He couldn't help it. The idea of his mother going on a date, though he knew she deserved it, disturbed him. Maybe it was jealousy because he had not found the nerve to ask Molly for the same thing. Each time he posed, he vowed that next time he would ask her out. But the next time he saw her, he was again struck speechless by uncertainty.

As the summer drew to a close, the time with Molly became Herman's heaven. But each time they were together, Betsy would appear at some point and begin to tug on her sister's arm and ask when they could play tennis or insist it was time to go back home and dress for tea. Molly would pack up her art supplies, flash one last smile, and turn her attention to her sister.

One day, Molly held up a finished drawing for Herman to see, and he felt like he was gazing into a mirror.

A triumphant smile lit up her face. "I've done it! Your patience has made me a portrait artist. Next I'm going to try doing my mother." She laughed. "Getting the fine wrinkles and worry lines will be a new challenge, but don't you dare tell her I said that!" She stood up and spun around. "When I sit too long, I need to get up and move about."

She shook her arms loosely and raised them to the sky in a sinuous stretch. As she moved, Herman's eyes were drawn away from her face to the swell of her breasts under her thin summer blouse. He could feel his body respond.

Seemingly unaware, Molly reached out her hand to him. "Come on. I'll show you the place Betsy and I used to hide when we were children."

He pulled his eyes back to her face. "Yes, I'd like that." Tentatively he took her fingers in his.

"This way," she said. She moved her hand to grasp his firmly and pulled him along the path, out of the rose garden.

In the kitchen garden, hidden from the main house by a hedge, they walked down the rows of overripe vegetables and past the wheelbarrow filled with fertilizer. She swung her arm gaily. "It's been a glorious summer, hasn't it?"

Herman could feel a warm tingle creep up his arm from where her palm nestled in his. He was afraid to speak.

She stopped and looked in his eyes. Her fingers slipped from his, and she ran ahead. "Catch me if you can?" Her silver laughter pulled him forward, his eagerness building as they approached the garden shed. Something new was happening.

The shed door was open, and she slid inside. When he followed her, the cool darkness enveloped him. He looked around. It took a minute for his eyes to adjust to the dimness. She seemed to have disappeared. Suddenly he felt the warmth of her fingers over his eyes, and her moist breath on the back of his neck. "Guess who?" Her soft voice was near his ear.

Herman turned in her arms, and her hands slid down to his shoulders. He could feel the slight pressure of her breasts against his chest and smell the lavender scent of her soap. Slowly he leaned forward until his lips grazed her cheek. She turned her head and their lips met for an instant. Too soon, she dropped her arms and stepped back. It was so quiet he could hear her breathe. He reached out in the dim light and clasped her shoulders. He pulled her toward him and smothered her face and neck in kisses. His hands moved to her breasts, and for only a moment, he felt their softness. Then she twisted away.

"I think we better go outside," she said. "This is not the place." She reached out for his hand, wrapped her fingers around his, and pulled him toward the door.

In the bright sunlight, Herman felt lightheaded. He wasn't sure if what had happened was an accident or a promise. "Molly . . . I . . ."

She put her fingers to his lips. "Shhh . . . Don't say anything. It was a sweet moment." She lowered her hand to his chest and pushed him away gently. "Look. My summer break is over. The semester starts next week, and Betsy goes back to boarding school, too. I won't be able to come home much anymore—only an occasional weekend."

Herman's heart dropped. "I'll miss you," he whispered. In a firmer voice he continued, "I'll look forward to the weekends you can come home. We can see each other then, right? Will you show me the portraits you do of your mother?"

"Yes, naturally." She caressed his cheek with her fingers. "I'll miss you, too."

It was almost a whisper, but the sound of it made his heart feel like it would burst. Her face lit up with a tantalizing smile, and she tapped his chest with a bossy gesture.

"You call me when you're in London visiting your sister. Surely you can get away from her long enough for us to meet somewhere."

"I'd like to . . ." He hesitated. Did she mean she'd go out with him?

Just as he was about to kiss her again, Betsy bounded up the path, breathless. "I've been looking all over for you!" Her cheeks were flushed, and her plaits bounced when she came to a stop in front of them. "And here you are hiding among the vegetables! Hi, Herman. Want to come for tea? Mum says we must eat early today, and it's all on the table.

Come on!" With a gesture of impatience, she turned and skipped away.

"I must go." Molly's eyes were sad as she turned toward the house. After a few steps, she turned and ran back to place a quick kiss on his cheek. Then she walked away and did not look back again.

THE LAST LONG DAYS OF summer moved slowly. Without afternoons spent with Molly, Herman felt lost, especially on the weekends. He again filled his morning hours with Aunt Nelly and Gracie, who distracted him with walks and puppet plays. He wrote letters to his mother, read more books, and perfected his English.

He wanted to take Molly on a real date, to treat her to something nice like dinner in a restaurant. For that he needed money. The only way he could think to save a few pounds out of the little spending money Uncle Bruno gave him was to not go into London on the train to see his sister. He stayed at The Wilderness and dreamed of the day he would be able to take Molly out to dinner at the Ritz or to dance at the Savoy or hold her again in his arms for a lingering kiss. For the first time in his life, his dreams were not of adventures in the deserts of Morocco as a French Foreign Legion officer.

CHAPTER 6

# LOVE AND WAR

AT THE END OF AUGUST, Clara finally fled Germany. She arrived by airplane at the Croydon Aerodrome with one tightly packed suitcase, fifty marks, and everything else—even her treasured violin—abandoned in the apartment in Meiningen. On her first night in England, Clara confided in her daughter, who shared the story with Herman the next day while their mother slept fitfully next to her dozing grandbaby.

"We sat right here in this tiny living room and shared a bottle of wine," Edith told him as they sat on the sofa sipping strong English tea. "Mutti was tired. The wine loosened her tongue. She forgot I was her daughter and spilled her heartbreak, woman to woman."

"Should you tell me then? A man?"

"You're her son. You need to know. She's a different woman than she ever was with Father." Edith's voice was low and confidential. "It was her love of music and her loneliness that first pulled Mutti into a friendship with that Jewish doctor. His name is Albert. Albert Fiedler. I think she feels deep affection for him. She and Albert became close. They saw each other almost every day."

"Does she love him?" Herman wasn't sure he wanted to know the answer.

"She thinks she does. She actually said to me, 'Edith, I have finally found love after years of living with your father who cared nothing for me.'"

Herman shook his head at the truth of the statement. He knew his father had been distant and seldom home. "If she loves this Albert, we must count ourselves lucky that she came away without him."

"I think she would have stayed. But Albert insisted she flee to us." Edith wiped away tears that threatened to slip down her cheeks. "Mutti told me that last week everything changed. Last Thursday, after going to a piano recital at the home of one of Albert's patients, he begged her to leave. He walked her home. It was late, almost curfew. Mutti said Albert had been quiet all afternoon, then suddenly he stopped her in the darkened street and spoke, low and urgent, in her ear. 'You must join your children in England . . . as soon as you can.'

"Tears were running down her cheeks. I've never seen Mutti cry before. 'I told him I didn't want to leave,' she said. She told me that Albert pulled her into the shadow of the theater building, gripped her shoulders, and made her look him in the eye. He declared his love for her, but then pleaded with her to leave. She said he told her he would never be able to forgive himself if she were to stay in danger to be near him. She told me he said, 'Our country has gone mad. All of us who can must leave. I need to know you are safe.' She wanted him to come with her, but his mother is ill and dependent on him. I guess Mutti begged him to follow as soon as possible. He has applied for visas to the United States, to Australia, even to Shanghai. But nothing has come through."

Edith paused to drink the last of her tea. "Mutti told him she would try to find someone in England to assist him. She thinks surely someone will help get a doctor a transit visa for himself and a dependent. I hope she's right." She stood up and began to clear away the tea things. "Herman, in the end she was sobbing. She told me he kissed her, a kiss like she never had before. The last words he said to her that night were, 'Go home, my love, my sweetheart, and begin packing.' She was sobbing when she told me this."

"So she came. We owe him that."

"I think she still would have stayed except for what happened the next day when she went shopping." Edith sighed. "I think Mutti is more like me than I ever knew. She can be stubborn . . . and she certainly is a romantic."

"What happened that pushed her to leave?"

"The next day, Mutti was walking through the market square on her way to the bakery in the old Jewish section. Frau Mueller, you know, the police chief's wife, walked near her among the crowd of shoppers. Mutti said she recognized her old friend but didn't speak to her. They hadn't spoken since Herr Mueller joined the Nazi party five years ago. She said Frau Mueller walked right next to her and matched her pace.

"Mutti can be very dramatic. She told me the whole story as if it were a play, imitating Frau Mueller's harsh whispers so well it sent a chill down my neck. 'Hisssst . . . pay attention. I am still your friend in my heart.' Mutti's eyes looked at the floor as she imitated Frau Mueller, as if she studied the stones of the street. The police chief's wife dropped a folded piece of paper into Mutti's shopping basket. Mutti opened her mouth to say something then, but Frau Mueller had already turned away and strode across the square.

"Mutti hurried to the safety of the house, her bread forgotten. With the door closed behind her, she unfolded the paper and read the note scrawled on the scrap of paper. She memorized the words and recited them to me.

*Leave now. Tonight if you can—by dawn without fail.*
*I have seen a list of Jews to be picked up tomorrow and*
*taken to a labor camp. Your name is on it. Godspeed.*
*My heart is with you.*

"Oh God," Herman breathed. "So close . . . and the Muellers again."

"Yes." The stack of tea cups rattled in Edith's hands as she carried them into the tiny kitchen and set them on the counter. She returned and sat on the sofa next to Herman. She smoothed the cushion to steady her trembling. "It was very close. Mutti burned the note over the flame of the gas cooker. She watched it turn to ash, then went to her bedroom and packed."

Later that night, while Edith nursed the baby, Clara confided in her son. "I called Albert after I read Frau Mueller's note and begged him to try again to get a visa for anywhere in the world . . . to leave Germany. He promised me he would apply for a transit visa to come to England as soon as possible. I want for us to be together—so we can marry. If I would agree to marry, he would leave everything else, he said. My heart is promised to him now." Clara paused a moment and tried to hold on to her composure. "But he must get his mother settled somewhere. Find someone to care for her and that won't be easy. Of course, he can't hire a Gentile, and all the Jews are trying to leave themselves. He told me not to worry. At the worst, he will wait for me," Clara explained, the tears spilling over. "He said that Hitler's madness will end someday, and he will see me when I return to Germany after it's all over. But I don't believe it will end in time." She wiped the tears from her cheeks. "I'm afraid I won't see him again."

Herman hugged his mother but was unsure what to say to calm her. This newly emotional, love-struck woman was strange to him. As he held her, he noticed a few strands of silver that rose from her temples and twisted through her dark braids. Worry and life in Germany had taken its toll.

She struggled to make herself useful in the tiny apartment with Edith, whose English husband was gone much of the time on maneuvers in the army. Clara found comfort in helping care for her grandbaby, and like her son, she anticipated a long wait in England for her United States visa.

Almost immediately, the world collapsed. Germany

invaded Poland, and on September 3, 1939, France and England declared war on Germany in response.

Herman watched as his mother became more desperate each day as she waited for news from Albert, who was suddenly trapped in a country at war. Mother and son now found themselves not only refugees, but also classified as enemy aliens in a foreign land.

For the first several months, nothing more seemed to happen—no invasion, no bombs, only angry talk. The only signs of war were English children who went to school with special gas mask boxes strung around their necks and lines of ladies who bought heavy, dark cloth to sew into blackout curtains.

Herman waited for the infrequent weekend afternoons when he might glimpse Molly at the tennis court. He longed to touch her and talk to her, but they had few chances to be alone, and those moments were only long enough for their fingers to entwine and for her looks to convey her pleasure at his touch. As they kissed quickly behind a hedge or in the dark of the shed, she whispered in his ear, "Can't you come to London soon?"

"I can't. I'm an enemy alien now, and I'm not allowed to travel." His voice was low with frustration. He mentally counted the few shillings and pounds he had set aside and decided that if he were allowed to go into London again, he wouldn't worry about where he took her. The neighborhood pub and a dark corner booth would be enough.

"It's all stupid," she sighed, and he could hear her disappointment and desire.

In November, finally and almost unexpectedly, Herman received his visa to the United States, but now he didn't want to leave. Molly and his mother were here. But the new visa triggered expiration of his British permit. He had no choice. The war was heating up, especially in the shipping lanes, and it was increasingly difficult to find passage to New York.

One evening after dinner, Uncle Bruno asked Herman to come to the library. "I hate that you will be leaving soon," he said. "We'll all miss you, especially Gracie."

Herman stood with his back to the warmth of the fireplace and looked at his uncle, who slowly lit his pipe. "Isn't there some way I can stay, Uncle? Could I get my papers changed?"

Uncle Bruno shook his head. "I'm sorry. I've already inquired and the visa department was firm. You must go to America as planned." He took several puffs on his pipe, and the smoke hovered over his head. "My biggest concern has been to find you safe passage to New York," he said. "Of course, British and French ships are being harried by German U-boats. Even ships that travel in convoy aren't safe these days. But the Germans have also declared they'll sink any American ship they can get their torpedo sights on. Hitler's angry at the Yanks for transporting war materiel to us in Great Britain."

"I'm not afraid, Uncle." Herman tried to sound confident, though he didn't like the image of a watery grave that flashed through his mind.

"Of course, my boy. But I've found a better option. The shipping agent for my company reminded me we sometimes use a Japanese steamship line to transport our products to America and on through the Panama Canal to the Far East. He says its ships are safe and well-run, but more importantly now, they have a few passenger cabins on each ship. We have inquired about getting you a berth on the next ship to New York, and I'm sure they'll make room for you." He walked over and put his hands on his nephew's shoulders. "Herman, it leaves in ten days. I'm sorry it's so soon, but you must take this opportunity. The Germans consider Japan a friendly nation, and a ship flying the Japanese flag will be safe from U-boat attack."

With his departure for the United States only days away, Herman was finally cleared to travel to London. He quickly wrote Molly a note. Would she meet him for dinner or a movie? He would visit his sister for a few days before it was time to board the ship. He thought he could get away in the evening when Edith and his mother were busy with the baby. Molly's answer arrived in the post the next day, written in clear script on creamy stationery.

> *Yes! Of course, I'll see you. A special good-bye is mandatory. Call me. You have been in prison at The Wilderness too long. Shall we see a film first? The new American animated movie, Gulliver's Travels, is in London, and I'd love to see it. Afterward, we can go to a quiet pub near my flat for a farewell drink.*
>
> *Soon you will be my American friend . . . much better than a German friend right now, don't you agree?*

Herman could hardly concentrate on anything else but the promise of being with Molly, his nerves jittery with anticipation. As he packed his suitcase, he was so distracted that he suddenly realized he had folded and refolded his best blue shirt two times. On his next-to-the-last morning in England, he stood in the grand foyer of The Wilderness and looked around. The room no longer seemed cold and foreign. Gracie was in tears and she hugged him with such force he was afraid for his ribs. Even Aunt Nelly was misty-eyed as she told Herman to continue to perfect his English.

Uncle Bruno first clapped him on the shoulder. "Good luck to you." His voice was husky, and he spread his arms and clasped his nephew in a smothering hug. When he released Herman, his words caught in his throat. "It's been my honor to give you a temporary home in this world gone crazy. When you see your mother this afternoon, tell her to call me if she needs anything. And come and visit when she can."

Later that evening, Herman sat next to Molly in the darkened movie theater. His shoulder tingled and throbbed where it touched hers. When he glanced over, their eyes met in the flickering gray-and-white light reflected from the screen.

On the screen, cartoonish Lilliputians danced to a jazzy number about bluebirds in the moonlight. She smiled and whispered, "Thanks for not thinking me silly to want to see a cartoon." Her fingers rested lightly on his thigh. He covered her hand with his and savored the feel of his thumb as it gently moved up and down her smooth fingers. He didn't care what the movie was about. The cartoon figures danced with Gulliver's giant hand. Herman could only think of Molly's hand in his own.

On the walk from the movie theater to the local pub, a cold wind flapped her coat and twisted its icy fingers between his woolen scarf and leather jacket. Her gloved hand rested in the crook of his elbow, and he steadied her on the uneven sidewalk. When they entered the pub, the warm moist air and subdued light felt safe and cozy.

Herman stepped up to the bar, ordered himself a pint of beer and a sherry for her, and followed Molly to a dark corner booth where they settled into the leather seat. They held hands and talked of the war, what would happen next, and Herman's plans. As they ordered a second drink, Molly nestled close, and Herman could feel the heat of her body against his.

"It has been a long time since our last kisses in the garden shed." Her voice was soft and edged with disappointment. "Tomorrow you'll be gone, and we have no time. Why didn't you ask me out before this crazy war began?"

Herman fiddled with his napkin. "I thought you'd say no. I couldn't imagine a girl like you wanting to go out with a nobody."

She reached up and ran her fingers down the side of his cheek. "No, my darling, you're far too good-looking and charming for any girl to turn down." She leaned back and smiled at him.

He looked at her bright red lips. His chest felt ready to explode, and he blurted out what was trapped there. "If I asked you for more than a kiss, would you say yes or no?" Molly leaned forward. With her eyes closed, her lashes lay like butterflies on her cheek. It was as if a powerful magnet pulled him toward her. Their lips touched and lingered. How he wished he had more experience. He moved his lips against the softness of her mouth and slowly it opened to him. The tip of her tongue brushed his lower lip, its touch a lick of fire. The sigh of her breath entered his mouth. Surely this was better than heaven.

Molly pulled back for a moment. She loosened the barrette that held her thick hair and shook it out in a cascade over her shoulders. She moved impossibly close and nibbled little kisses on his ear. The longing of all his virginal years surged through him, and his arms surrounded her. He could feel her breasts crushed against his chest. Her fingers caressed his shoulders and trailed up the back of his neck and into his hair. "We have so little time left to be together," she whispered. "Let's do it right." And she leaned forward and her mouth covered his again, her kisses warm with passion.

Suddenly she pushed herself away from him, stood, and grabbed his hand. "Come to my flat," she said. "My roommate is visiting her family." Drinks forgotten, Herman allowed himself to be pulled away. He did not feel the frigid wind or think of anything beyond the promise of her embrace.

The walk-up flat was cold, and Molly turned the knob on the radiator. Two doors opened off the sitting room, and Herman glimpsed a small bedroom with a single bed. There was a tiny kitchen and a sagging divan covered with a knitted blanket.

Molly laughed at his expression. "Did you expect a penthouse? My parents say if I must study art, then I should live like a starving artist." She laughed again. "But I love it here. And I have a special place. Come see."

She took his hand and pulled him in the direction of a dark green, velvet drape suspended from a heavy wooden rod. She swept open the curtain and revealed an unmade bed that filled the hidden alcove. Three tall windows looked out to the dark night.

"This is mine," Molly announced. "I like it better than the dark bedroom. And I like it even better now that you are here." She pulled him down into the tumble of bed linens and pillows that smelled of her perfume. The bed springs moaned with their weight, and he felt the length of her against him as he enclosed her in his arms. Their mouths were hungry, lips and tongues discovering the tastes of ale and sherry. His hand thrust under her blouse and found her breasts, delicious and soft. The hardness of her nipples surprised him, and he felt awkward and inept. He wished for finesse but didn't know how to achieve it.

Molly put her hand over his. "Slowly," she whispered. "Let's go slowly and enjoy every moment."

He groaned and relaxed his hand but did not remove it from her breast. "Yes. Tonight must be special. Show me how to bring you pleasure. Show me everything."

Molly propped herself on her elbow and looked down at him. "This is your first time, isn't it?"

"Yes, but don't worry. I'm a fast learner. I promise you."

Long after midnight, Herman struggled to leave.

"I must go," he said, though he longed to stay. "I must go, but I don't want to."

Molly wrapped herself in her winter coat. "I'll go downstairs with you." Her voice was soft, and her eyes shone with tears. "One more kiss." They lingered in the foyer of the building, the embrace between them filled with the sorrow of parting. Still they clung together and moved to the front stoop, overlooking the quiet of the deserted street. A few lonely snowflakes drifted down. "It's the first snow. Winter is always long and cold." She pulled her woolen coat tight, and he wrapped his arms around her. The feel of her warm body made him forget the need to leave. "Who knows what will happen this winter?" she said. "I wish you weren't leaving." The whisper of her warm breath brushed his ear. "It's cruel that you have to leave now, just when we are starting—"

He kissed her mouth again to stop the sad words she spoke. "Will you write to me?" He wanted to make the moment last. "I'll write you from America. I promise."

"Yes, I'll kiss the stationery before I send it. I hope you remember my kisses every time you read a letter from me."

"Will you be my girl? Will you wait?" He knew this was a crazy question to ask, but at that moment, his need for her to be his was like a fever. "I'll come back to England as soon as I can. I don't want to lose you."

Molly held her hand out and caught a few snowflakes in her palm. They melted instantly on the warmth of her skin. She looked up at him. "You are very special . . . but . . ."

Her hesitation was heartrending.

**A gift for you**

Hey Mr Simpson! I saw a segment on "The Ritchie Boys" and it was so interesting I thought you would enjoy reading about it! You probably already know about them, but hope you havent read this! Love yoU! xo amy From amy zambrano

"Who knows what will happen? There's the war. And you're young. It could be a long time." She kissed him again—a kiss of lingering sadness rather than passion. "I'll write. That's all I can promise. Then, I don't know. Honestly." She shrugged and pulled out of his arms. "I'll always remember this night." She turned and went inside, leaving him immobile, enveloped in the falling snow.

"I will, too." Only his heart could hear his words.


IN THE DARK OF EARLY morning, Herman tossed on the small cot in his sister's vestibule, his dreams filled with visions of Molly. When the baby cried out at 6:00 a.m. and then the hawking and spitting of Edith's husband in the tiny bathroom, he knew he wouldn't sleep again. He couldn't face the squalor and confusion of morning in the apartment. He mumbled an excuse to his sister and slipped out into the gray morning. The snow had stopped and murky puddles edged the street as he walked aimlessly, his thoughts turbulent. He wished he could stay. But he knew it was too late. He was an enemy alien in Britain, and the war was expected to turn ugly any day. London wouldn't be a good place to be a German, even a so-called Jewish one.

As he headed back to Edith's flat, he passed a beauty shop. In the window was a display of face creams, perfume, and lipsticks. The row of golden tubes with the reds and pinks of lip color turned up reminded him of Molly's lips. One caught his eye, a bright, raspberry red lipstick in a silver case with gold filigree decoration. As he gazed at the display, the closed sign in the window flipped over to read "Open." The money Uncle Bruno had given him to get to Chicago burned in his pocket.

The sales lady wrapped his purchase carefully in tissue. "Would you like a gift card?"

On the pink card he wrote, "I will never forget your lips, even in America." The tissue-wrapped lipstick and note went into a small red box.

The sales lady tied the box up with satin ribbon. "Your girlfriend will like this," she said.

That afternoon he gave his mother Molly's address and asked her to mail the package. "Just send it to her. Don't write who it is from or anything."

Clara opened her mouth to ask why but remained silent.

# CHAPTER 7
# A GERMAN CHILDHOOD

THAT EVENING, HERMAN BOARDED the *Husima Maru*. The freighter, flying the flag of the Rising Sun, carried twenty-one assorted passengers, its captain, and crew into the stormy Atlantic.

Four days later, he huddled in a teak lounge chair on the ship's upper deck, a knit cap pulled down over his ears and a heavy wool blanket wrapped tightly around him. It was a relief to get away from the retching of his cabin mate, who spoke only Yiddish and Polish. As the ship plowed through the frigid waves, Herman felt a certain pride in being one of the few passengers well enough to appear in the salon for meals. Still, the tossing of the ship made it impossible to hold a book steady, and the deck was too unstable for walking. With nothing else to distract him, Herman pulled the blanket over his head and thought about what had brought him to this point—not yet twenty years old and a refugee heading alone for America.

His happy childhood had known only occasional shadows. He remembered his father's deep voice grumbling about the price of bread at the dinner table.

"Exorbitant," he had fumed. "If prices keep rising, the family's wealth will be liquidated to put bread and butter on the table!"

"Hugo, please don't frighten the children." His mother reached toward her husband and spoke in a soft, soothing voice.

But as usual, Herman's father didn't pay attention to his wife.

"If this situation gets worse," he ranted on, "there will be upheaval. Political unrest always follows hard times. Mark my words, evil will follow."

But Herman was young, only a schoolboy, his mind filled with kicking a ball around the yard and reading adventure comics. The hard times in Germany didn't seem to affect his father's wholesale leather business, which had been in the family for two generations and remained strong.

Their new home in the theater district was the center of Herman's young life. He remembered his favorite room, a glass-enclosed front parlor Mutti called the winter garden. How welcome its warmth would be now. As a small boy, he would lie on the tiled floor heated from below by hot water pipes and ignore the snow falling beyond the glass window panes. Surrounded by ferns and the drooping blooms of his mother's white orchid, he imagined the potted palms were four times taller, with parrots and monkeys among the fronds, and he an African explorer.

The other downstairs rooms were the realm of adults, but the attic was the children's kingdom. There he, his brother, his sister, cousins, and friends enjoyed a place where grown-ups seldom ventured. Whole afternoons were spent curled up on the sagging, discarded chairs, or sprawled over piles of pillows. They thumbed through forbidden movie magazines and played cards. The dormer windows were left ajar except on the coldest nights to allow the smoke from his older brother's stolen cigarettes to curl out the opening.

When he was still in primary school, the family business moved to the basement of the home on Bernhardstrasse. The converted basement became a storage space for the leather inventory. On afternoons when delivery trucks were expected from Switzerland, Herman would run home after school to watch the driver and his helper unload the cargo of leather. The stiff bundles of hide, flat and wrapped in burlap, were added to the shelves and arranged by type. Heavy leather for shoe soles was almost as thick as Herman's little finger and had a distinct toasted smell. Soft and supple, the finer, top-grade leather felt like butter between his fingers.

On the tossing deck of the *Husima Maru*, Herman pulled the blanket tighter and smiled to remember how Uncle Martin, who kept the books for the business, would come out of his office cubicle to greet Herman when he came to the basement rooms. The old man taught him how to tell by the feel and smell what kind of animal the hides came from and how to find blemishes. Herman sighed and pulled the blanket away from his face. The icy wind tugged at his hair and the cold, salty sea spray dripped off the end of his nose. He closed his eyes and thought of his mother, his comfort and anchor, a quiet, gentle lady always willing to listen. As much under Hugo's autocratic rule as her children, Clara formed an especially strong bond with her two youngest children, the two most in awe of their father. He knew his mother had never found happiness as a wife, and he thought now of her brief time of joy with Albert, hoping they might somehow be reunited.

Among the easy days of his childhood, Herman remembered a visit from his father's American-born cousin, Mae Spiegel. She arrived in a shiny touring car driven by a chauffeur who held the door for her and clicked his heels when she stepped out. Only nine years old, Herman thought she looked like a great actress or a duchess.

She had brought wonderful gifts. Herman would never forget his—a small, but authentic, Sioux outfit, complete with feather headdress and fringed, buckskin trousers.

He ran to his room to try it on, then returned to the salon where he danced around the adults, whooping and prancing. The feathered headdress flew out behind him as he circled the room.

Mae laughed and touched Herman's shoulder to slow down his encirclement. "My son, Arthur, chose your gift himself while he was home from Dartmouth for the summer. He used to have one just like it when he was a boy. He would gallop around the parlor and the kitchen, making chilling war whoops and getting underfoot as Cook tried to prepare meals. Once he borrowed table linens from the butler's pantry and used them and the dining chairs to build a teepee." She smiled. "Cook complained bitterly about having to send the linens to the laundress again, but I thought he was terribly creative."

Hugo's face turned stern and he glowered at Herman who knew the look meant, "Don't you dare try such behavior."

Now he was heading to America because his father's wealthy cousin and her brothers had vouched for him and guaranteed he would not become a public burden. Herman rubbed his cold nose and cheeks and snuggled deeper into the deck chair. The ship continued to toss and pitch as his feelings for his brother and sister welled up.

Friedel, the oldest and their father's favorite, was always considered the family's golden boy, his many talents gaining him the admiration of family and friends. Edith became the family bad girl. Her saucy attitude and the defiant toss of her long, blond braids revealed her rebellious nature. Herman was the baby, and because of that, the forgotten child. He didn't earn the criticism that went to Edith or the praise that fell to his brother. He dreamed of adventures, became deft at going unnoticed, and discovered this gave him unexpected freedom. Protected by his invisibility, he hung out with his own friends, rode his bike, and read about explorers and adventurers. Like many younger siblings, he watched his older brother and sister, and he was a good observer.

Now he pulled the blanket around him and felt the vibrations of the ship's engine through the wood of the deck chair. It was difficult to be confident when he could not make sense of the forces that had pushed his life to this point.

Herman's father made sure they were immersed in all things German. The only stories Hugo would take the time to read to his youngest child were from *Struwwelpeter,* a book of rhymed nightmarish stories illustrated with black-and-white drawings. Herman remembered especially the tale of the thumb-sucker with the drawing of the boy, blood dripping from his severed thumbs, and the tailor who had done the job, dancing in glee across the page. At Christmas, Hugo bought an enormous evergreen tree and set it up near the front window where the glimmer of the candles in its branches could be seen by anyone passing. But Hugo soon learned that neither *Struwwelpeter* nor Christmas would make his family German enough for Hitler.

Herman shivered under the heavy blanket and shook his head. He would not think of the Nazis. Better to remember the good times and adventures of boyhood, like when he had turned eleven and was hit hard by wanderlust. One summer morning he'd fearlessly pedaled his bicycle across the Werra Bridge, out of town, and into the countryside without telling anyone where he was going, each pocket stuffed with an apple and his heart ready for anything.

Long after darkness descended, Herman returned home, certain he'd get a beating from his father.

When he sneaked into the house, his father waited in the vestibule, arms crossed over his solid chest, legs planted firmly. In a low voice that allowed no response, his broad face devoid of expression, Hugo issued punishment. "To your room. Alone. No dinner. You will stay there until I say you can rejoin the family." Then he turned his back and stalked away.

Herman scurried up the stairs. In his darkened room, he sat on the edge of his bed and listened for the sound of heavy footsteps on the stairs. All was quiet. He threw himself down on his bed, somewhere between laughter and tears. He expected it would be days before he was released from solitary confinement. His father might forget about him entirely. It might be weeks until he remembered he had a second son. *I will be like the prisoner Phillipe, the king's brother, in Alexandre Dumas's book, The Man in the Iron Mask,* Herman imagined. *No one will even know I am imprisoned.*

Herman turned on his bedside lamp and hugged his knees. He let the memories of his day flood over him. The countryside had been full of wonders. Streams tumbled over stones and small fish swam in the shadowed pools. Roads led up to steep hillsides with a breathtaking view at the crest, and golden fields were planted with wheat or alfalfa or the twisted vines of potato plants.

He wondered if Friedel might still be up and listened for sounds, but the house had settled into nighttime quiet. All he heard was the growl of his hungry stomach. As he reached to turn off his light, he heard a soft footstep in the hall. His door opened a crack, and his mother stepped silently into his room. She carried a tray covered with a tea towel.

"Hermanle, are you still awake?" Her voice was barely audible. "I thought I saw a light under the door. I've brought you something to eat."

He began to speak, but she shook her head and set the tray on the top of his dresser. When she lifted the cloth, the pungent steam from cabbage and pork was released and made him salivate. His mother handed him the plate and a glass of milk. She smoothed back his hair with her gentle hand. "There's a piece of cake, too. Hide the tray under your bed when you finish," she whispered. "I'll get it in the morning after your father goes downstairs to work."

The next afternoon, as Herman lay on his back reading, Friedel and Edith slipped into the room. His brother looked at him with mock severity, his voice a stern imitation of their father. "What a bad boy you are."

Edith shoved Herman's outstretched legs to one side and bounced onto the bed. "It's about time you did something naughty," she said. An impish grin spread across her face. She crossed her legs and sat with her elbows resting on her knees. "Father says no one is to talk to you until he gives permission. It's such a shame. You're not even missing school because it's summer holiday!" She took the ends of her blond braids in her hands and wiggled them in a saucy way. "Right now father is in his office in the basement. Mutti is taking a nap, but she made you a sandwich before she went to her room."

"Keep it down." Friedel gave Edith a stern look. He reached up under his shirt and brought out a small parcel wrapped in brown paper. The smell of ham and pickle filled the room. "A little something for the prisoner from his mutti." He tossed the package to his brother, sprawled on the floor, and looked seriously at Herman. "I told Mutti to let me feed you from now on, except for the jail rations, of course. No need for her to get into trouble."

Herman nodded solemnly, his mouth full of sandwich.

Edith reached into her pocket and brought out a cookie. She waved it under Herman's nose, took a bite out of it, and handed the rest to him. "I am the dessert assistant, but I'll be taking a percentage." She giggled, clapped her hand over her mouth, and quieted down. "Now tell us what you did," she said. "We want to hear everything."

"I traveled for miles and miles, all on my own. I stood on top of a haystack and could see all the way to the horizon. All I had to eat was some apples I took from the kitchen, but most of the time I was having too much fun and I forgot to be hungry." Telling the story to his sister and brother was almost as delicious as the original bicycle adventure.

Six days later, Hugo issued the release order, but during those days Herman talked to Friedel and Edith more than he had since they became teenagers. They had been like the Three Musketeers in a conspiracy against an evil tyrant. He had a fine big brother to look up to and a sister who was a mischievous bandit. Afterward, his father continued to treat him with icy indifference, and Herman was surprised to find he no longer cared.

## CHAPTER 8

# JEWS CAN'T BE GERMANS

HUDDLED ON THE STORMY DECK of the *Husima Maru*, Herman wondered why he had paid so little attention to the changes that took place in Germany after Hitler came to power early in 1933. In his schoolboy innocence, he had believed none of it applied to him.

He remembered his father at the breakfast table, angry and frustrated by what he had read in the news. Hugo had scowled and slapped the morning paper down on the table sharply enough that the coffee cups rattled against their saucers. "Burning books! Thousands of books by great thinkers. The works of Albert Einstein, Sigmund Freud, and Heinrich Heine were burned at the University of Berlin last week."

Clara looked frightened, but Herman couldn't make out if it was her husband's anger or the news that upset her.

"Those damned National Socialists have only been in power for six months, and already the crazy man Hitler is head of state. Democracy is dead in Germany."

"Shh . . . shh . . . not so loud, Hugo," Clara whispered, and for once he did not contradict his wife.

By the following winter, a concentration camp for political prisoners had been set up outside Munich in a small town called Dachau. In February, Clara received a letter that brought fear and sorrow into their home. Her second oldest brother wrote that his son, the hope of the Kohn family, had been taken to Dachau as a political dissident. Herman vividly recalled his mother's anguish when a phone call a month later brought the news of her nephew's death soon after his imprisonment.

"Bloodlines! That's what the Nazis look at," Hugo said on a morning when snow still clung to the eaves. He spoke in a low tone though his eyes reflected his anger. "They are using terms like 'The German Master Race.' Anti-Semitism is back with a vengeance." He waved the paper under Clara's nose. "Look at this article. They are defining Jewishness on bloodlines. They care nothing for religious belief or practice. We must blend in. Do nothing Jewish. I'm glad my mother didn't live to see this."

Clara looked dumbstruck. Herman knew she must be thinking of her own family—her elder brothers and her three sisters who went to synagogue on the High Holy Days every year.

Hugo continued, oblivious to his wife's distress. "The Austrian keeps talking about racial purity. The Jewish race. The Aryan race. He knows nothing."

Friedel boldly looked up and tried to get into the conversation. "But Father, we aren't Jewish. Not since Grandmère."

"Tell that to the Nazis." Hugo's response was curt. He continued to rant. "Let me know how far you get. The newspapers are spewing the Führer's hatred and contempt. He talks of ridding Germany of all Jewish elements. He claims the Jews have dominated the nation's intellectual and financial life. The newspaper publishers follow his lead and write about Jews as ugly, ape-like, subhumans and picture the perfect German as a blond, blue-eyed ideal of pure Aryan stock. The typical Aryan looks like you, my dear son. But Hitler doesn't think of you when he talks of Aryans." Hugo pointed to the ugly cartoon on the front page of the paper. "Look at his lying cartoon. People will begin to believe this rubbish because they want to blame someone for their troubles."

Herman peered at the drawing. It showed a long-nosed, evil-eyed Jew robbing the pockets of a tall man in a top hat.

Friedel stood. "Father, I must go to school. All I care about is getting into university. Hitler is uneducated and a clown. He won't last long, don't you agree?"

Hugo grunted and pushed back his chair to stand. "We must hope so," he said. He flung his napkin on the table and stalked out of the dining room. Clara, Edith, and Herman sat in silence, nibbling on their cold toast.

But Hitler did not go away. Soon Jewish shops were boycotted and anti-Jewish graffiti smeared their windows. New laws prohibited Jews from being attorneys or holding jobs in civil service. Worst of all for Herman's brother, laws were passed that restricted the number of Jewish students in schools and universities. In rapid-fire succession, Jews were forbidden by decree to be journalists, artists, writers, farmers, or radio announcers. Jewish doctors were restricted to Jewish patients, and Jews were not allowed to employ Gentiles as servants. Suddenly Clara was doing all the cooking, though she was able to find a Jewish widow who needed the work to come and help with the cleaning of the big house once a week.

By spring, Hugo's voice was hushed at the family dinner table when he talked about the news. He warned Clara and the children that the laws required their family to live differently now. "We all need to be careful," he said. "Clara, stay home as much as possible. You must do the shopping yourself with no maid, but try not to go out otherwise. Edith, no pranks and devilment at school. If I get even one more call from the headmaster, you will be confined to the house. And Herman, be a good student, but not too good. Do not draw attention to yourself." He laid his hand on his oldest son's shoulder. "Friedel, I know you are looking forward to university and you've signed up to sit for the examinations next month, but you may as well forget about all that for now."

"But Father, I must take the exams. They can't stop me. I've paid the fee and studied hard for the last four months."

"Boy, be quiet and listen. I received a letter today from the Department of Education stating that even if you sit for the exam, your scores will not be recorded."

Friedel stared at his father in disbelief but held his tongue.

"As long as the current government holds power, no institute of higher learning in this country will accept you," Hugo said. "You may as well find something else to do with your life."

A few days later, Herman sat comfortably propped up on his pillows, reading by the glow of his bedside lamp. It was late, close to midnight, but he wanted to finish one more chapter. As he read the last sentence and closed the book, his brother quietly entered his bedroom and pulled the desk chair over next to the bed. "Listen, little brother," he whispered. "I'm leaving Germany as soon as I can."

Herman was taken by surprise. He opened his mouth to speak, but Friedel laid his hand on his shoulder. "Nothing you say will change anything. I can't stand it here. I've already applied for a visa and passport. And I've written to Father's uncle in America. I'm going. If I can't go to college, I'm going to America."

"But, Friedel, what about Mutti? And the rest of us? What should we do?"

"You'll be okay. Maybe it'll all blow over before you need to think about college." A troubled look clouded his face. "Hitler is evil. Surely the public will realize that soon and throw him out. I hope . . . ." After a moment he shook his head and forced a smile. "Anyway, Edith doesn't care about college. She's too busy thinking about boys to concentrate on her studies." He stood and continued. "I depend on you to look out for Mutti and Edith when I'm gone. Father will probably stay holed up in his office, protecting the business." He pulled his brother toward him and gave him a swift, tight hug. "Don't worry. I'm not leaving tomorrow. But as soon as my visa comes, I'm leaving. I wanted you to know." At the door he turned. "I'll write to Mutti, and you too, of course. And I'll tell you about all the exciting things I see in America."

Herman had always looked up to his older brother, so smart and talented, so popular. He was always surrounded by girls at parties who sat on his lap kissing him when they thought no one was looking. As a young teen, Herman watched and memorized Friedel's moves and hoped some-day he, too, would be surrounded by pretty girls to kiss. A warm glow washed through his body as he remembered the kisses he had shared with Molly—more than kisses. He laid his hand over his crotch and savored the hardness this memory created. He rolled to his side, removed his hand from between his legs, and curled up under the blanket. He would think of her again, later.

Now he was on a ship that steamed toward the United States. Like his brother before him, he headed for Chicago and the sponsorship of his father's relatives. The letters from Friedel after he left Germany had been infrequent, the messages hurriedly written. Herman remembered clearly the short letter that had arrived after Friedel had been in Chicago for barely a year.

*Dear Family,*                                    *March 3, 1934*

*Chicago doesn't suit me, though I like the art museum and the lakefront. Cousin Mae is very nice and has me for dinner once a week. Her brothers like being called "Onkel" rather than cousin, I think because they are so much older than me and it seems more respectful. The work Uncle (that's the American spelling) Walter gives me is easy enough, but I spend most of my time in an office in front of a typewriter. I'd rather be outside.*

*Next month I plan to leave here and travel west. I have gotten a chance to drive a car to California for a friend of Uncle's who is moving to Los Angeles, but first I must learn to drive. As soon as I finish the driving class, I am off to the Golden State.*

*I'll send you my new address when I have one. I am now using my American name of Frederick. Please address my letters that way from now on.*

*Love to you all,*
*Fred (That's what my friends in Chicago call me.)*

Herman had been allowed to remain in grammar school until graduation. But suddenly he had no social life. Even his best friend, Otto Warner, deserted him. As young boys, they had spent countless hours together, riding bicycles and playing games in the attic, but Otto, tall and blond, soon joined the Hitler Youth, an organization that not only excluded Jewish boys, but taught the membership to hate them. For a while, he continued to visit in order to brag about his adventures, but before long, he wouldn't even nod when they passed on the street. Herman still felt the sting of betrayal when he thought about it.

He spent his lonely afternoons at home, often in the attic room where he nurtured his fantasies of the French Foreign Legion, a place where background was not important. Lost in a world of books, he made himself ignore all the harsh changes outside, and he became adept at blotting out unpleasant thoughts. He would not acknowledge the ugly graffiti or the signs that shouted, "No Jews allowed." He ignored the low grades he was given for good work. He refused to think about how Holm, an Aryan accountant, forced his way into the family business and soon began to treat it as his own.

Left with little to live for, Hugo had died of heart failure one summer afternoon two years into the Nazi regime. Clara came home from shopping to find her husband sitting very still in his favorite chair on the front porch. His cigar dangled from his fingers. She had thought he was simply asleep until she smelled a curious acrid odor and noticed the cigar was burning the flesh of Hugo's fingers.

Only days later, Holm took over full ownership of the leather business, offering no compensation to the widow. All the hides were moved out, and he set up his newly acquired business in shop space recently vacated by a Jewish grocer.

Three months after Hugo's death, the Nazi Party issued the first of the sweeping Nuremberg Laws and it became difficult for Herman to ignore the changes. He was denied German citizenship, and equally distressing to him, it became a crime to date Aryan girls, the only girls he knew. The new laws defined what constituted a Jew and such designations as *Mischlinge* or mixed race "half-Jews." Herman vividly remembered the feelings of confusion and anger that swept through him when he read the laws in the newspaper. Jewishness was legally determined by the number of full-blooded Jewish grandparents a person had. Herman's cousin Max, whose father was a Bavarian Catholic, was designated a *Mischling* because he had only two non-Jewish grandparents. But all four of Herman's grandparents were Jews. He was, by law, 100 percent Jewish.

Now everything happened rapidly. The family home was sold to the architect who had designed it. A fair man, he converted two of the second-floor bedrooms into an apartment for Clara. Edith was hired at a Jewish youth camp caring for children who were boarded there while their parents tried frantically to arrange immigration to any place safer than Germany. At the end of the summer, she was issued a work visa for England, and believing anything, even being a housemaid in London, was better than staying in a place where it was a felony to walk hand in hand with her Aryan boyfriend, she left.

Barely fifteen, Herman was sent to live near his cousin in Suhl. There he enrolled in the local business school and worked at the hardware store, a pleasant job, counting nails, selling pots and kettles to farmer's wives, saws to their husbands, and nuts and bolts to buyers from the local bicycle factory. He boarded with the horse dealer and instantly developed a crush on his wife, the beautiful and kind Frau Mannheimer, who convinced her husband to hire Herman for the early morning job at his stables. Each morning, Herman cleaned the stalls and groomed the horses until their broad backs and powerful flanks glistened like satin.

But all of this was a world removed from the adventure Herman had dreamed about.

## CHAPTER 9

# A NEW LIFE BEGINS

THE CLANG OF THE SHIP'S dinner gong shook Herman out of his reverie. He stood up and made his unsteady way to the dining room. All the memories brought only grief and longing, hate and misery. He would bury them and enjoy the American life awaiting him.

A few days later, as the ship entered New York harbor and sailed past the Statue of Liberty, he stood at the railing and let the sensation of new beginnings wash over him.

The bus ride through the snow-covered country to Illinois took him farther and farther into his adventure, though concerns about the future pulled at him. What could he expect in Chicago surrounded by Jewish relatives who actually attended temple? And what would he find when he finally reached California? It had been six years since he had seen his brother, and there was Bonnie, the American sister-in-law, and a baby niece, too.

When he stepped from the bus into the pale light of

the Chicago Union Bus Depot, he felt the early December wind whip under his leather jacket and cut through the sweater beneath. Determined to stay positive, he pulled the jacket closed, zipped it, and bent to pick up his battered suitcase from the line of luggage the driver pulled from the underbelly of the Greyhound.

When he turned, the first sight greeting him was Fritz Meyer striding through the doors of the station building. It was as if the last year of waiting had never happened. Here they were, together again, safe in the dream place—America.

"Hermanle, Hermanle! You're finally here." Fritz swung his arm over Herman's shoulder, gave him a squeeze, and reached to shake his hand. He pulled Herman through the warm station and onto the street where a taxi waited, its engine idling. Inside, the cab smelled of stale cigarette smoke, sweat, and old upholstery.

The driver turned and smiled, extending his hand in greeting. "Meet my friend Rudi," Fritz said. "In Hamburg, he was a surgeon, but in Chicago, he drives a cab."

Rudi reached over the front seat and shook Herman's hand. "Welcome," he said. "And don't worry about me. Soon I'll get my Illinois state licensing. Then back to the white walls and bright lights. For now I actually enjoy driving people around." He laughed and added, "What better way to get to know Americans and this great city by the lake. These days, I'm almost as good a driver as I was a surgeon, and proud of it." He grinned, then turned to his task. Waving his arm energetically out the driver's window to slow the traffic, he pulled the cab into the busy street. "This is Wabash," he said. "Lake Michigan is off to the left. Did you see it coming in?"

Herman relaxed, surrounded by his cousin's excited, nonstop talk. "Everyone is waiting to see you! Well, except for Klairle's husband —he had to work—and our Anna. She didn't want to go to school this morning, but she must improve her English, and school with American kids is the best way. She is very quiet these days, but she soaks up everything. We hope. We have a one room apartment over a bakery. The smells in the morning are divine. It's not far from Isaiah Temple." He paused to take a breath, then rushed on. "Klairle and Hilda are preparing a special lunch for you at the Kleins' apartment. They live in Hyde Park. You'll stay there. Their kitchenette is bigger. Two bedrooms and a comfy couch for you. And Leonora is beside herself to see you again. She insisted on staying home and you know how stubborn she can be. But she must do her volunteer work this afternoon. She's a freshman in high school and after her classes she goes to help at the hospital. She wants to be a nurse, you know. She's very much the young lady now. You won't recognize her. She's grown up in the last few years. Cousins Herbert and Walter are expecting you tomorrow. I have to work, but I'll tell you later how to get to their office. Tonight you are stuck with the poor relatives. It will be cozy and very gemütlich. We want to hear everything."

At the door of her apartment, Klairle Klein, who had always been Herman's favorite older cousin, greeted him with a glowing smile and a kiss on both cheeks. Hilda came out of the tiny kitchen, wiped her hands on her apron, and enveloped him in a hug that smelled of onions.

The apartment was warm and comfortable, with a mix of new and secondhand furniture. The smell of good, German cooking filled the air. Klairle and Hilda could not restrain their questions. "How is Tante Clara? Is she finally safe in England? What do you hear from the Kohns? Is everyone safe?" During a lull, Cousin Klairle handed him a letter from his brother, which he slid into his pocket to read later.

"Any other letters? From England?" But there was nothing—not from Molly and not from his mother. He knew it was silly to even think about mail from Britain so soon.

He had barely taken off his jacket, when Leonora bounced into the room and gave him a huge hug, almost knocking him off balance with her enthusiasm. She was no longer the little girl Herman remembered. She stepped back and gazed up at him with her deep brown eyes. "You should go to Hollywood and be in the moving pictures. Ooh-la-la, with your stunning British accent you'd beat out Douglas Fairbanks, who's too old for my taste anyway."

As a girl, Leonora had been, by turns, both funny and serious, and she was always bursting with life. She hadn't changed. Four years younger than Herman and not blood related, she was the stepdaughter of Klairle Klein, her husband Felix's daughter by his first wife, who had died in childbirth. Herman and Leonora had been the two youngest in the family, and they were often thrust together at family gatherings, relegated to the attic while their parents talked about the changes in Germany. Herr Klein was one of the first to move his family to America soon after Hitler came to power. He had been a successful businessman, but now he worked as a manager in the mail-order business of their Chicago relatives.

In the five years since he had seen her, Leonora had blossomed into a fifteen-year-old flirt. Herman had to admit that her dark curls and tiny figure in her pink nurse's aide uniform charmed him, but she was still very young and couldn't compare to his sophisticated Molly.

Hilda and Klairle had prepared numerous traditional German dishes and they presented them proudly. Fritz poured coffee into Herman's cup while Hilda piled the table with dishes of German-style potato salad, chopped chicken livers on toast, pickled herring, and beets in sour cream. Leonora, sitting next to him, leaned over and whispered in his ear. "Bet you didn't eat like this in London. Mom and Hilda are full of plans to tempt you to stay with us in the apartment . . . and I'd like that too," she said. "I miss your stories and your naughtiness."

Herman leaned back in his chair and sighed with contentment. The rich food had made him drowsy. Leonora reached over and gave his arm a jerk. "Don't be falling asleep now," she said. "Not like your father used to do." She slid out of her chair and ruffled his hair as she passed behind him.

Klairle looked stern and shook her head. "Don't be fresh, young lady. You'll scare him all the way to California."

Leonora laughed and grabbed her coat. "Oh, Mother. Herman knows I'm kidding around." She turned to him and beamed. "I'm off for a few hours to pretend I'm a nurse. Cousin Mae got me such a wonderful chance to help at the Michael Reese Hospital. She is practically famous there for starting their volunteer program. I love it!" She went to a small mirror hanging by the door, twisted her thick curls into a chignon, poked in a few hairpins, and topped it all with a pink starched nurse's cap. She turned to cast another effervescent smile his way. "But don't worry, Cuz. I'll be back to torment you this evening." She slipped her arms into her heavy coat and flung herself out the door and into her Chicago life.

With her young exuberance gone from the room, the others began talking seriously of events in Europe, their elbows on the cluttered dining table as they leaned forward, eager to hear Herman's news. They asked him about life in London with its blackouts and war preparations, discussed what they had heard was happening in Germany, and shared news of relatives now dispersed all over the world—from England to Palestine, South America to Shanghai. During it all, Klairle jumped up to offer him more coffee and another slice of cake.

When Anna returned from school, Herman saw she had changed from the carefree little girl he remembered. He opened his arms to her, but she did not climb onto his lap. She came close, leaned against his thigh, and rested her hand softly on his knee. But she did not say a word. Occasionally she looked up at him, her large brown eyes serious and her smile tentative.

The afternoon turned to evening, Leonora returned, the women cleared the table of the afternoon's detritus, and

Felix returned from work. The aroma of roasting chicken filled the apartment, and Herman wondered how he could eat another bite. But when Klairle marched triumphantly out of the kitchen with a golden bird held high on a large platter, his appetite revived.

His cousin grinned when she set the plate in the center of the table. "The American president promised a chicken in every pot," she said and handed her husband the carving set. "Tonight we will help him keep his word."

Later, after the Meyers had smothered him with more hugs and returned to their nearby apartment, Herman lay on the living room sofa, thinking of all that had happened. The hall light filled the room with a soft glow. "I'll leave it on," Klairle had said, "so you won't feel lost in the dark."

Herman touched his cheek where the warmth of Leonora's good-night kiss lingered. "I'm glad you are here," she had whispered before she kissed him. "Now we will be Americans together. I'll teach you some American slang when I get home from school tomorrow. I've learned lots of great new slang from the kids in school." She had planted the impulsive kiss, giggled wickedly, and disappeared down the hall and into her bedroom.

Suddenly he sat up. He opened his suitcase, reached into the side pocket, and pulled out his German passport with its Nazi stamps and permissions. As long as he stayed in the United States, he would use his American immigrant identification card, stamped and sealed in New York. His German passport had gotten him into the United States and that was the main thing. He no longer cared about the rules and regulations of his native government. It had disowned him, and he would disown it. He had no intention of returning to his homeland until Hitler was gone. Herman searched through the drawers of a little desk in the corner of the living room until he found a fountain pen with a thick nib—just what he needed. In the dim light, he studied the document cover with the offensive "J" stamped on the upper right. With the pen, he carefully obliterated the letter until there was nothing to see but a black rectangle. He opened the passport to the first page with his name and picture. With bold strokes, he obliterated the phony middle name, "Israel," assigned by the Nazis.

Earlier that evening, while Klairle, Hilda, and Leonora cleaned up the dinner dishes, Herman had opened his brother's letter, reading it over twice before he could accept what it said. Short, to the point, and written in English, the letter from his brother was a shock.

*Dear Herman,*                    *November 20, 1939*

*Now is not a good time for you to come to us. Our house is small. With the baby and the long drive to work each day, Bonnie has a lot to worry about. Stay in Chicago until summer. Bonnie does not teach then and it will be better.*

*Your brother,*
*Fred*

Herman's eyes stung with hurt and anger. He felt put off and abandoned but had made the effort to hide his distress from the others gathered in the room. Fred had written previous letters saying he was welcome in their home, and Bonnie had often added her greetings. She had even signed papers declaring that, along with Uncle Herbert, she would give him financial support, a condition for his getting an immigrant visa to the United States. Now Herman could see something had changed. It appeared they no longer wanted him to live with them. Still, he was determined to go to California. He would make it on his own and not cause his brother or his wife any hardship.

First he had to visit with his father's cousins.

Herman had never met this pair of wealthy, bachelor brothers, but he remembered Cousin Mae talking of them affectionately when she had visited Meiningen. They were both successful merchants. Uncle Walter owned the large mail-order firm where Fred had been so dissatisfied, and Uncle Herbert, also an officer of the mail-order business, was involved with paints, plastics, liquor distribution, and investment counseling as well. They and Cousin Mae had generously contributed to the safety of many German relatives besides him, including the Meyers, the Kleins, and Friedel.

The next morning, following Fritz's instructions, Herman walked two blocks west to the Cottage Grove Line and took the streetcar north. In the downtown area, which Fritz had called "The Loop," he transferred to the elevated train that crossed the river and got off at the second stop. The day was clear and sunny, but a chill wind blew between the buildings. Herman held his fedora down with one hand and pushed the other deep into the pocket of his leather jacket.

Fulton Street was crowded with trucks loading up with meat and produce from the wholesale market. The air reverberated with the noisy shouts of men giving orders and the odors of exhaust, raw meat, poultry, and smashed onions. Among the hubbub, he found the brick pillars of the entrance to the offices of the Walter Field Company. Inside, it was quiet compared to the street, and he located Herbert Oberfelder's office without any trouble.

Herman was announced to the gentleman by a secretary. His elderly second cousin greeted him with a warm smile, shook his hand firmly, and looked him up and down. His gray eyes probed deeply and assessed the young man in front of him. "Welcome to America," he said. He seemed to consider what to say next and finally sighed. "Is that all you have to wear?" he asked.

Herman was startled. What was he supposed to answer? His clothes were not shabby and he had taken care to be clean and well-dressed. "No, sir, I have enough," he said. "Several more pairs of trousers and three shirts. But I don't have a suit jacket or a tie."

"That's not what I meant, son. You look fine. But it's cold here. The winter is bitter in Chicago. Don't you have an overcoat?" Herbert's voice was gentle, and now Herman could feel his concern.

"No, sir. No overcoat, but my jacket is warm enough, really. I have my sweater too, sir." He was determined not to appear needy or troublesome.

"You need an overcoat! This is Chicago, after all." Uncle Herbert walked across the room and took his hat off the rack near the door. "Let's go get you one."

"But, sir, I want to go out to California. My jacket should be enough there, don't you think?"

The old man turned to Herman. "It's still winter in California, my boy. Still winter. The wind in San Francisco can be icy, I'm told."

"But sir, Friedel, I mean Fred, is in Southern California."

"Never mind. If you are warm here, you might stay a day or so longer." He led the way out of the office, Herman following in his wake. Herbert stopped on the way out to speak to his secretary. "Cancel any afternoon appointments. Have the car sent round. Herman and I are going shopping," he said. "And remind Walter we'll see him tonight at Mae's. Dinner promptly at eight."

Herbert's chauffeured car pulled over in front of the State Street entrance of the Marshall Field and Company Department Store. They walked between four gigantic Ionic columns and into the store. Herman had never seen anything like it. The five-story, open central hall was crowned by a magnificent mosaic and dome of iridescent stained glass. Late morning sun streamed in through the skylight like honey. Uncle Herbert followed his gaze to the sparkling ceiling. He put his large hand on Herman's shoulder. "When the sun is out, this is the most magnificent place in the city," he said. "Created by Louis Comfort Tiffany. Simply splendid, don't you think?"

Herman continued to gaze in awed appreciation. "Like a rainbow after a storm," he said softly.

They walked through the store with its gleaming glass display cases, high ceilings supported by white columns, and aisles filled with chattering ladies in furs, their high-heels clicking on the tiled floors. When they finally reached the men's shop, the salesperson greeted the old man by name. "Mr. Oberfelder, sir. What can we do for you today?"

"We're here for an overcoat for this young man."

Herman tried on one coat after another, luxuriating in the soft warmth and classy styling. Once he glimpsed a dangling price tag. The cost made him gasp. He turned from his image in the full-length mirror and spoke. "Uncle, I can't let you buy me a coat like this. It's far too expensive."

Herbert chuckled and looked very pleased with himself. "Nonsense, son. It's something I want to do." He came over to stand behind Herman and straightened the shoulders of the camel hair and wool coat he was trying on. "This one fits perfectly. Even without alterations. It's too long though. You might want to get it shortened a bit when you get to Los Angeles . . . to be in style. What do you think?"

"I like it, sir. I like it very much, but the black wool is nice, too, and less expensive."

"No, my boy. The lighter-colored coat will be more suitable in Los Angeles." Herbert picked up the old leather jacket from the chair in the fitting area and handed it to the salesman. "Put the camel hair coat on my account, please. He's going to wear it. Please wrap his jacket in a parcel for us and have it sent to this address on Ingleside in Hyde Park." He jotted down the street number on a notepad the clerk offered. Herbert turned, ready to move on. "Are you hungry?" he asked. "I am! It's past noon and there is a lovely grill on the seventh floor."

The Men's Grill was a male sanctum with a circular domed, mosaic ceiling and round tables luxuriously covered with linens and silver flatware. "I highly recommend the famous corned beef," Uncle Herbert said. "Though I have to eat more lightly. At my age, a meal like that can sit heavy on the stomach."

Herman nodded in agreement and gave the waiter his order. Herbert ordered the codfish cakes for himself. When Herman's rose-colored meat arrived with perfectly round potatoes and wedges of tender cabbage, he was surprised by its succulence.

After the meal, they left the store and walked to the lakefront. They strolled toward the Art Institute and back again. Herman, wrapped in the warmth of his new coat, no longer felt the icy wind off the lake.

Uncle Herbert asked questions as they walked, and Herman poured out his disappointment at the withdrawal of Fred's invitation to live with him and his own determination to go to California, with or without his brother's help.

"He's still my brother," he tried to explain. "There's a special bond with family, even when they disappoint you. I appreciate all you're willing to do, but I long to see California. The sunshine, the movie stars . . . I've read all my life about Hollywood, and I'd like to see it."

Uncle Herbert smiled and patted Herman's shoulder. "I do remember what it's like to be young," he said.

"I used to dream of the sands of North Africa. Maybe the sandy beaches of California will be better." He hoped the elderly gentleman wasn't offended that he was eager to leave Chicago. "I'd like to get to know my sister-in-law and niece, too," he added.

After a while, Uncle Herbert's black car and driver rolled up to the curb. Herbert was delivered to his office, and Herman was driven back to Ingleside, where the driver reminded him he would be picked up for dinner.

That evening, he found himself in the midst of the elegant company of his wealthy relatives. Cousin Mae's home took up one entire floor of a stately building north of the Loop. The living room, with a fireplace at one end and a row of windows that overlooked the lake, was bigger than the Kleins' entire apartment. Besides Uncle Herbert, Uncle Walter was there, and Mae's son, Arthur Spiegel Jr.

The younger man greeted Herman warmly with a friendly smile. "I heard you liked the Indian outfit I helped Mother choose for you that summer she visited Germany. She told me that you made a fine, loud Indian."

"I was just a boy," Herman said, somewhat flustered. "But yes, I loved it. My mutti could hardly get me to wear my regular clothes for a while." He laughed softly when he remembered how Clara had finally hidden the tattered costume from him but had allowed him to tack the feather headdress to the wall of his room. He wondered what had become of it.

"It gave me such pleasure to see you wear it. You reminded me so of Arthur," Mae said. "My son will soon have a baby of his own. But we won't know for some weeks if it will be an Indian princess or an Indian chief."

The group laughed politely at Mae's humor.

Uncle Walter put his arm across Arthur's shoulder, their heads together, sharing confidences as the group walked into the dining room. "Those two are almost like father and son," Herbert whispered to Herman. "Especially now that they are cohorts working side by side at Walter's catalog company."

Over dinner, Herman had to tell everyone the same story about how much he wanted to go to California. "I hoped to keep you here in Chicago longer," Mae said. "But I can see you, like your brother, have a longing for the adventures of the West. After you dip your toes in the Pacific, you might come back one day and visit again."

Uncle Walter looked glum and said nothing. Herman had heard he was disappointed when Fred left. At least now he seemed to have Arthur as a protégé.

"A young man needs a dream," Uncle Herbert announced at the end of the meal. "I intend to do as I promised, wherever Herman chooses to go." On the drive back to Hyde Park later that evening, the old man promised to send Herman fifty dollars each month until he found a job, starting with three fifties he tucked into his nephew's pocket as he spoke. "This is spending money for your trip west," he said. "As soon as you get settled, send me your new address. Take your time finding a good job, and don't get married right away like your brother."

As they parted, the older man shook Herman's hand. "I know you'll do well wherever you go. You have a way about you that will attract good luck and good friends." A smile lit up his eyes. "You won't have much use for that new overcoat in Los Angeles, you know, but still I'm glad

I got it for you. Maybe it will remind you to come back, at least for a visit."

After only four days in Chicago, with the western sunshine and remembered cowboy stories luring him on, Herman bought a $40 ticket on a Trailways bus, less expensive than Greyhound, leaving the following morning for a trip that would take him south through St. Louis, Missouri, west across Texas, New Mexico, and Arizona, and finally to California. He sent a curt telegram to his brother.

*Arriving by bus Santa Ana 2 p.m. Dec. 22.*
*Short stay before going to Los Angeles.*

That evening, the dinner at the Kleins' apartment was subdued. Everyone gave him advice on managing in America and sent their greetings to Friedel. Unusually quiet and serious, Leonora sat next to Herman on the sofa after dinner, resting her head back against the cushions, her eyes half-closed. After a while, she turned toward him and sighed. "I'm going to miss you. I had hoped to have you here as my friend for a long time." She wiped the back of her hand across her face. "I love America, but I miss Germany, too. Sometimes I want to be the little girl in the attic again—the one who used to snuggle in your arms listening to the stories of Tarzan." She leaned forward, her elbows on her knees, her hands clasped together. "Will we always be friends?"

Herman took her slender hands in his and squeezed them. "Of course. We're family. And we'll always be friends."

Later that night he wrote his first American letter to his mother. Starting with news from all the relatives, including details of the fine dinner at Cousin Mae's home, he then copied out the words of Fred's letter and confessed his frustration and determination to go to California anyway. Finally he tried to reassure her and tested one of the slang phrases that Leonora had secretly taught him.

*Don't worry about me, Mutti. I can take a room in Los Angeles and find a job. If Fred doesn't want me, he can kiss my ass! Sorry, Mutti, but I feel that angry. Leonora says this is something all the boys in Chicago say when they think she can't hear. I must learn the latest American language so I will fit in.*

# CHAPTER 10
# LIKE PARADISE

THE LONG BUS TRIP ACROSS deserts and mountains dissipated Herman's anger toward his brother. Soon he would be in California. He imagined a place where a mild breeze filled the air with the aroma of orange and sage.

Fred, tan, his blond hair tousled, waited in the bus arrival area at the Santa Ana station and waved enthusiastically when Herman came down the bus steps. This older brother, who had been suave and sophisticated, who he had looked up to as the ultimate lady's man, was unshaven, dressed in denim jeans with wide rolled cuffs to accommodate his short legs, a well-worn khaki shirt, and scuffed leather boots. He seized Herman's suitcase and clasped his hand in a strong greeting.

"Well, little brother," he said, his blue eyes twinkling, "You are a stubborn one. But, actually, I'm glad you're here. I've missed you!" Fred strode through the building toward the sun-flooded street where an old Ford was parked at a red-painted curb. "Your timing is good," he said over his shoulder. "Bonnie is off for Christmas vacation, and her family loves these holidays. You are in for a big American celebration."

"I don't want to cause trouble," Herman said, once they were in the car, his suitcase, his overcoat, and fedora thrown in the backseat. "I can manage fine on my own." Fred's warm welcome didn't match his memory of the letter, and he plunged on. "I can only stay for a few days. I want to get to Los Angeles as soon as possible. I need to find a job."

Fred glanced over at Herman as he fiddled with the starter button. "Nonsense." His voice was firm. "Christmas time is different. You'll stay until New Year's for sure. Bonnie can drive you to Whittier when she goes back to teaching. That's where her school is, and it's more than halfway to Los Angeles."

Herman shrugged. He would decide once he had met his sister-in-law. Maybe she would be as easily charmed as the stern Aunt Nelda.

The drive to Laguna was both beautiful and perilous, the car in such bad repair Herman feared it would fall apart any moment. Yet Fred drove with abandon on the narrow road. They passed orange groves and wound into a canyon, the hills on either side covered in golden grass and blue-gray sage. Occasionally they passed a herd of brown-and-white beef cattle, munching contentedly on dry stubble. The beasts lifted their heads and moved away from the road when Fred tooted his horn. The gray-white twisting sycamore trees, their leafless branches sometimes adorned with greenish bundles of mistletoe, were the only hint that it was winter.

The road emerged from the close standing hills and burst into the little town of Laguna Beach. The Pacific Ocean glistened ahead. Blue water sparkled in the sunshine. There was a broad sandy beach, fronted by a wooden boardwalk with a bowling alley, several shops, and a big signboard that read "Benton's Café, Best Apple Pie." They rattled south, down Pacific Coast Highway, past the Spanish tower of the Hotel Laguna and clapboard beach cottages with flowers spilling around their gardens.

His brother's Spanish-style cottage was near a creek that trickled down Bluebird Canyon and into the sea. A poinsettia with dozens of wide, deep-red flowers grew near the front door. Behind the house stood a thick grove of eucalyptus trees. Their peeling, dun-colored bark covered straight, thin trunks and their silver leaves fluttered in the breeze, spreading a medicinal scent.

Bonnie was tall with chestnut hair and quiet eyes, her welcome reserved but friendly. She smiled as she offered Herman coffee or tea. When Fred insisted on opening a bottle of wine to celebrate, she walked to the living room and resumed work on the half-decorated Christmas tree without further comment. Precisely and carefully, she draped its branches with long strands of shiny, foil tinsel that resembled icicles. The baby, little Marie, stood in the playpen and waved her chubby hand. She made burbling sounds in greeting and her bright eyes took in everything.

Herman and Fred sat at the kitchen table and sipped an inexpensive red wine from jelly glasses. The rooms gradually filled with delicious smells that promised a good meal and Herman relaxed. He was welcome here—maybe not as a permanent houseguest but certainly for a few days.

He soon found that Christmas in California was not a holiday of goose and snow. The day was warm and balmy. His sister-in-law was up early to get a small turkey stuffed and in the oven. In honor of Herman's visit, she had prepared a German Stollen. It was her first attempt at making this traditional holiday yeast bread studded with dried citron and raisins and topped with a light dusting of powdered sugar. She placed it on a pretty glass plate and smiled shyly when she set it on the table at breakfast.

In the late morning, Fred appeared downstairs ready for the beach. He strode into the living room in his bathing suit, his chest bare, a striped towel slung over one shoulder. Herman was on the floor playing with the baby. Fred squatted next to them and built a tall pile of blocks. Marie swatted at the tower, then looked at her father, her eyes wide. Fred laughed and stood up. "Come on, brother," he said. "Do you have a swimsuit? If not, I have an extra, but it's got a hole in the ass." At Herman's puzzled look he added, "My new Christmas tradition is a plunge in the Pacific."

Five minutes later, Herman struggled in the tiny bathroom to pull on the old suit. He tried to check the rear to make sure the hole wasn't too big, but he heard his brother's impatient call from downstairs. "Come on, Hermanle. Come on."

The brothers walked the two blocks to the beach, scrambled over some rocks, and jumped down to the sand. In spite of the dazzle of the sunshine, there was a chill to the air. Fred spread his towel over a boulder, ran to the water's foaming edge, and dove under a cresting wave. Herman followed, amazed to find the sea cold, though not icy. His brother swam straight out through the waves, seemingly headed for the island that floated on the horizon. Herman stayed where the swells carried him up and down with the surge and surveyed with wonder the houses perched along the rocks overlooking the sea. He was living an adventure as good as any in a book.

After the swim, they sat on a rock wrapped in their towels.

"I met Bonnie on a beach near here." Fred ran his fingers through his wet hair. "I had hitchhiked to Laguna and couldn't wait to plunge into the Pacific. It was almost evening when I came out of the water, nearly frozen. I didn't have a towel, and I was so chilled I had to slap myself to keep warm. I saw the glow of a bonfire down the beach and headed toward it, elated to see a group of girls sitting around, roasting marshmallows on sticks and singing. Each lady was more gorgeous than the next—their faces aglow in the firelight. They seemed like nymphs of the sea, waiting for a man to enchant . . . me!" He laughed at the thought of that fateful evening. "I went right over with as much brass as I could muster, all blue and practically naked, and asked if I could sit with them and warm up."

Herman was delighted by the picture that formed in his mind. "I'm sure you charmed them all."

"They fell in love instantly with my shivering body and stunning German accent. It was hard to decide which one I should seduce."

"Was Bonnie the prettiest of all those girls?"

Fred chuckled. "Well, they were all pretty. Bonnie seemed the most intelligent, which attracted me, and the most adventurous, in spite of being shy and quiet."

Herman hadn't noticed any adventurousness in Bonnie but was willing to see his brother's perspective. "What dreams of adventure does she have?"

Fred shook his head a bit sadly. "Well, we both have our adventures on hold for a while. My seduction was a bit too complete." He looked away for a moment and turned back with a determined smile. "Now we have our beautiful surprise baby, and it's time to make a home." He looked out to the distant horizon and the profile of Catalina Island. "Bonnie traveled to Europe on her own a few years ago and loved it. She is more sophisticated than her sisters. She was fascinated by my foreign ways and fell for me totally. That, in itself, may be a bigger adventure than she counted on."

Adventures and love. Herman thought of Molly, left behind in London while he had traveled halfway around the world to land in paradise. It seemed to him that adventure and romance didn't mix very well.

THOUGH HERMAN SAW THE CHARMS of the beach town and was gradually making friends with Fred's quiet wife, he stayed only two weeks, anxious to move on and start his new life. His letter to his mother told it all.

*Dear Mutti,*　　　　　　　　　　　*December 28, 1939*

*The temptation to live here is huge. That is the danger of this place. Many people come to Laguna and don't* ever go away again. They live happily here for the rest of their lives because it is so beautiful. This is probably what will happen to Fred. He is perfect for Laguna, and it is perfect for him. He fits right in with the ocean and the artists. There is even a small local theater, and I'm sure he will soon be a part of that, too. He is still good with words and is writing stories in English which he tries to get published. If only he can find a way to make a living here, he will push down roots. For now he is dependent on Bonnie's income as a teacher, and he takes care of the baby. A funny activity for Friedel, don't you think? In this situation I can understand why I might be an unwelcome addition.

I have made up my mind. I want the excitement of city life and in a few days I will go to Los Angeles to find a room and a job.

Hugs from your loving son,
Herman

# CHAPTER 11

# IMMIGRANT IN A GOLDEN LAND

LOS ANGELES WAS THE THIRD bus station Herman had arrived at in the last month, but this time there was no one to meet him. He collected his suitcase, bought a copy of the *Los Angeles Times*, and sat on the hard waiting-room bench, the paper spread across his knees. He was tired of living in other people's homes and wanted a place to call his own. He turned to the rental section and scanned the page for an inexpensive room.

By evening, he had used half of what remained of the advance from Uncle Herbert to pay the first month's rent for a small furnished studio apartment on Alvarado Street. It had everything he needed—dishes, one cooking pot and a small skillet, a few utensils, a two-burner gas cooker, and hot and cold running water in a little sink. There was a phone in the vestibule and a shared shower and toilet down the hall.

That night, Herman sat at the tiny table in his room, the newspaper open now to the help-wanted pages. Soon penciled circles were scattered up and down the columns of newsprint as he found ads that sounded possible—office clerk, busboy, stock boy at a Bullock's Department Store, and hospital attendant. He hoped he would find a job as easily as a place to live.

The next day he took his first ride on the "Red Car," one of the city's electric streetcars, and started going to interviews. At several places they said they would call him back, but he couldn't help wondering if this was a way of brushing him aside. The jobs weren't very exciting anyway. The hospital was way out in Pasadena, far from the downtown area where he had already paid a month in advance on his room. The clerical job would be like his work at Fritz's Hardware in Suhl—inside too much, filing and copying figures into a book, always bored and isolated. Still, he needed to take it if they called back.

On his fourth day in LA, Herman waited again at the streetcar stand, the folded classifieds under his arm. He wondered if he should consider hitchhiking. Fred had done it, and he noticed a lot of young men used this as a way of getting around town. They stood on the curb and casually flung their thumbs toward the oncoming traffic. He was amazed to see how many cars stopped to give rides to strangers. It looked like a fun way to get from one place to another and certainly a way to meet people. He decided to give it a try. He walked to the edge of the street and watched the cars as they moved down the avenue. Finally he took a deep breath and stuck his thumb in the air as a shiny, green convertible came toward him. To his surprise, it pulled over to the curb, and the driver, a lanky, freckled man with a rust-colored mustache and red hair, leaned across and beckoned. "Need a ride, buddy? Where're you headed?"

"To Broadway, downtown, sir. Are you going that way?" Herman was thrilled by the idea of riding in a big American car with the top down, and in January, too, something impossible to do in London or Chicago.

The driver reached across and opened the passenger door. "Hop on in. Broadway, it is." The driver maneuvered back into the traffic, then turned to Herman and gave him a steady look. "Are you new to Los Angeles?" he said.

"Yes, sir. I arrived four days ago. This is my first time accepting a ride." Herman was unsure of the protocol but decided it was best to be friendly. "My name is Herman. Herman Lang. I appreciate you picking me up."

"William Bauer. Pleased to meet you." With his left hand on the wheel, the driver reached out and clasped Herman's hand with a firm and vigorous shake. "I'm cruising around looking at the female scenery," he said. "You looked like you might share my interest."

"Yes, sir. Pleased to meet you, sir." For a few moments, Herman felt nervous to hear the man's German name, but soon he settled into the creamy leather of the seat. Its familiar aroma reminded him of his father's storeroom. He allowed his hand to caress the dashboard, painted the same pale green as the car itself, the radio knobs shiny chrome. "Your car is beautiful," he whispered.

William nodded his head in thanks. He had a nonchalant way of driving with only one hand on the wheel. He looked to the left and right as he drove, admiring the girls who strolled along the sidewalks. Once he even gave a low whistle when a tall girl in heels, her skirt swishing in the breeze, passed in front of them on the crosswalk.

Herman was enjoying the ride. "This is my first time in a real California convertible. I spent the last year in London and most of the cars there are black."

"Guess you left London just in time. The news says things are getting a bit rough over there."

"I'm glad to finally be in the US, that's for sure," he said. In the moving car the air felt chilly, and Herman pulled his leather jacket closer. His warm, camel's wool overcoat hung in the back of his small closet, unused since his arrival in California, and he was sorry not to have it with him. The sun shone down brightly and he wished he had darkened glasses like William wore. The street they were on now was different from the neighborhood where his gray apartment building rose from a dirty sidewalk. The boulevard was lined with palm trees and Spanish-style stucco buildings painted white, tan, light green, and pale pink, their tile roofs glowing red and their arched entranceways offering a peek beyond to lush gardens and hidden patios.

William slowed and stopped at a traffic light. "Where did you start out? I detect something other than British in your accent."

Herman hesitated a moment. He wondered if Americans disliked Germans as much as the English did, but he swallowed his doubt and decided to be honest. "I grew up in Germany," he said, "But I don't like what's going on there now, so I left."

"So right! But I thought your accent had something familiar about it. My parents came over from Germany forty years ago. Both of them still have an accent."

Herman didn't know whether this was good news or bad, but he thought it was probably okay. If William's parents had left Germany that long ago, they would, most likely, think like Americans and not be Nazi sympathizers. It was obvious that William was more American than German.

"My parents were from near Frankfurt. That anywhere near where you're from?"

"No, Meiningen, my town is farther north and east. Not very close at all. But I went through Frankfurt on the way to England. It was several hours by train from my home."

"By US standards, that's practically neighbors." William had a hearty, friendly manner. "By the way, where exactly do you need to go? We're almost downtown."

Herman checked the notes he had scrawled in the margin of the newspaper. "Seventh and Broadway," he read. "You can let me off anywhere that's easy for you."

"Job hunting? What kind of work are you looking for?"

"Actually I'm not sure. In Germany, I went to business school and worked in a hardware store, but I'd like to try something more exciting. I found I didn't like office work."

"So what do you think would be exciting?"

"Well, my brother was an exercise boy for the horses at the race track when he first came to Los Angeles. That was pretty exciting, I guess. But I want to be in the city . . . downtown or in Hollywood . . . anywhere there are lots of people. I want to practice English and get an American accent instead of an English one." He looked at the circled ad on his newspaper again. "Today I was going to apply for a stock boy job at a department store. Bullock's. Do you know it?"

William shook his head. "Sure. It's a big place but stock boys spend most of their time in the basement. Not many people to talk to there, except other stock boys, maybe a stock girl or two."

"Oh . . . well . . ." Herman didn't like the idea of working in a basement, though working with girls would be nice. "I need to start somewhere soon. I have to pay my rent and stand on my own two feet. Stock boy won't be very exciting, but it's Los Angeles. Nothing here could be totally boring."

William smiled broadly, showing his white, evenly spaced teeth. "This may be your lucky day. I'm the head bartender at a place on Wilshire Boulevard, the Zebra Room in the Town House Hotel." The traffic was getting thicker and he paused to downshift, slowing the car. "I'm friends with the manager of the hotel's restaurant. He's always looking for busboys. There's a lot of turnover because the work is hard." They were stopped at a red traffic light, and William turned in his seat to face Herman. "It's not downtown, but it is one of the best hotels in all Los Angeles. There's another Bullock's out on Wilshire, too, a much fancier one than downtown. If you're interested in working at the Town House Hotel, I can check with my friend and see if he needs someone."

Herman was able to nod his head and clear his throat. He didn't want to sound too excited, in case this was a jest of some kind. "That would be great!" He added because he hoped to sound more businesslike, "What kind of pay, do you think?"

"That I don't know exactly. I make forty dollars a week, but bartenders are highly trained and have a lot of prestige in this town. Being a busboy is at the bottom of the ladder, so it'll be a lot less. Our clients are upper crust at the Town House. They give good tips. I think you could manage . . . depends on your rent though. Most of the waiters are German or Swiss, and they'd help you get started." The light changed to green. William put the car into gear and moved forward. "If you're interested, I'll look for a pay phone and we'll give my friend a call. What do you say?"

"Yes, sir! I'd like to check it out."

After that, everything happened so fast he could scarcely take it all in. An hour later, William dropped him on the sidewalk in front of the Town House Hotel. "Just go inside and through to the restaurant. Ask for the manager. He's expecting you." Herman crossed the sidewalk. Still feeling a bit hesitant, he looked back nervously at his new friend.

"You're a shoo-in for the job," William called as he prepared to drive away. "So, I'll see you tonight. I come on at five p.m."

Twenty minutes before noon, Herman stood at the back of the Wedgewood Dining Room. The tables that filled the restaurant were covered in fine linen and set with real silver. A bud vase with a single red rose adorned each table. He glanced down at his worn brown shoes, the scuffed leather looking out of place with the spotless white uniform he had been given to wear.

The manager had been clear. "Get yourself some white shoes by tomorrow."

Herman ran his hand down the front of the white jacket with its gold buttons and "Town House" embroidered in gold letters above the pocket. The waiters had warned him lunch hour would be crazy, and he was nervous as he waited for the crowd to appear.

By noon, more than half the tables were filled and Herman was on the run. He had to concentrate in order to remember all he had been told before his shift started. Give the bread, butter, ice, and water right away. There must be three pieces of ice, two pieces of butter, and two rolls. When a patron left, he must clear the tables quickly and quietly. He had to use a small silver scraper to clean off all crumbs or change the linen if it was stained. The fresh silver and napkins had to be placed a certain way, everything according to Town House standards. In addition to all that, he was the attendant to the waiter and must pass him each plate to be presented to the diner.

He learned quickly, and by the third day, the waiters sometimes asked him to serve the orders when they were very busy. Until recently, the Town House had been an apartment hotel and some of the long-term tenants remained as guests. They expected personalized service, and he memorized their idiosyncrasies quickly, greeted them by name, and cheerfully served them what they wanted. The Saudi prince demanded extra green olives and the Duchess wanted her coffee black—she would not tolerate cream or sugar at her table.

He worked the lunch and the dinner shift and returned exhausted to his room after 11:00 p.m. with only enough energy left to set his alarm and fall into bed. It wasn't until the middle of his second week of work that Herman was able to write to his mother during a meal break.

*Dear Mutti,*　　　　　　　　　　　　*January 15, 1940*

*I'm now a "busboy" in the best hotel in California. It's on Wilshire Boulevard, the best street in Los Angeles. The work is hard but exciting. I never knew I could be so popular. I'm the youngest guy working in the dining room and at first they called me "Liebling." Most of the waiters speak German, which is not good for me learning English.*

*From morning to night, everywhere I hear, "Hallo, Herman. Wie geht es Dir? Hallo Liebling! Hallo Herman!" Everybody offers to help me learn the job. Yesterday they have given me a new nickname. They now call me Blitzkrieg because I'm like a lightning bolt in the dining room!*

*Of course, it's hard work and a lot of hours. I start before lunch and usually don't get off until nine in the night, and sometimes not until after midnight. But then I get overtime pay. No other busboy lasted very long at this job because it is too much work. Usually they leave after a few weeks. I know I can do it longer because I love it!*

*Hugs to you and Edith and baby Hazel.*

*Your son,*
*Herman*

# CHAPTER 12

# MAN ABOUT TOWN

*Dear Mutti,*            *February 10, 1940*
*(or Mom, as we say here in California),*

*Last week I was down to visit Fred, and I found three letters from you. I was very glad to get your news and to hear that everybody is well. I had the day off and it was raining. When it rains here they call it "liquid sunshine." It only snows in the mountains, which I could see from the bus on the ride to Laguna Beach. It is funny to look over palm trees and see the snowy mountains not far away.*

*I like to visit Fred's little family. Baby Marie is cute and smart. She is barely two years old and already very stubborn. She reminds me a bit of Edith because she likes to be naughty.*

*I wrote to you in my last letter about my job in the dining room in the best hotel in LA. This is finished, but don't worry, I have a new and better job.*

*After only three weeks in the dining room, I was moved to the nightclub! I guess they like that I learn so fast and stay happy. My friend William works in the bar, too. It is called the Zebra Room. There are only carefully selected men serving in the bar. There are four waiters and I am one of only two busboys. Only very international and experienced men who have worked a long time for the hotel usually get promoted to the cocktail bar. And I got the job already! I can't serve the drinks because I'm not yet twenty-one. That is the law here. But I can serve the special dinners. I almost didn't get this job because I'm too young, but the manager applied for a special permit for me. He said he absolutely wanted me.*

*Say hello to Aunt Nelda when you see her, and thank her for teaching me such good English.*

*Your busy son,*
*Herman*

Herman was sure he had landed a job in one of the most exciting nightclubs in Los Angeles. The Zebra Room Cocktail Lounge, its tall chairs upholstered in zebra skin, hummed with action from afternoon until long after midnight. Film stars and wealthy socialites came to be seen and to dance to the sounds of a big band and the latest crooners. Live dance music from the Zebra Room was broadcast every night by radio to listeners around the city.

In the late afternoon, the darkened rear booths offered seclusion for couples, while other booths filled up with chatty groups of rich, sorority girls from the University of California up Wilshire Boulevard. In the evening, ladies dressed in long, flowing gowns arrived on the arms of their dates. Diamonds and pearls glittered on their slender throats, ears, and fingers. Their upswept hair shone in the lamplight, the curls held with combs adorned with sequined butterflies or jeweled flowers.

These women mesmerized Herman. He always carried one of the zebra-striped match packets in his pocket and watched for the flash of red nail enamel as a lady gestured with an unlit cigarette between her fingers, a signal for him to rush to her table and hold a flaming match in his steady, cupped hands. As she leaned toward him, he could smell the heady scent of her perfume until the first puffs of smoke rose and he had to wave out the match and back away.

Later, movie moguls and other important business types came to enjoy the music and to relax after a day of big decisions. They lounged at the rear tables, smoked cigars, sipped brandy, and left big tips.

It was Herman's job to make everyone happy. He helped the waiters, served dinners, cleaned ashtrays, carried away empty glasses and dirty plates, and smiled. Sometimes it seemed his infectious smile was the most important qualification for the job. His grin was natural because he had never been happier. He enjoyed working with William Bauer, watching the glittering women, and talking to all the famous people, even if it was only to say, "May I take your coat, sir?" Within a few weeks Herman was promoted to head busboy. The work was hard and his shift was from 5:00 p.m. to 3:00 a.m., but he was making about $25 a week including ample tips. Every evening he got a good meal at the club and he was proud to see his shoulders and chest fill out from lifting the heavy dish-laden trays.

He made friends easily at the Town House and in the Zebra Room. Two of the good-natured waiters were older Germans who had come to America as children and they took him under their wing. They mainly ignored the news from Europe and he wrote his mother, "They're German, but not a bit like Nazis." They owned cars and property, and one owned a large chicken farm in the San Fernando Valley. Their success was Herman's new inspiration, though he definitely didn't see himself raising chickens.

His mornings were leisurely. After a late breakfast, he listened to concerts on his new radio, read the *Los Angeles Times,* or wrote letters until it was time to head for work in the late afternoon. Most nights he collapsed in bed by 4:00 a.m., though often he went with his new friends to the bowling alley that was open around the clock. On his weekly day off, he usually went to see the latest cinema. He leaned back in the cool of the darkened theater, nibbled popcorn, and watched the screen for actors whose cigarettes he may have lit the night before at the Zebra Room.

The romance and love stories of the movies reminded him of Molly. When he looked at the movie posters or the billboards of pretty girls posed with a bottle of Coca-Cola, he longed for her touch. At night he sometimes drifted to sleep full of imagined futures in which she joined him in California and they lived by the ocean in Malibu. He wrote long letters to her, filled with stories of Los Angeles and Hollywood.

He hoped she would follow him to America but knew she could not as long as the war raged. Her letters to him were always sealed with a lipstick kiss. "I keep the lipstick you sent in a special place (I know it was from you, silly boy) and wear it only when I write to you," she said in one letter.

He was only able to visit his brother every month or so. The bus trip was long and involved a transfer in Santa Ana with a bad connection that made it difficult for him to get back to work in time the next day. When he did make it to Laguna, he and Fred always went for a walk on the beach in order to talk out of Bonnie's hearing. Whatever they started talking about, it always came around to the same subject in the end.

"I'm worried about Mutti and Edith," Herman would find himself saying. "The news from England is bad. Besides the bombs and air-raids, Mutti writes about the shortages and how difficult it is to get milk for the baby."

"Edith should have thought of that before she got pregnant again." Fred sounded impatient with their sister.

"I don't think she meant to. You should understand how that goes."

"Okay. Don't remind me. But twice? That's stupid. And from what you've said her husband is a—"

"There's nothing for her to do now but manage . . . or leave him. But I doubt she will. It looks bad to leave a soldier during war time. The trouble is Mutti's in the middle of it." He stood a moment and let the cool water from a wave flow over his toes. "She's fighting all the time with Edith and her letters sound desperate." The two brothers stood together in the sand and watched the surf as Herman continued. "And she keeps asking for us to do something to help Albert."

"There's nothing we can do. It's war now, not politics." Fred sounded angry again.

"I know. I know . . . but I'm worried that she'll try to go back to Germany to be with him."

"Not damn likely! Don't be overdramatic." His brother was rough these days but he still always managed to sound confident. "Mutti's not stupid. She knows it would be suicidal to go back, and while the war rages, it would cost a fortune through Spain. Besides, she knows everyone else is trying desperately to get away from Germany. She won't try to go back."

"But Friedel, we need to do something to help." Herman hoped using his brother's childhood name would soften him. "Mutti's waited so long for her US visa, and now she's stuck in England at the worst time."

Fred combed his fingers through his hair. "When she gets her visa and comes," he said, calmer now, "I promise she can live with Bonnie and me in Laguna. She can take care of Marie. Then maybe I can get more work." He shook his head and added, "But for now, I can't help financially. I don't have much that's mine, you know. I give Bonnie what little I make from the paper route. I've begun to get a few gardening jobs. Maybe I can help a little if that picks up."

Herman knew his brother's situation was tough because it was Bonnie who supported their family, but still he was disappointed. He would have to smile more and make more tips so he could help their mother on his own.

When he returned to Los Angeles, he wrote his mother a long letter.

*Dearest Mom,*                    *April 10, 1940*

*You know I always try to tell you only pleasant things because I want to cheer up your life. I hope I can do this for you as long as I live! Right now I am listening to my favorite radio station, and I think how nice it would be if you were here to listen with me. They are playing the Concerto in D by Paganini. It's grand.*

*But you are not here, and I'm awfully sorry about your troubles and your sorrows. I often think how sad it is that, though you are the mother of a very happy son, you can't do anything to banish your own unhappiness. Please try not to worry about everything and enjoy some of the small pleasures. Kiss and hug your granddaughter and knit a bobble-hat for the new baby. Can you still get knitting wool? In America they call it yarn. I can send you some if you can't. Shall I send blue or yellow?*

*Can you find a job for yourself? Maybe as a nanny or baby nurse? Then you could find a place of your own or live with some rich family. You would be away from Edith's cramped flat and the turmoil there. Please think about this idea.*

*And think how lucky you are not to be in Germany now!*

*When you come to California, you will see that this is a place that makes everybody happy and carefree. Life here is all singing. The popular songs are only about happy feelings, but mostly love! The people of Los Angeles hardly notice that Europe is at war. They talk of money and horse races, tennis, and the latest moving pictures, and what famous person has gotten divorced. I am very enthusiastic about California. Everyone here is happy! I know when you are in Laguna and living with Friedel and Bonnie, your life will be bliss compared to London.*

*Remember what Cousin Renata said to do to stay happy? We used to think she was silly, but she always had a smile on her face. She said, "Look into a mirror and say three times to yourself, 'Hilwerbobo!'" A nonsense word will cheer you up every time.*

*Your loving son,*
*Herman*

A week before his birthday, Herman moved to a better apartment closer to the Town House. It was carpeted and furnished with a sofa, a table, and a wall bed. Best of all, it had a modern bathroom with a shower and toilet, "everything included." It only cost an extra $10 a month over what he had been paying. He was making such good tips that he was able to begin to send a little money to his mother regularly, too.

He had been watching the mail and had told his old manager to forward whatever came. Finally, a birthday package arrived from London. It had only a small dent in one corner and the all-important lipstick print below the address. He cut the twine with his pen-knife and ripped the brown paper off in great hunks. He hoped the gift would be something with romantic promise.

Inside, wrapped in tissue, lay a pair of handsome driving gloves and a note. He unfolded the pink stationery and was disappointed to find only a few impersonal words.

*For when you get your car. Happy Birthday!*
*Your friends, Molly and Betsy.*

From both of them? No special note to him from Molly? He searched through the tissue twice but found nothing more. He was turning twenty, and he still felt like a teenager mooning over a distant girlfriend.

On his birthday, he went to work as usual. The last hours of his nineteenth year were spent lighting cigarettes and serving meals to rich tycoons and their jewel-covered ladies. He brought cherry-decorated drinks to spoiled college girls escorted by equally spoiled boys his own age. He could not help feeling sorry for himself—he longed for a girlfriend of his own, one he could touch and hold in his arms.

At midnight, the band master stepped up to announce the next set and spoke into the microphone. "Please join us for a special musical arrangement in honor of our favorite bar boy." He searched the crowd in the dimly lit room and pointed toward Herman when he spotted him among the tables. "For the one and only Herman who is twenty years old today," he said. He turned back to the band, raised his baton, and tapped his foot. "One, and two, and . . ." With elaborate fanfare, the dance band broke into a lavish rendition of "Happy Birthday."

Herman could feel his chest swell with joy, and he was ashamed of feeling sorry for himself five minutes before. The band finished the birthday song, and some of the customers stood and clapped. When the band began playing "Bluebirds in the Moonlight," the strains of the song filled the room, and the rich ladies and gentlemen he admired rose to dance to the fast, jazzy music. He couldn't help but tap his foot as the vocalist began to sing the lyrics.

It was truly a silly song, but every time he heard it, he remembered his last evening in London, holding Molly's hand in the cinema and watching the cartoon characters dance, and then afterward . . . How had the bandleader known the song was special to him? He looked toward the bar and William smiled, made a flamboyant sign with his hand, and gave him a small bow.

With his pocket full of the extra tips he made on his birthday, Herman decided to celebrate. Some weeks before, he had paid a deposit on his first car and now he had enough money to pick it up. It wasn't much of a car—a ten-year-old black Buick—but it ran and would make getting around LA and down to visit Fred much easier. He would be carefree again like he had been with his motorcycle.

AT THE CAR LOT, HE paid the salesman, slid behind the wheel, and pulled on his new driving gloves. He cruised Mulholland Drive and drove down into Westwood Village where pretty co-eds from the nearby university campus filled the sidewalks, then he joined the traffic moving westward toward the beaches. He stopped only when he reached the Pacific Ocean and parked the car near the sand and the Santa Monica pier. He walked out the long pier, the orange disk of the setting sun casting a golden glow on the water. The waves curled beneath the boards under his feet, their white foam rolling relentlessly to the shore. It was like his life—he was on a firm footing now but the crashing waves of war were always in the background.

At work the next day, he was suddenly thrust into becoming an entrepreneur. The Zebra Room Cocktail Lounge and the adjoining hotel dining room enforced a formal dress code that required all men to wear a tie, and the management kept a few well-used, loaner ties at the coat-check counter. Usually wrinkled, often stained, and certainly not the latest styles, they were all that was available to a patron who appeared without a tie.

That evening, the film director Busby Berkeley, a regular at the bar, appeared in casual dress after a long day shooting one of his famous dance scenes. With a rumpled, borrowed tie around his neck, Berkeley settled exhausted into a booth and signaled Herman for his usual martini.

Herman knew exactly what he wanted and made it appear in minutes. "That's what I needed tonight. Thanks, Herman."

"No problem, Mr. Berkeley." Herman enjoyed serving the director. "Can I get you anything else, sir? Would you like something to eat?" He knew the man tended to drink too much and forgot to eat.

"No, thanks. I'll have another martini when you get the chance." Berkeley ran his hand over his slicked-back hair and tried to adjust the rumpled tie as two young la-dies entered the lounge and perched on the high zebra-skin covered chairs at the bar near where he sat. The handsome and flamboyant director was known as a ladies' man, but tonight he wasn't at his best. He put his hand on Herman's sleeve to hold his attention. "See those lovely girls, my boy? They have class. If I had on a decent tie, those two beauties would soon join me. All I'd have to do is wink and wave my hand. But this old choker makes me look like a reprobate. I'd have to get up and sweet talk them, and honestly, tonight I don't have the energy. The Zebra Room ought to supply better ties for us regulars."

Herman bobbed his head in agreement. He felt bad for the man who had recently been through a nasty divorce. Suddenly he had an idea. "Sir, on a night like tonight, would you be willing to buy a new tie, if it wasn't too expensive?"

Berkeley raised his martini glass in salute. "Absolutely. Do you have a blue one to match my eyes?"

"Sorry, sir. I just this minute thought of the idea." Her-man saw the disappointment in the patron's face. "But I promise next time you're in, I'll have a brand new blue tie set aside for you to buy."

Herman went to Woolworth's the next morning and bought a dozen inexpensive ties. His selection included mainly blues, grays, browns, and neutral designs that would look good on any shirt, but he also bought one red tie and one with diagonal stripes. He knew these ties were noth-ing like the $25 silk ties his customers had at home, but they were far better than the wrinkled, overused ties behind the coat check counter. Herman coiled his selection of ties neatly in a flat box so that it looked like a mini-display from the men's department at Bullock's. He made a small sign which the manager allowed him to display.

*Look like a Million!*
*A brand new tie, picked especially for you*
*by Herman Lang.*
*$1.00*

Word got around quickly and his business took off. Usually none of the wealthy men who came to the Zebra Room wanted to keep a forty-cent rayon tie, so at the end of the evening, they often handed them back to Herman. With no feelings of guilt, he was able to sell the same ties over and over. The minute they showed even a small spot, he took them home to clean and iron or throw away. When the selection ran low, he returned to Woolworth's and bought more with his clients' individual tastes in mind. His customers were happy, he was happy, and the manager threw out the disreputable ties the coat check girl had been offering.

Selling came easy to Herman. He was always cheerful and seemed to attract people like a magnet. When he handed out ties or cleared tables, he chatted to the patrons, flashed his smile, and was soon requested by the regulars. One patron, a radio announcer who befriended him, took Herman to his first baseball game and gave him a crash course on the sport.

No matter how busy he was, he tried to find time to write his mother at least once a week.

*Dear Mom,*                                   *May 2, 1940*

*I am doing well. I get great tips at the Zebra Room because all the clients like me. And my tie business was a brilliant idea. Lots of regulars don't worry anymore and come to the bar right after playing golf or tennis. They show up and buy one of my ties to look good. Sometimes this makes me as much as $10 a night!*

*I am now able to send you money regularly. I know things are tough in London, and I want to help you and Edith. I want to please Uncle Bruno, too. He has done too much already, and I think it is time for me to do my bit.*

*I know you and Uncle Herbert would like me to get a more respectable job, one that uses my business training, but truly, I would make a lot less money at an office job, and I wouldn't be able to send you as much as I do now. The only drawback of this job, as far as I'm concerned, is that I only meet rich girls here, girls on the arm of a wealthy date. I can't compete with that.*

*Do you ever see Molly when you go out to The Wilderness to visit Uncle Bruno and Aunt Nelda? I don't get many letters from her any more. Has she found a new boyfriend?*

*Your loving son,*
*Herman*

CHAPTER 13

# WORLD IN UPHEAVAL

WHILE HERMAN ENJOYED THE INTOXICATING scene at the Zebra Room, the news from Europe continued to spiral downward. His worry and fear for his mother and sister grew each day as he read the *Los Angeles Times* front page news and listened constantly to the radio for updates on the situation in Europe. Every day the broadcasts brought more bad news.

Like many others in America, Herman found himself drawn to President Roosevelt's popular "Fireside Chats." Herman was calmed by the striking contrast between Roosevelt's quiet voice and Hitler's rants on the German radio a few years before.

One afternoon on his day off, he went to a movie matinee where he had watched a cinema newsreel showing footage of German troops overrunning Holland, Luxemburg, and Belgium, then goose-stepping into Paris. Later that evening, Herman huddled next to the radio in his apartment and listened intently to the news and the scheduled "Fireside Chat."

"My friends," President Roosevelt began as usual. "At this moment of sadness throughout most of the world, I want to talk with you about a number of subjects that directly affect the future of the United States. . . . Tonight, over the once peaceful roads of Belgium and France, millions are now moving, running from their homes to escape bombs and shells and fire and machine gunning, without shelter and almost wholly without food."

Herman thought of the thousands of Jews who had believed themselves safely out of Germany and were now caught again in the Nazi web. His coffee grew cold on the table in front of him while he listened intently. The president told his audience that all branches of the military must be built up in order to insure the national defense—just in case.

Herman shook his head. Strengthening the military had been Hitler's answer to problems, too. Roosevelt was different from Hitler, yet his solution sounded uncomfortably familiar.

A few days later, headlines blared the harsh news of the massacre at Dunkirk where tens of thousands of British soldiers had been trapped on French beaches and slaughtered by German guns. Under heavy fire, a Navy flotilla, joined by British civilians in fishing trawlers and anything else that would float, crossed and re-crossed the English Channel in a superhuman effort to save the English troops. As Herman read his copy of the newspaper, his mind filled with worries for his mother and sister in London. Soon the Nazi armies might follow the retreating British troops across the Channel to England. His family would be caught in a trap as surely as the Jews who had moved to Holland had been.

That summer, with most of continental Europe now under German control, Roosevelt openly endorsed the conscription bill under discussion in Congress. In the Zebra Lounge, patrons clustered in the booths and expounded on a variety of views based on no logic Herman could understand. The German-born waiters argued that only a strong military could stop Hitler's megalomania. Well-dressed movie tycoons shouted that the draft was the first step toward the loss of American freedoms. Women with diamonds in their ears whispered that their husbands had pulled their old army uniforms out of the closet. Sorority girls listened to their boyfriends declare that the United States would soon go to the aid of Great Britain in the war against Germany, and the young men swore they would go to England themselves and join the Royal Air Force if the US government didn't act fast enough. Even though they would be the ones called to duty, many young men supported the draft bill, while others, mainly older men who had served in the First World War, vehemently opposed it because this time they wanted to stay quietly neutral on the American side of the Atlantic.

By September, the news from Britain was ominous. Herman began to have trouble getting to sleep at night. He would lie in bed for hours, his mind a jumble of worries, watching the dawn light creep through his apartment window. He could not banish thoughts of his mother and sister trapped in London while German planes thundered over the English countryside, their bombs a nightly rain on the capital city.

The papers were full of news about London under siege and Edward R. Murrow broadcast radio reports from the thick of it. He always began his report with, "This is London," and ended it with, "Good night, and good luck," but it was the words in between that riveted Herman's attention. "The Blitz" brought massive destruction and sudden death to thousands of civilians. And his mother, Edith, and her sweet babies were in the middle of it.

Clara wrote that the underground passageways of London's subway system had become bomb shelters, while sirens wailed and bombs exploded above. She described the masses of mothers, fathers, and grandparents like herself who wrapped themselves in blankets, drank tea from thermos bottles, and comforted the nightmares of their children. Clara and Edith, with a toddler and an infant in tow, were down in the crowded tunnels with their neighbors almost every night. Then a letter from his mother arrived with news that sent chills of fear down Herman's spine.

*Dear Herman,*                              *October 2, 1940*

*All is well here, but I want to tell you a story. One night when Edith was out with the babies to visit a friend, I ran to the Underground alone. Halfway there, I heard a hissing sound, something like the movement of air. Then there was a crash in the bushes near the sidewalk not more than two feet from where I ran in the dark.*

*The next morning on my way back to the flat, I decided to investigate. I poked about in the bushes and there it was—a large piece of jagged shrapnel lying in the weeds right where I remembered hearing the noise. It was a piece of heavy twisted metal about the size of my hand, but it could have killed me nevertheless. I picked it up and brought it back to the apartment where I have placed it on the mantle as a reminder of how lucky I am to be alive.*

*Edith thinks me daft, but I will never run in fear through the streets again. I am finished with being afraid. From now on, I plan to stay in my comfortable chair in your sister's basement flat. When the sirens begin their warnings, I will make myself a cup of tea and add a thimble full of Schnapps. I will wrap myself in blankets and pick up my knitting. I will not budge when Edith gathers the babies and runs to the shelter. Nothing you or she can say will change my mind. If I must die by a German bomb, it will be in comfort.*

*But do not worry. I feel lucky.*

*Your Mutti*

While London was suffering through nightly bombings, Congress passed the first peacetime draft bill in the history of the United States. Herman was again glued to the radio the night in September when the president spoke to the nation.

Roosevelt declared that it would be the duty of "every male citizen of the United States, and every male alien residing in the United States, who is between the ages of twenty-one and thirty-six, to submit to registration." Herman felt like the president talked directly to him and wondered how much longer after his next birthday his carefree life in LA would continue.

Roosevelt ended his speech with words designed to inspire patriotism and support for the military in the months to come. "In the military service, Americans from all walks of life, rich and poor, country-bred and city-raised, farmer, student, manual laborer, and white-collar worker, will learn to live side by side, to depend upon each other in military drills and maneuvers, and to appreciate each other's dignity as American citizens. Universal service will bring not only greater preparedness to meet the threat of war, but a wider distribution of tolerance and understanding to enjoy the blessings of peace." Herman knew he didn't need to become a soldier to gain appreciation for the benefits of democracy and peace. His experiences in Nazi Germany had taught him that.

Still, when he thought of his mother, his sister, and her little ones caught in the bombings, when he remembered how he and all his family had been humiliated and forced to leave their homeland, he longed to join the fight against Hitler. But not yet. He needed to be able to send money to his mother so she could pay for most of her own expenses. The soldier's pay that Edith's husband earned was barely enough for their growing family. When Mutti was safe in America, in Fred's care in Laguna, then he would run to join up.

CHAPTER 14

# A GREAT SETBACK

"YOU NEED TO FORGET ALL the troubles you hear on the news," William said as he wiped the bar counter after closing one night. "Have you been to Mexico yet? How about a night of carousing in Tijuana?"

"I haven't been that far south. I've only been to my brother's. Nowhere else."

"Tijuana is totally unlike Laguna." William laughed in a slightly lewd way. "It takes about twice as long to get there, but you, my boy, need the diversion." The twinkle in his eye promised hot Mexican senoritas. "It's over the border from San Diego. Cross that invisible line and you're in a completely different world. I'll arrange everything so we have a day off together. We can leave right after work and be there in time for breakfast. We'll spend a day and a night in Mexico and be back in time for the five o'clock shift."

"Is Tijuana that different from Olvera Street?" Herman

had visited the touristy Mexican area near downtown Los Angeles.

"You won't believe how different. Wild nightlife, gambling, bullfights, cheap booze, and easy women. Stuff that's illegal in California can be bought by anyone with a little cash." William clapped Herman on the shoulder. "I guarantee you'll forget your troubles. Leave it to me. I'll arrange everything."

In the early hours of the following Monday morning, Herman, William, and Arne, one of the waiters from the Zebra Room, piled into William's car and headed south on Highway 101. They drove in the dark for several hours, stopping only to sleep beside the road on a sandy stretch of beach somewhere south of Oceanside. The glare of the late September sun, hotter even than mid-summer, woke them. They cranked down the canvas top of the convertible and continued the drive south. The road hugged the coast. Herman relaxed in the ample backseat and enjoyed the view with the crashing surf on his right, and on his left, stretches of dun-colored hills, inland marshes, and avocado groves.

At the border, the Mexican guards smiled knowingly. "*Buenos días, jóvenes. Que tenga un buen día.* Have a good day." They winked as they waved the convertible into Mexico.

William was right. Tijuana was not California. Everything was cheaper, dirtier, and sleazier. Herman was fascinated by what he saw as they drove toward downtown. The roadway was clogged with vendors, their cheap pottery and colorful blankets spread across the sidewalks. Old, dusty cars moved slowly in the traffic and honked often. Barefoot boys hawked chewing gum, one piece at a time, and a few drunken sailors from San Diego with heavily made up girls clinging to them stumbled along the main avenue.

"Where first?" William wanted to know.

"Food!" shouted Arne. "Food and beer."

They ate a breakfast of beans wrapped in tortillas and fried eggs that swam in a spicy sauce, their bright orange yolks soft and creamy. They ate fast, impatient to get the party started. William downed the last dregs of his black coffee and wiped his mouth with the back of his hand. "I'm a lucky stiff. Let's do a little gambling. We might make some money."

"Or lose some," Arne said with a laugh as they walked out of the cantina and onto the blazing sidewalk.

William turned to Herman. "What'll it be? Horses or Jai Alai?"

"What's Jai Alai?"

"A game played in a tall three-sided court. The players strap a funny-looking basket thing to their arm and use it to catch the ball and launch it against the wall." Arne swung his arm around wildly to demonstrate. "The ball goes so fast you can't even see it. Whack! Whack!" He laughed. "They say the Jai Alai ball is the fastest in the world."

"And you bet on the players?" Herman was confused by Arne's animated description.

"I'm not sure," William said. "I think the players are on a team and they rotate. They're only in the court one at a time. But in the end, I think you bet on the team." He turned to Arne. "I never could follow it. How about you?"

Arne shook his head. "It's a bit strange. But fast . . . an extremely fast ball."

Herman shook his head. He wanted to understand what was happening. "Horses are fast, too," he said. "And I love horses."

"Great! To the racetrack." Arne swung his legs over the door of the open convertible and plopped into the passenger seat. He leaned over and honked the horn. "Come on you guys. Let's go see the horses."

Two hours later, Herman was twenty dollars richer. The horses at the opulent Agua Caliente racetrack had been good to him. Now he was ogling a pretty senorita in a white sundress and broad-brimmed hat. She had made shy, sidelong eye contact with him and smiled. He was ready to move from horses to senoritas, but Arne, who had lost every bet he placed, was ready to leave. He grabbed Herman's arm and pulled him toward the exit.

"Come on, buddy. Let's go see the bulls. That's Mexico for real."

"Not yet," Herman protested. He turned back and searched the crowd for the girl, but she had disappeared. "Darn. She was there a moment ago, her smile like sunlight."

"Forget that girl." Arne slurred his words. "She's too snooty anyway. High-class girls down here won't give gringos the time of day, and they always come with a *duena*."

"A what?"

"A chaperone. Some old auntie with big ears. Come on. Willy's waiting for us." Arne turned toward the exit again, and Herman followed reluctantly.

At the El Toreo de Tijuana, the sun beat down on Herman's head. The smell of blood and the snorts and groans of the poor dying beasts made him queasy. The countless bottles of beer he had been drinking didn't help, and he was glad when they left the arena.

It was well past noon, and they were hungry again. William took them to a café where he promised they could eat the best *carnitas* in town. "The pork is both crispy and moist," he said. "It comes with chopped tomatoes and that mashed avocado guacamole you like so much. And all the freshly made tortillas you want."

The sun was dipping below the surrounding hills west of town when they walked out of the restaurant. William fanned himself with his used bullfight program. "It's time to check out the local nightclub competition," he said. "We're off to where the action is."

The three friends walked down the street and into an area dominated by nightclubs and bars, the air aglow with neon. Though a breeze from the nearby Pacific trickled into town, *Avenida Revolution* was the part of Tijuana that never cooled off.

Herman realized his sheltered life had not prepared him for the local bars. Shills stood on the sidewalks and offered free shots of tequila for anyone who entered. Inside, the lounges were dark and noisy, and the acts on the stage were flagrantly crude. Sailors shouted lewdly from the audience, nearly naked girls gyrated, announcers made suggestive gestures, and lights flashed. Herman was dazzled and disgusted at the same time. The friends traipsed from one bar to another, guzzling tequila with beer chasers. All the places swirled together in Herman's mind. The booze he had consumed was taking its toll, and sometime after midnight, he began to feel dizzy and nauseous again. He put his head on a table and closed his eyes—just for a minute.

He was aware of nothing more until he woke up in the back seat of the convertible parked on a side street. William and Arne were asleep in the front, and it was already bright morning. Herman closed his eyes again. His temples throbbed, and the sunshine sent daggers deep into his skull.

William began to move. He shambled out of the car to piss in the gutter, then slid into the driver's seat again. "Breakfast. We need *menudo*. Best cure for a hangover."

Arne stirred, groaned, opened the door on his side, leaned out, and vomited. Then he sat up straight and gently closed the door. "Okay. *Menudo*," he grunted and leaned his head back against the seat.

By midmorning they were in the line of cars waiting to get across the border and back into the United States. William Bauer was at the wheel, his elbow on the door frame. The fresh air that wafted through the open car was a welcome balm. Herman's head still felt fuzzy as if it were filled with cotton. Surprisingly, the breakfast of hot spicy soup, afloat with chunks of tripe and potatoes, had calmed his stomach. As far as he was concerned, chilies were better than Alka Seltzer. He slumped in the back seat and tried to remember exactly what he had done the night before.

When the car reached the border gate, an American immigration officer rested his hand on the window ledge of the car and looked them over carefully. "I see you fellows have been enjoying yourselves." He smiled in a toothy, not very pleasant way. "You boys all Americans?"

"Yes." William's voice was firm.

Arne straightened up and answered clearly. "Yes, sir." The others had answered. Herman looked up and answered "Yes! For sure." with all the enthusiasm he could muster. Maybe it was a bit too enthusiastic, or maybe there was something in his inflection that made the officer pay attention.

He looked at Herman. "You in the back. What were you guys doing in Mexico?"

Herman sat up as straight as he could and looked at the officer. He decided that truth was usually the best. "Ve V'ere drinking, sir. Vay too much, sir."

William looked at him with an expression that seemed to say "be careful" or possibly "shut up." Too late Herman heard the echo of his own voice slurring the W's into V's. He clamped his mouth shut.

The officer continued to stare at him, but his voice still seemed jovial. "If you're American, please tell me the name of the home stadium of the Dodgers."

"Ahh . . ." Herman knew the Dodgers were a baseball team, and he searched his mind for the little bit of knowledge he had learned from his radio announcer friend. "The Dodgers are from New York." He hesitated and tried to talk without using any Ws. "Not exactly. Brooklyn, I think." He paused again to get his thoughts straight. "They play in Brooklyn, but I'm not sure of the name of the stadium.

Maybe it's Fenway?" He was very careful to say each letter correctly.

The officer did not smile at Herman's mistake. "Fenway's in Boston. A funny place for a Brooklyn team to play, don't you think?"

Herman looked at his lap without saying another word.

"And where were you born, young man?" The officer's voice held not a hint of friendliness.

"Germany, sir. But I'm living and working in the United States."

The officer held out his hand. "Let's see your passport and your work papers."

Both William and Arne were looking at him now. Unspoken concern hung in the air. Herman felt sudden panic. How could he have been so stupid?

He knew exactly where his passport and his work card were. Not in his pocket. Not in the carryall bag on the floor. But tucked under his freshly pressed shirts in his dresser drawer. "I don't have my passport with me, sir. I'm in the US on a legal visa. All my papers are in order. Work papers and everything." Herman knew these explanations were useless, but he didn't know what else to say. If he were in Germany he would be arrested and carted off to jail or even Dachau. But this was America. Or was it Mexico? He wasn't sure what would happen next. He looked up at the border agent, a sense of hopelessness engulfing him, and pleaded, "I have to be at work this afternoon, sir."

"I can vouch for him," William interjected. "He works with me, and I know he's got all the papers he needs."

"Sorry. This man can't enter the United States until I see his passport and his visa." The officer stepped back from the car and rested his hand lightly on the holster of his gun. "We can't be too careful these days. We have orders to be especially careful about Germans. Who knows what kind of Huns or communists might try to sneak in and stir up trouble. Lots of paperless refugees coming out of Germany these days, too."

Beads of perspiration stood out on William's forehead. Arne stared directly ahead and thankfully kept his mouth shut. "What should we do, sir?" William appealed to the US officer. "We all have to get back to work tonight. We can't leave him here."

"You'll have to. First, I'll need to check your IDs before you leave, and your friend's name will go on the watch list. But after that you can take him to some hotel. He can't come into the US. If he has a passport and papers, get them to him because without them, he'll be living in Mexico. And for a very long time."

An hour later, Herman was alone in a room that smelled of mildew, old cheese, and dirty socks. Large flakes of bilious green paint peeled off the wall, revealing the dull burgundy of a previous era. He lay on the sagging mattress of the single bed, the rough, brown blanket scratching his arms, and looked at the ceiling. Over his head, a large, rusty stain blotched the stucco to one side of the light bulb hanging from a frayed electric wire. Beside the bed, the sparse furnishings consisted of one wooden chair and a dresser with the bottom drawer missing. On the wall over the dresser, the framed picture of a bullfighter painted in iridescent colors on black velvet hung at a slightly lopsided angle.

He still had about half of his racetrack winnings from the day before, enough to cover the cost of the room in this dilapidated hotel for eight days, the earliest that William said he could return without missing work. Herman gave him the key to his apartment and an exact description of where his passport and work papers were hidden. His friends dug deep into their pockets for stray pesos to give to him, hopefully enough to keep him from starving. If it took William two weeks to return, he'd be out of money for sure, wandering homeless in Mexico.

The hours of each day stretched endlessly. With almost no money, he walked the streets and ate cautiously from the push carts that sold *tacos de cabeza*, a cheap meal made with small corn tortillas wrapped around chopped meaty tidbits taken from a pig's head. He avoided the salesmen who came out of the shops waving dirty, pornographic postcards and tacky souvenirs. The main streets smelled of manure from the bedraggled donkeys painted with zebra stripes and harnessed to colorful, two-wheeled carts where tourists had their pictures taken. The side streets reeked of urine and garbage. The foul odors and blatant hawking of the vendors on the sidewalks depressed Herman so much he returned to his room every day with a sense of doom.

He lay on the bed in his room for hours every day, studying the shape on the ceiling. Each day he saw something new in the stain until finally he felt he might go mad. He couldn't stop kicking himself for leaving his passport behind and putting his wonderful California life in jeopardy. What if something happened to William—a car accident or amnesia? Herman's thoughts spun into worst-case possibilities. He might be stuck in Mexico forever, his mother without support, his brother too busy to even worry about him for months. He felt close to panic. Even going down the hall to the bathroom was an ordeal. Cockroaches scurried across the cracked tile and disappeared down the drain in the middle of the room. The shower was a handheld contraption that came out of the wall near the grungy sink, emitting only a thin stream of warmish water. He stood with his toes curled and washed down as fast as he could.

At night he listened to the noisy celebrations of sailors off the ships anchored in San Diego bay. Their drunken steps, accompanied by the laughter of girls, echoed on the stairways. On those nights, Herman seriously considered joining the US Navy in order to be back on American soil and wondered if there was an enlistment office in Tijuana.

The fourth afternoon, as Herman walked the streets, he turned in a new direction and suddenly saw something familiar and welcome. The marquee of the local cinema announced an American movie with Gary Cooper and Ray Milland. Herman had seen *Beau Geste*, a film about three brothers who joined the French Foreign Legion, the year before in Los Angeles, and it was one of his favorites. For twenty cents, Herman could go into the darkened theater and forget his troubles. He counted his coins—he had enough left to see the movie every day, eat cheese and onion

tacos, and pay his room bill for another seven days. He decided to take the risk.

He paid for a ticket, entered the dingy theater, and settled into a lopsided seat. The place smelled of popcorn and
sour wine and the floor was sticky under his feet, but he sat
through two showings of the movie. The swashbuckling adventures of the Geste brothers involved the mystery of the
disappearance of a giant, blue sapphire and how the men at
Fort Zinderneuf had died. Each of the next four days, he
returned to the theater to lose himself in the action. Soon
he had memorized each twist of the plot and could recite
dialog along with Gary Cooper. He booed the cruel and
sadistic Sergeant Markoff and felt tears on his cheeks when
John, played by Ray Milland, said good-bye to his true love,
Isobel. *Beau Geste* was his lifeline until William arrived
on the promised day with the passport and work papers
and took him back to Los Angeles. The French Foreign
Legion—and William—had come to his rescue after all.

# CHAPTER 15

# ARMY TIME

WHEN HERMAN RETURNED TO HIS apartment, he found letters from his mother with more news of her hardships in London. He immediately sat down at his kitchenette table and wrote to her.

*Dear Mom,*                      *October 8, 1940*

*I know things are tough for you, and I wish I could do more to help. I will keep sending you what money I can, but you need to be patient. Fred and Uncle Herbert are doing all they can to expedite your visa, but the American government is slow and stubborn. They won't change the quotas, even in these hard times.*

*Sorry I haven't written sooner but I just returned from a big adventure in Mexico but now I am back in LA and working hard. Every day I think of you and Edith.*

*Love,*
*Herman*

It had been more than a year since his time with Molly, and he found his memories of her were fading like an old photograph exposed to the sun. Probably it was the same for her, he thought. Her letters dwindled in both length and frequency, the last two coming three months apart, the scarlet lipstick mark of her love notably absent. In early February, another letter arrived. Herman ripped open the unadorned envelope and extracted a single page of blue notepaper. Her slanting penmanship slid across the page and reminded him of her smooth limbs and enticing smile. But her news hit him like cold water.

*Hi Herman,*

*Hope all is well in California. Betsy and my father send you their greetings.*

*I think I should tell you that I have been spending quite a bit of time with the son of one of my father's business associates. Hugh is great fun and keeps me from being lonesome. He takes me out to dinner, and we go dancing on nights there are no raids. He was wounded at Dunkirk and released from the army because he lost his foot. He has a prosthesis, but he can still dance the slow dances. We are on the same civil defense team. It is exciting to stand on the roof of a building and watch the flare of bombs in the distance. Hugh has a way about him that keeps me from being afraid.*

*I remain your friend,*
*Molly*

Herman realized that for some time he had been expecting something like this. The words on the blue paper finally extinguished the fire of his infatuation, and he put off writing her again because he didn't know what to say.

Content with his job and sending money regularly to his mother, he felt like he had found a home in Los Angeles. He was beginning to feel like a real American, so it was with a sense of pride, he registered for the draft before his twenty-first birthday.

Then like a house of cards, everything fell apart. On May 27, 1941, President Roosevelt declared the nation to be in an "unlimited period of national emergency." In July, the term of enlistment for all draftees was extended from one year to eighteen months and before the summer was over, Herman received his draft notice and his classification—1A, eligible for immediate service. He wrote his mother with the news.

*Dear Mom,*                    *August 20, 1941*

*My papers for the army came last week. It happened quickly, and I'm afraid I have to go. This will be such a great setback for me. I will lose my wonderful job and my new car!*

*I have tried everything I can think of. I told the draft board that you need my full support because I'm the only one who is able to help you. But dependents like you, living in another country, are not considered important.*

*You have asked me many times to help your friend, Albert. Please believe me, we can't help him. The*

*United States has totally broken all connections with Germany. Now, with Hitler at war with his ex-allies, the Russians, it must be worse than ever at home. There is nothing that can be done for anyone still there.*

*This war will last a long time. I only hope the Russians can hold out against the Nazis. If only they can, and the Brits can gain strength, and Roosevelt can make up his mind to help, then—and I say this filled with American hope—Mr. Hitler will be out of luck! Try to believe that Albert will find a safe way to last out the war. Perhaps someday you will be together again.*

*Please write soon again. The army may call me up to report any day. If you don't hear from me for a while, don't worry. If I have to go, William will forward my mail.*

*Love,*
*Herman*

Only days later, Herman's orders arrived. Within a week, he found himself at Camp Roberts, 240 miles north of Los Angeles, near the city of San Luis Obispo.

Herman and the other new recruits in his group began basic training. He was assigned to artillery, given a bunk in the two-story barracks, and issued his uniform, two pairs of boots, and a rifle, which his sergeant declared was now his best friend. His days began at 5:00 a.m. with reveille and ended at 5:00 p.m. unless there were nighttime training exercises.

He suffered through bayonet drills, jogged to the rifle firing range, memorized the difference in the damage caused by a 105 mm and a 155 mm howitzer, ran and crawled through obstacle courses, wiggled under barbed wire barricades, and marched. He learned to clean his rifle, the best way to hit the dirt when meeting enemy fire, and how to stack mortar shells. He enjoyed the quiet of predawn guard duty, but not the tedium of KP or the endless hours of marching.

Herman managed to find the time between all the training to write his mother.

*Dear Mom,*                                    *November 3, 1941*

*I'm in the artillery and like it very much. It is a rough and healthful life, and I suppose it does me a lot of good. Every night I am so tired I fall into my bunk and I'm asleep in about two seconds. Every Saturday we have inspection and then march in the hot sun on the parade ground which is enormous. And sometimes we have night marches too. It is hilly country with lots of beautiful oak trees here, but at night the air is cold. Unless there is a full moon, we march in the pitch dark and come back to barracks muddy and bruised from bumping into trees and tripping over rocks! I am only half joking.*

*You ask how long I will be in the army. I have no idea! The camp is full of rumors. The enlistment time for a draftee should be eighteen months, but everyone knows that if the US joins the war in Europe, anything could happen. I could be a soldier for as long as the war lasts.*

*I miss my friends and the good money I made at the Zebra Room. The pay I get from the army is very* low. I will be able to send you and Edith only a little money sometimes. Not regular like I used to, and I feel bad about it, believe me.

I will write again if I can,
Herman

In early December, after graduation from basic training, he was ordered to report to Fort Ord, south of San Francisco. Before his new assignment, he intended to make the most of the three-day leave he had earned. He called William to ask if he could sleep on his couch for a few days and boarded the next bus to Los Angeles for what promised to be a continuous party with his friends.

When he arrived Friday evening, William handed him a letter postmarked two months earlier and forwarded from his last apartment. Molly's words fell from the page.

Herman,                                    October 15, 1941

I'm sorry. I can no longer write to you. The truth is that I'm engaged to Hugh, and we plan to get married next month.

I know you are happy in California, and you have been steadfast, but I am an English girl and could never have left my country, especially in this difficult wartime.

I wish you the best. If you are ever in England, come see us.

Your friend,
Molly

Herman crumpled up the letter and tossed it in the trash. "Finished! The end," he said. "It's way past time for me to find a girl with kisses to spare." He squared his shoulders and set his uniform cap at a cocky angle. "Tonight is the night. Let's go hit the town."

William had managed to swing a night off that evening, no small feat for a Friday night, and they spent it eating, drinking, and gathering girls by the cluster. On Saturday evening, Herman was alone but not for long. At the first nightclub he visited, a tall blonde introduced herself as Gloria and clung to his arm the rest of the night. In the wee hours, they were still together. Her lips were paler than Molly's, her mind a bit dimmer, and her kisses not as sweet, but her ability to wrap her long arms and legs around him triggered a feeling of affection that lasted until Sunday morning.

The glow of dawn edged the Hollywood hills as he woke among the crumpled sheets of a hotel bed. Gloria stood over him, fully clothed, her curls again restrained by a clip. She leaned down for a lingering kiss. "I must go," she said. "You are really lovely." She turned and walked toward the door. Before she left, she paused and held up a scrap of folded paper between two fingers for him to see, then bent and tucked it into the pocket of his uniform jacket, which was hung over the back of the desk chair.

She turned toward him with a hopeful smile. "Write me?" she whispered, then slipped out the door.

He rolled over in bed and swung his bare feet to touch the chilly floor. What had possessed him to take so long to move on?

Late that morning, he sat at one end of the bar in the Zebra Room while William stocked liquor bottles and wiped down the counter in preparation for opening the bar. Herman nibbled at the last crusts of a ham sandwich and nursed a strong coffee as he stared at the scrap of paper Gloria had given him. The fragrance of her perfume still lingered. She had made a lip imprint like Molly used to, but hers was strawberry pink rather than scarlet. Below the kiss she had scrawled her name and address. He wondered if he would ever see her again. In a few hours he would be on the bus back up to Paso Robles and from there to Camp Roberts. Monday morning he would be transported to Fort Ord. There was no way of knowing when, or if, he would return to Los Angeles.

William paused in front of him, the disinfectant-smelling counter cloth stopped in mid-swipe. "Everyone misses you around here. The patrons keep asking for you, especially the ones who come in without ties." His friend grinned and slapped the bar with his hand. "Come on, soldier boy. You should be too tough by now to have a hangover."

Herman looked up. He ran his hand over the top of his head. The close-cropped stubble of his army cut reminded him of the haircut his mother had given him in Meiningen. He shook his head to dispel the memory.

"Not a hangover exactly. I'm not sure what to expect any more. It's depressing. My life keeps changing, and I don't seem to have any say in it. Every time things get good, something else happens. Everything turns on a dime and I have no control. Sometimes I don't know who I am or where I belong." He took a sip of the now cold coffee. "I'm proud to be in the US Army and I want to help kick that damned Hitler into hell. But I love LA and . . . well, especially the parties and the girls . . . finally, the girls!"

"Hey, guys!" One of the bellhops from the hotel burst in from the lobby. "Turn up the radio. All hell's breaking loose in Hawaii."

William reached under the bar and turned the knobs of the small radio he kept there. "What's happened?"

Before the bellhop could catch his breath, the radio blared and an excited voice filled the room. The announcer was in midsentence. ". . . in flames. It's terrible. Jap planes everywhere. Bombs like rain. The USS *Arizona* is at the bottom of Pearl Harbor . . ."

Another announcer's voice, this one speaking with deadly calm, broke into the report. "All military personnel are ordered to return to their stations immediately. All leaves and passes are cancelled indefinitely. Repeat. All military personnel . . ."

Herman's hand shook as he set down his cup unevenly. A single splash of coffee landed on his cuff, but he hardly noticed. "Jeez . . . God!" He stood up. His knees felt shaky. "I have to go. We're in the war for sure now." He grabbed his jacket from the back of the bar stool. War could bring anything. He might never return to Los Angeles, not alive anyway. He reached his right hand over the bar. "Thanks, William. For everything."

His friend grasped Herman's arm and palm in a two-handed shake. "Good luck. If there's war, I'll join up in spite of my flat feet. They won't be able to keep me out."

William squeezed his hand hard. "I'll be thinking of you. Keep in touch."

"I'll write." Herman bolted toward the lobby and the street. The small scrap of paper with Gloria's lip print floated from the bar counter and settled gently to the floor.

ON DECEMBER 8, 1941, THE United States declared war on Japan and two days later, the country was at war with Germany and their treaty ally, Italy, too. Herman found himself classified as an enemy alien again. Yet this time, he was in the army, and he had sworn an oath to serve the United States.

Promoted to corporal, Herman was immediately sent to Idaho with orders to help a National Guard battalion transport heavy artillery across the snow-covered Rocky Mountains to the Pacific Northwest where Seattle's strategic harbor and modern aircraft plant would invite attack by the Japanese.

Herman was assigned to drive a behemoth wrecker tow truck as part of the convoy. He was the shortest man in the unit and he drove the biggest truck, but he had little time to enjoy the humor of the situation.

The dangerous, icy road seemed endless. He had to go back and forth, pulling heavily laden trucks out of the slush of ditches from one side of the mountain pass to the other. One of the last to arrive at Fort Lewis, Herman towed a disabled truck full of explosive shells through the barbed-wire and machine-gun fortified gates of the biggest fort of the Pacific Northwest.

FOR CLOSE TO A YEAR, Herman waited with everyone else for the expected Japanese attack on Seattle that never came. During the tedious months of expectant waiting, he was promoted to sergeant and was put in charge of the maintenance section of his artillery unit.

Herman was getting impatient. More interested in the fight in Europe than the battles of the Pacific, he wanted to be in Africa where Americans battled German and Italian troops. He needed to take action, but as long as he was classified as an enemy alien, getting out of the mud and sleet of Seattle seemed unlikely. Only as a US citizen could he hope for an overseas assignment. He applied for expedited citizenship, which was sometimes granted to men in the service with the proper recommendations and a good record. Uncle Herbert, always eager to help, wrote letters for him, as did his commanding officer. By the spring of 1943, Herman proudly became an official citizen of the United States.

# CHAPTER 16
# THE LETTER

HERMAN TRAMPED THROUGH THE THICK, springtime mud on his way back to the barracks. He didn't want to be with the other men as they huddled around the radio that squawked constantly with war news. He had been part of this intense group every other night that week and during most lunch hours, too. The men cheered at the news of British or American victories and hissed and booed when Hitler or Tojo were mentioned. Herman was tired of it all. He didn't want to stand on the sidelines and cheer—he wanted to be in the midst of the action. He knew what the bombings in Europe meant to his friends and relatives still there, and he needed to be part of the efforts to free them from the terrors of war.

The British Royal Air Force had started to drop bombs on German territory in 1940, long before the Americans arrived to help. By now, more than a year after Pearl Harbor, the US Army and Air Force had joined RAF pilots in a mutual effort to obliterate German cities, power plants, railroads, and radar stations. Berlin, Hamburg, Cologne, Kassel—cities Herman had hoped, in his boyhood innocence, to visit someday—all were being reduced to rubble. The German Luftwaffe had lost control of the European and North African skies. Russia was now an ally of Britain and the United States, and in the Pacific, the Japanese were slowly being pushed back, one island at a time.

Herman had received several letters from William, who had joined the navy and was assigned to a submarine. His allusions to dancing girls in grass skirts made it past the censors, and Herman believed his friend was in the Pacific.

Now, as he walked toward the barracks in the cold darkness, he was frustrated. The next day was his twenty-third birthday, and he still felt like a boy with no control over his life. Getting his citizenship hadn't been enough—he needed to do something radical. He entered the dimly lit barracks and stood a moment, looking around. The long space, filled with crisply made beds and the solid shapes of footlockers, was quiet. None of the usual sounds and smells of men filled the room—the loud talk, laughter, shuffle, and jostle of bodies and equipment eerily absent.

The small corner office where he and the other staff sergeants did paperwork for the unit was deserted. An idea began to form in his mind—something outside usual procedure, but he figured he had nothing to lose. He entered the darkened room and lowered the Venetian blinds across the windows that looked out to the barracks hallway. The office reeked, as always, of mold and cigarette smoke.

He switched on the green-shaded desk light and settled into the chair in front of the typewriter, his fingers poised above the keys. Slowly, he began to type.

*Dear President Roosevelt,*          *April 14, 1943*

*I hope you can help me to serve my country in a more useful way. I know the invasion of Germany is near. I think my skills can be better used than by driving a truck.*

*I was born in Germany and lived there for nineteen years. I would still probably be in Germany today if the Nazis had not decided that my Jewish blood made me unfit to be a citizen. Since December of 1939, I have lived and worked in the United States. I love my adopted country for what it has done for me, and for the wonderful place it is.*

*I have been in the US Army for more than two years. I am proud to be a naturalized citizen since March 12 of this year. Since that day, I see the world in a different light. I am fluent in both German and English. I know a lot about the people of Germany and how they think. There are German prisoners of war being held right here at Fort Lewis. Several times I have been asked by the officers in charge of the prisoners to help with translating instructions to these Germans. Isn't there something like this I could do for the army when we invade Europe?*

*Please help me to get in a unit that will fight in Germany. I would do anything. I want to help my new country, which I love, and to rid the country of my birth of that devil, Hitler.*

*Sincerely,*
*Staff Sergeant Herman L. Lang*

Herman addressed an envelope to "President Franklin Delano Roosevelt, the Commander in Chief, The White House, Washington, DC." Carefully he folded the letter in thirds and slipped it into the envelope. Probably nothing would come of this, but maybe . . .

Three weeks later, Herman was called into the office of the post commander. He stood at attention across the desk from the full colonel and saluted.

"Staff Sergeant Lang, you want to be knocked back to private?"

"Sir?" Herman was caught by surprise. What could this be about?

"You have some nerve. Don't you know enough to go through the proper channels to make a request?"

"Yes, sir! I've filled out the proper paperwork."

"Is that so, Staff Sergeant?"

"Yes, sir. I applied for the Air Cadets. I was denied, sir. I applied for transfer overseas, but I've heard nothing, sir."

"We need you here, Sergeant. You're valuable to the defense of this post."

"Thank you, sir."

"Don't thank me. I have half a mind to demote you for your audacity. And I could do it, too." The colonel took a breath and slammed his fist down on the desk causing the top sheets on a stack of papers to flutter and shift. "Who gave you permission to write directly to our Commander in Chief?"

"No one, Colonel." Herman could not believe his ears. Someone had read his letter. Was it only a censor on the base, someone in the War Department in Washington, or the president himself? Whoever had read the letter had contacted the colonel, and the result was not good. Now he would be stuck stateside forever, driving trucks, cleaning howitzers pointed toward the Pacific, and translating orders to clean the latrine to the German prisoners quartered at Fort Lewis.

"Report back to work, Lang. And don't forget how lucky you are to still be a staff sergeant."

"Yes, sir. Thank you, sir."

"And, Staff Sergeant Lang. No more letters to the President that don't come over my desk first. Follow the proper chain of command the next time."

Herman figured he had come off lucky in the colonel's office and didn't write another letter. He hoped the first letter had gotten through to someone in Washington, DC—someone who would do something.

Within a week he received orders that his entire battalion was being sent to Camp Young in the Mojave Desert. Now he would be driving trucks in sand instead of mud. He hoped it was the first step toward being sent to North Africa.

Before he left, he had time to write another letter to his mother.

*Dear Mom,*                     *May 10, 1943*

*I received your letter today. I hear London is not so*

*heavily bombed these days, and I am glad to know you are safer than before. I am sorry you no longer get news from Albert. The Allies are bombing most of the cities of Germany, and maybe the mail is just not going through. Try to be happy. Your visa will surely come soon. It takes such a long time to get through the famous red tape of Washington, but when your number comes up, you'll get it.*

*This will be my last letter from Fort Lewis as we are being moved to another location. I will be glad to leave the rainy weather. It reminds me of England too much. Since I last wrote, I have been promoted again and am now a staff sergeant. My job is one of the most responsible in the battery as I am in charge of about fifty men and trucks. The army depends on its vehicles and if my section didn't function, everything else would go haywire. Our new assignment may lead us to overseas duty.*

*I hope we won't be late for the fighting, because I have a score to settle with Hitler, that son of a ##%%#. I wouldn't spell it out in a letter to my mother, but I'm sure you know what I mean.*

*I send my love to you and Edith. Please stay safe.*

*Your son,*
*Herman*

The hot, dry air of the California desert was the exact opposite of Seattle's wet northern climate. Herman found he was almost constantly soaked in sweat. The fine silica dust of the desert blew up, plastered his skin, and formed a gritty film on his tongue. There were no barracks, only canvas tents and pit latrines. Drinking and washing water was brought in by tank truck.

During the day, the men practiced desert warfare. Within weeks of their arrival, every man could run a mile in ten minutes, even under the weight of full battle gear that included backpacks and rifles. Between the daily runs and simulated battles, Herman and his men maintained the trucks. They cleaned sand from the engines and checked radiators, tires, batteries, and air filters.

On evenings when there were no impromptu card games or friendly boxing matches in the makeshift ring, Herman sat cross-legged on his cot, awash in the dim moonlight that filtered through the canvas roof of the tent, and wrote letters by lantern light.

*Dear Mom,*                                    *May 28, 1943*

*I sometimes think I am living a daydream right out of my boyhood books about the French Foreign Legion. The desert surroundings suit me, in spite of the sand and the dust and all the running and training. The scuttlebutt is that we are getting ready to fight Hitler in the Sahara.*

*We men do find time for high-jinx between the work details. Desert snakes are everywhere, but don't worry, most are harmless. We watch out for rattlesnakes and some of the men make a sport of using them for target practice. Gopher snakes are our friends because they keep the population of kangaroo rats and lizards* under control. They do it without biting but squeeze the breath out of the poor little creatures. I have to admit that I found it a bit disgusting to see the first time, but now these snakes are like pets to me.

I hope you like the enclosed picture of me with a few of my "pets" as a bracelet and necklace.

Give my greetings to Hazel. Start packing your bags. I'm sure that soon your visa will come through and you will be leaving jolly ol' England.

Your loving son,
Herman

Dear Fred,                                    June 2, 1943

I hope you and your family are well. Mother will soon be traveling to the United States. It has been difficult for her, and I can't do much to help any more. Please do what you can to make her happy.

Desert training is hot and difficult. We soldiers enjoy a good laugh now and then. Last week some new recruits arrived, and we initiated them by hiding a harmless little snake under one of their cots. What a ruckus that caused! I think the poor snake got the worst of it. One of my buddies here is not too keen on snakes. Yesterday, I draped a harmless King snake over the enclosure of the outdoor shower while he was inside covered only in water and gray soap suds. The result was much swearing and a running nude.

*I am finally a desert fighter just like I dreamed as a boy. When I get out of the army, I think I will look for work as a snake charmer in the circus, like in the picture I have sent.*

*Give my greetings to Bonnie.*

*Your brother,*
*Herman*

Just as the days in the Mojave began to reach temperatures well over 100° F and the men started talking about frying eggs on the hoods of their jeeps, Herman received classified orders from the War Department in Washington, DC. The message was cryptic, his final destination not revealed. Even his superior officer would not, or could not, tell him anything.

"Just follow orders," the captain told him. "We are at war. That's all you need to know."

He was the only soldier in his unit to receive the top secret orders, which sent him first to Yuma by truck and then by train to Baltimore, "Where you will get further orders." He had no idea where he might end up or what to expect. Had the army decided they didn't trust Germans, or was he being sent to Europe in answer to his letter to Roosevelt?

Herman's nerves were wound tight as he set off—a solitary soldier ordered on a mysterious mission.

CHAPTER 17

# THE RITCHIE BOYS

FOR SEVERAL DAYS AND NIGHTS, the train clacked over the rails. It crossed the Rocky Mountains, the flat plains of the Midwest, planted with new, green corn, and finally, the Mississippi, brown and flowing toward the Gulf of Mexico.

There were delays along the way. Sometimes the train pulled onto a side spur and a loaded troop train rushed past. Herman imagined that the men he glimpsed outlined against the steamy windows would soon be in Africa or the Pacific, fighting the enemy. He chafed at the thought that he still didn't know where he was headed. Slowly his train rolled through the forests and farmland of the eastern states—Ohio, Pennsylvania, and south into Maryland—where everything was lushly green in early summer and reminded him of the wooded hills near Meiningen. A wave of nostalgia caught him by surprise.

In Baltimore, he was directed to board a local train with only two cars, each marked with a large **R**. He stacked his duffel with several others in a baggage area at the rear and looked around. The car was inhabited by other uneasy men in uniform, each apparently traveling alone, no two sitting together. As the train pulled out of the station and wound into the countryside, the soldiers started to talk to their neighbors, gradually coagulating into clusters. They were mostly privates, but there were also a few noncommissioned officers and one or two lieutenants. Herman found two sergeants standing in the vestibule at the end of the car. They compared orders. Their cryptic papers had them puzzled.

Herman became aware that both sergeants spoke with German accents. He excused himself and walked the length of the car and back again, listening carefully. Among the babble of whispers from the other groups, he detected a variety of accents coloring the English words spoken. He was sure that most of the soldiers on the train counted German as their first language, but he also detected a few other accents—the lilt of Italian and the staccato of Polish. When he returned to the rear vestibule, he considered injecting this observation into the hushed conversation of his new friends. But the talk was already charged with doubts, and he decided to wait and see what happened when they reached their destination. If they had noticed the profusion of accents, the other men didn't mention it either.

Herman knew of the Japanese detention camps set up in the deserts of California and other desolate spots. The thought that the US Government had decided it would be safer to sideline Germans, too, revolved in his mind. He forced himself to think of a positive reason for these foreign-born soldiers to be together. Maybe they were to be formed into a special fighting unit for the European invasion, similar to the all-Japanese battalion Herman had heard whispers about.

Finally, the engine with its two cars pulled into a dead-end spur. The men piled out, and a lieutenant waited on the platform.

"You have arrived." The officer's words offered no hint of what lay ahead. "Form up. Two lines," he ordered.

They marched past low stone walls, the crenellated design reminiscent of a European castle, and through a wrought iron gate. At the top of the gate, worked in iron bars, were the words Camp Ritchie. Herman glimpsed a lake, several clusters of tents, and farther back, wooden barracks, many still under construction. They were led into a theater plastered with posters for upcoming movies. The men bunched together in the rear, unsure of what they were meant to do. The lieutenant, flanked by two sergeants, mounted the stairs to the stage.

"Men, come down front and sit," he barked. The soldiers settled into the front rows while he waited, his legs slightly parted, his hands clasped behind his back. As the last man settled into his seat, the lieutenant spoke. "Gentlemen, you have been selected for a very special program." His voice was firm and could be heard across the auditorium, even without the aid of a microphone. "You have arrived at Camp Ritchie, the United States Military Intelligence Training Center. Some of you are United States citizens, either by birth or naturalization. But many of you are not.

Don't worry. Your loyalty is understood or you wouldn't be here. For the next eight weeks, you will be students. After that we will see that you all become citizens of this great country so you can join the fight overseas. That is where the army needs you."

A sigh of relief and a quiet ripple of anticipation passed through the audience. The officer continued. "You are members of the ninth class to attend this school. I think you will find it a challenge and an honor to be here." His enthusiasm was contagious and the men sat up straighter in their seats. "You will notice that Camp Ritchie is different in many ways from other training facilities. You will discover these differences over the next few days, but one thing I want to make clear from the beginning. Most of you are privates or noncoms, but some of you are officers. Regardless of your rank, you are all students together. In the classrooms, higher ranks will receive no special privileges. All students will be graded on the same scale, privates the same as generals, if there are any." The men looked around expectantly, some laughing and shaking their heads. "More importantly," the lieutenant resumed as the buzzing settled down, "you may have an instructor that is below you in rank. Do not misunderstand. In the classroom the instructor is always to be treated as the soldier of highest rank. All our instructors are specialists and deserve your respect and attention."

After this speech, the lieutenant took a deep breath and the men shifted in their seats. He looked from one side of the auditorium to the other and waited for absolute quiet before he continued. "Men, this is a top secret facility and you are not to talk to anyone outside of Camp Ritchie about what you learn here. Do not write home about your classes, the school, our location, or our mission. No one outside Camp Ritchie is to know our real function." He then boomed out, "Is that understood?"

The hall filled with the echoes of male voices.

"Yes, sir."

"Understood, sir."

"More men will arrive to join your class in the next few days. On Monday you will become serious students," the lieutenant said. "You will need to study hard and well. Not all of you will pass the courses, but those of you who do will have earned a special place in the waging of this war. Your contribution will be invaluable. Remember, knowledge is power. You will be the ones helping the generals gain the knowledge they need to plan a victorious campaign against the Nazi and Jap aggressors."

At the end of the indoctrination, the new students were given barrack assignments and their class schedules. Then they proceeded to the infirmary for a physical checkup and to the supply room, where they were issued books, study materials, and new uniforms. They had two days to make themselves comfortable in their quarters and get familiar with the layout of the area. Then the serious work of learning would begin.

That evening in the barracks, Herman wandered around, talking to as many of the men as he could. They were a most unlikely group of soldiers with a wide range of ages. There was a preponderance of college students, even one professor, as well as clerks, bookkeepers, musicians, artists, and literary types. But there were also several boys just out of high school, as well as an auto mechanic, a butcher, a greengrocer, a tailor, and a jeweler. They soon discovered all the men in Barracks 4 were German speakers—mostly born in Germany, and like Herman, refugees. And they were, all but two, Jewish. Some had come as young boys, fleeing Nazi anti-Semitism with their families. Others, like Herman, had been sent on their own, their parents desperate to find safety for their children, even if they couldn't or wouldn't leave themselves. Many had relatives—aunts and uncles, cousins, even parents and siblings—who had disappeared in the maelstrom that was now Europe at war. One of the non-Jewish men had been born in the United States and spoke English without an accent. However, German was his first language, learned from his parents, who had come to America twenty-five years before. The other American-born soldier had earned a master's degree in German at Columbia University before he enlisted. His German was flawless, though he had an American accent.

In the mess hall the next morning, the men were served their breakfast by several German and Italian prisoners, who seemed happy to be slinging scrambled eggs and passing out biscuits rather than fighting with their comrades in North Africa where they had been captured. Herman and the men from his unit lingered over their coffee and talked of their families and their experiences.

Suddenly Jacob Mittleberg, one of Herman's new barracks mates, jumped up, almost knocking over his half-empty cup. He made his way between the tables and benches, waving his arm in the air and calling out, "*Hallo,* Bernie. Hey, hello." At the far side of the room he embraced another man, the joy on his face evident. They couldn't seem to stop hugging each other and laughing, but finally, the two men walked arm in arm back to the table.

"Fellows, I want you to meet Master Sergeant Bernie Levinson," Jacob said. "He and I went to grade school together and our fathers were doctors together at Berlin Hospital." He clapped his school chum on the shoulder and grinned at his new friends. "Haven't seen Bernie for six years. Last I heard his family was in Belgium."

"And last I heard Jacob was still in Germany." Bernie's grin was as wide as his friend's. "What a relief to find him here."

Herman and all the other men stood and shook hands with the sergeant. For a moment they were not soldiers, but simply refugees who understood the wonder of finding a friend who they had feared was trapped in Nazi Germany.

Finally, Bernie stepped back and gave a smart salute. "At ease, men. I've been at Ritchie for seven weeks already." He sat down at the table and pulled his friend onto the bench next to him. "Let me tell you what to expect."

ON THE STREETS OF THE CAMP, the men usually spoke English, their one common language. Anything else would have been bedlam. Not all the men at Camp Ritchie spoke German. Their native tongues came from all over Europe, though many spoke Yiddish as well. Herman heard Hungarian, French, Polish, Russian, Croatian, Dutch,

Italian, and Greek. The barracks were divided by classes and the classes were divided by language emphasis, and they learned later, sometimes by special areas of study. New classes started almost every week, thus some of the men were finishing up their courses, while others were just getting started.

Herman soon made friends with Jacob, who preferred the American nickname of Jake he had been given by school chums at his American high school. He was also a staff sergeant and only a year younger than Herman, though he had been in his first year of college when his adopted country joined the war and he was drafted. Another man, Walter Stern, a corporal who bunked near them in the barracks, was only nineteen and had been in the army barely six months, but his youthful exuberance and sense of humor appealed to both Herman and Jake, and they took the young soldier under their wing.

The second afternoon at Ritchie, the three new friends wandered around the camp. Officially dedicated as a training center just a year before, it still had the feeling of the summer recreation camp it had been before the war. At the edge of the blue lake, boats bobbed at their moorings, and in the distance, the surrounding hills were lush with trees. But the camp also had the raw new feel of a place undergoing change and development, with rows of new, wooden, two-story barracks. There were officers' quarters, countless freshly built classrooms, five mess buildings, and a string of new structures that comprised the hospital and medical center.

Not far from the gate, they passed a small white church surrounded by flower beds. Walter pointed to the notice board in front of the chapel. "Look, Sergeant. They have more Jewish services listed than Christian ones."

They all looked at the sign.

*Jewish Services—Friday: 7:00 p.m. 9:00 p.m.*
*Saturday: 8:00 a.m. 10:00 a.m. 12:00 noon*

*Catholic Confession—Saturday: 4:00 to 5:00 p.m.*
*Catholic Mass—Sunday: 8:00 a.m.*

*Nondenominational Protestant Service—*
*Sunday: 10:00 a.m.*

Walter stood reading the notice. "Are you going to go to services next Friday?"

Herman shrugged. "I don't think so. I wouldn't know what to do at a Jewish service. Maybe I'll check out the Protestant service one day. I used to go to the Lutheran church at home with my best friend."

"I wouldn't know what to do in a Protestant service or a Catholic mass either," Jake said. "My father wouldn't have permitted me to go with friends, even if I was invited, which I wasn't." He sighed. "We didn't often go to the synagogue, for that matter. My dad said they'd kick us out for all the bacon on our breath. He sure did love his sausage and bacon." A sad look passed over his face. "Wonder what he's got to eat these days?"

Herman heard the sadness in his friend's voice. "Are your parents still in Germany?" He wasn't sure he wanted to hear the answer.

"My mother died when I was six. But my father's still

there. He started making plans for my sister and me soon after the Nuremburg laws were passed. Our visas finally came in '38. My mother's brother lives in Denver, and my sister and I came together to live with him. My sister Sara was only ten, and it was hard for her to leave her friends. But my dad is stubborn. He insisted he would stay to help his patients and to remain near my mother's grave. I haven't heard from him in over a year. His last letter said he had been ordered to report to the train depot in two days. He thought he would be sent to a labor camp in the east. I don't like the sound of what I've heard about those places. But he just wrote, 'Don't worry. They will need doctors there.'"

Herman looked at the ground and kicked at a clump of grass pushing through at the edge of the road. He didn't want to meet Jake's eyes. "The rumors are bad."

Walter shook his head. "I heard those camps are just places to—"

Herman cleared his voice and interrupted. "Hey! Look over there!" The conversation had been about to take a dark turn. There was nothing to do anyway but get through the school and get over to Europe as soon as possible. He pointed across the road to where a large building was under construction. "That one looks like it'll be something special when it's finished. What's your guess?"

Jake made an effort to bring himself back to the present. "Don't know." He shrugged and wiped the sweat from his forehead with a khaki handkerchief. "I hope it's an indoor pool. I could use a swim in this heat."

Walter waved his arm in the direction of the lake. "What about that? Surely all that water isn't just for officers. Maybe we can swim there?"

Herman liked the idea of a cooling swim. "I think so. And I saw some guys out in canoes yesterday. Let's check it out."

THEIR TRAINING STARTED EARLY THE next morning. Herman soon realized that Camp Ritchie was not a place to fool around—the classes were intensive and fast-paced. His schedule included German language, German military organization, German military identification, interrogation techniques, tactics and field observation, map reading, and document analysis.

The schedule was arranged according to a special system devised by the Camp Ritchie commandant, Colonel Charles Banfill. The students attended classes seven days in a row. On the eighth day, called "Ban-day," there were no classes. Most students spent this day off deep in their books and class notes. This unique eight-day week allowed a supposedly "eight-week" course to stretch into what was actually just over nine weeks of study. Banfill's schedule was very confusing at first because "Ban-day" fell on Monday the first week, on Tuesday the second week, and so on, but gradually the men adjusted to the system.

The first few weeks were devoted mainly to memorizing. Though Herman and most of the other students in his class were native speakers, the German instructor set them to learning military terms and new Nazi slogans and titles.

"Your vocabulary must be current," he lectured, "and the new Nazi way of speaking must flow off your tongue naturally." Some of the students had not spoken German for five or six years, and they had to regain their fluency. Robert, the Columbia University graduate student, struggled to get rid of his American accent.

In a class called Order of Battle, they had to memorize the look of German tanks, artillery, airplanes, and other equipment, as well as the German names and terms for all these armaments, military ranks, and insignia. They were taught the structure of the German military and memorized the complete history of German units, as well as their insignias and the names of their officers. They were shown photos and had to memorize the faces of high-ranking Nazi officials and important generals. In another class they learned to read German maps of Europe, some so new they showed Austria as part of Germany proper and all the conquered countries as German possessions. They memorized the names and locations of mountain ranges, rivers, towns, and cities in Germany, France, and the Low Countries. There was a class in Morse code and another where they learned to read and analyze aerial photographs. And they spent hours translating documents from German to English, and sometimes, from English to German.

Not all the work was in the classroom. One hot afternoon they were called out of the map-reading class and told to line up in the central field. Perspiration dripped from under Herman's forage cap and down his cheek, and as he fought the urge to wipe it away, he glimpsed an enormous first sergeant striding toward them. Walter saw him too and whispered clearly, "It's Man Mountain Dean. I heard he was here."

This was the first time they had actually seen the famous wrestler. Now he stood in front of them and saluted. "At ease, soldiers. I am here to teach you how to kill with your hands."

The men shifted their feet on the grass and the hushed sound covered the low, strangled gasp of one of the men in the back row.

The first sergeant stood before them, well over six feet tall and close to 300 pounds of muscle. He had been in the army in World War I. Both showman and athlete, he had enjoyed a successful career, touring Europe as a wrestler and working in Hollywood as an actor. Now he was back in the army by his own choosing. Herman had seen him in the movie comedy, *The Gladiator*, with Joe E. Brown, but no one was laughing today as they faced his imposing figure. Herman, a full foot shorter than the sergeant, and nearly 200 pounds lighter, hoped he would not be selected to help with any hands-on demonstrations.

Luckily First Sergeant Dean chose a young private, the tallest man in the unit, to come forward. Still, he was inches shorter and visibly shaken, as he faced the instructor and did what he was told to help Dean methodically demonstrate various holds and throws of hand-to-hand combat. Later, the students were divided into practice teams. Within a few sessions, they felt comfortable working with the huge instructor who had a gentle teaching style to offset his giant size. They were taught the use of arm, leg, and back muscles, the power of surprise, and finally how to wield a knife, a small stiletto that killed in silence, and according to Sergeant Dean, without pain. Herman was agile, and by the end of the training, was able to throw a man bigger than himself. He hoped that he wouldn't need these skills—using his head seemed infinitely preferable.

After several weeks of classes and several supposedly free "Ban-days" devoted to studying the past week's materials, Class Nine was told it would join other classes for a special presentation. The instructors warned them to be prepared to experience what it was like to live in Nazi Germany, not a pleasant thought for many of the men who had done exactly that already. Rumors were rampant throughout the camp as to what they would see, and men who had been there a while refused to give full reports, creating more trepidation.

The next afternoon, when his group entered the theater, Herman's stomach lurched. The walls were festooned with Nazi banners. Red, white, and black bunting was draped from the rafters, a huge portrait of Hitler dominated everything, and gigantic Third Reich flags flanked the stage. These long, blood-red flags, centered by a white disk and the hated, black swastika symbol, brought back too many unpleasant memories—things Herman was determined to forget. He could not get the queasy feeling to leave his gut, even though he knew it was all a stage show.

Scattered throughout the audience were men in gray Nazi military uniforms, Brown Shirt uniforms, and the dreaded black of the SS. A ramrod straight officer in SS uniform stood at each side of the stage. Herman looked around and saw several men in his group were pale and trembled as if they had seen a ghost. Suddenly loudspeakers blared out with the German national anthem "Das Horst Wessellied."

The men dressed in German uniforms stood and sang loudly along with the music. A few of the students stood but did not sing, though most of the audience remained cringing in their seats. Herman almost stood, an automatic reaction to the sounds of the familiar music, then he gripped the armrests of his seat and waited for the song to end. As the last notes were sung, a voice from the front row yelled out, "Don't worry, guys! It's a reenactment. Be glad it's not real!"

A collective relaxation and audible sigh rippled through the audience. They listened to a fake Brown Shirt Nazi harangue the crowd while shills in uniform cheered and stood to give the Hitler salute. "Heil, Hitler!" they yelled.

An answering loud "Booooo" from the audience released the tension. Herman began to relax.

Finally, at the end, Colonel Banfill came on the stage. "Men, you are here in Maryland to learn how to bring this Nazi horror to an end. Our motto is, 'Know thy enemy.' Starting next week you will be seeing more of these men in Nazi uniform. They are a special battalion known as the Composite School Unit. Their mission is to help train you. They are so good at pretending to be Nazis that we have, on occasion, had some pretty scared locals hereabouts. The Composite Battalion will be your laboratory rats, and you will be graded on the way you observe and treat them. Occasionally you may be asked to wear German uniforms and help them out. Remember, it's all in order to make us better able to annihilate the enemy." The colonel saluted the audience. "Do a good job, men. It will be the only chance you'll have to practice before the big game."

# CHAPTER 18
# CARDBOARD TANKS
# AND FAKE GERMANS

THE NEXT DAY WOULD BE their fourth "Ban-day," a Thursday with no classes. That evening, after the reenactment, Herman and Jake went to the honky-tonk bar known as Chocolate Park, just outside the gates of Camp Ritchie. They sat on the high stools in the dim light, a pitcher of beer between them, hoping to drink away the tension all those Nazi flags had created.

Herman took a long draught from his glass. "I don't feel like studying tomorrow. It's past time for a day off and a little fun." He wiped foam from his mouth with the back of his hand. "I'm not interested in Sergeant Holden's whores in the shacks out back. I'd rather kiss a regular girl just once than pay a tart for the full job. Wouldn't want to give that pimp the satisfaction, anyway."

Jake seemed to be in agreement. "On principle I object to giving the sergeant my money, even if I have to stay a virgin 'til after the war." He lifted his glasses and rubbed the bridge of his nose. Herman, who had seen this gesture whenever his friend was contemplating an important issue, was not surprised by the admission of virginity. "I'd stop contributing the dime every week to Holden's retirement fund if I had the nerve," Jake added.

"He's old-school army . . . probably been in since the Spanish-American War." Herman laughed, though the joke held a kernel of truth. "He ought to be drummed out, but it won't happen soon enough to help us." Herman took another long swig of his beer. "Forget that bastard. We need a vacation. My brain is getting addled with all the memorizing. I need to relax. See something." He swallowed the rest of his beer. "Maybe if we find the right town, you'll get lucky. Best to ditch the virginity before you get sent to the front." He rubbed the beads of condensation from his glass. "I can speak highly of English girls if we get sent there first. I promise, some of them can be very different from their proper reputations."

Jake looked up with interest, a question in his eyes, but Herman shook his head and said nothing more. Finally Jake shrugged. "I'm for the best use of our day," he said. "If we get up at dawn, we might be able to have a full twenty-four hours away from camp." He scratched the dark stubble on his chin. "Where shall we go? We can agree that girls are on the top of our list, though I'd die for some good food . . . maybe a little live jazz, too. But that might be too much to ask for."

Herman shook his head and slapped his friend on the back. "Okay. Music and food. But mainly I want plenty of females and lots of drink to help loosen them up! I need to smell perfume. To run my hand up a shapely leg and feel the top of a pair of silk stockings. And so do you."

Jake grinned. "Well, sure. But we should decide where. We can't just walk out the gate at five a.m. and hop on whatever bus is out there with its engine running."

"Let's go back to the barracks and see if Walter wants to join the expedition," Herman said. "He's a party guy and always knows what's up."

They had just climbed the stairs to the second floor when Walter came out of the latrine, wet from his shower, his towel around his neck.

"Count me in," he said as soon as he heard plans were being made. "I have a map and bus schedule I've been saving." He strode across the room to his bunk, dried off quickly, pulled on a pair of trousers, rummaged in his foot locker, and popped up with a grin, a bundle of papers in his hand. He spread out a large map of Virginia, Maryland, Pennsylvania, and Washington, DC on Herman's mattress. The three friends leaned over and studied the creased paper.

"If we're going to get away," Herman said, "we may as well do it right. How far do you think we can get and still have time to see something when we get there?"

Jake swept his hand in an arc over the map. "I'd love to see Washington, DC. Some guys went there the two days before class started. But they said the bus didn't come by here until eleven in the morning. And besides, it may not be the best place to find girls."

"We'd lose half the day before we got anywhere. Jake's right, too. Probably more old men in DC than women,"

Herman said. "I heard the bus that goes north into Pennsylvania leaves the gate at six a.m. That true, Walter?"

While his friend studied the bus schedule, Herman ran a finger over the map, from Ritchie northward, up the highway, and into the neighboring state. "Here's a town. York! It looks big enough to be interesting. We could get there before noon and have the whole day."

"How about Hagerstown," Walter said. "I overheard the first lieutenant in my map-reading class tell his buddy about a hotel there that has a dance band and lots of girls."

Jake shook his head. "Too much competition from the officers. If that's their spot, we need to find some place different."

"Yep. We need a town where sergeants and privates are appreciated," Herman said.

Walter laughed. "Yes, sir. I'll ask around right now . . . see if anyone knows what's in York." He stood, walked down the row of cots, and joined a loud group of men with a reputation for wild evenings out.

Within thirty minutes he came back with his report. York offered German food, without any Nazi cultural overtones, and plenty of pretty girls.

"All right, team," Herman said. "Be prepared for departure at zero-six hundred hours."

In the pink light of a July morning, Herman, Walter, and Jake, as well as a handful of others, waited at the camp gate for the bus to York. By afternoon, they knew their choice had been a good one. They found girls who spoke a few words of German and a German-style beer cellar that served familiar food. The friends stuffed themselves with kraut and sauerbraten washed down with more than a few steins of beer. Best of all, the barmaids were buxom and friendly. Herman found one willing to offer a few kisses to a soldier out behind the restaurant after closing.

As agreed, he met up with his buddies at the bus depot at two in the morning. Jake's shirt was buttoned crooked, and his face was smudged with lipstick. "Pretty close," he said grinning broadly. "She gave me her phone number." He patted his pocket.

The station was crowded with soldiers. The 2:15 a.m. bus was the last transportation out of town before noon the next day. It would get them to the gate of Camp Ritchie well before reveille. Herman and Jake shoved their way into the already packed bus, with Walter stumbling behind them. They wedged themselves in the remaining aisle space as the bus started to move.

Herman, too short to get a good grip on the grab bar, was only able to keep his upright stance because of the close pack of bodies around him. He was standing nose to chest with a tall soldier who smelled of beer, sweat, and stale cologne. The idea of four hours in this position made him feel nauseated. He glanced down the aisle at Jake, also wedged between two soldiers, but couldn't locate Walter, though he knew he had seen him struggle up the stairs and into the bus. Herman looked up and saw the chrome bars of the luggage rack, empty except for one or two small shopping bags and a rucksack. He stood on his toes and stretched his arms until his fingers barely grazed the edge of the rack. He set his boot on the armrest of the nearest seat, and lifted himself up to hover over the startled soldier who occupied it.

"'Scuse me, Corporal," he said, "I'm going upstairs." With a little jump and the leverage of the armrest, he pulled himself up and slithered into the narrow luggage rack. He stretched out as best he could, bent his arm under his cheek to act as a pillow, and closed his eyes. If he had been any bigger, he wouldn't have fit in the open space—sometimes being short was a good thing. Within minutes he drifted off to sleep.

A couple of hours later, the jerk of the bus jarred him awake and out of a dream. He heard the different tone of the engine as it idled and lifted his head, his mind fuzzy and disoriented.

"All you Ritchie boys," the driver hollered, "you're home. Everybody off, or you'll end up where you don't wanna be."

Surrounded by groans and complaints, Herman managed to climb down and out of the bus. Walter and Jake waited by the gate.

"We made it," Herman said. "Great though it was, I don't think I'd have energy to do it again soon."

Walter gave a sleepy sigh. "Don't worry, we won't have time. Not until we graduate, anyway."

"Come on guys," Jake said. "We can get a much-needed cold shower before class if we hurry." He turned and strode through the gate into camp, Walter and Herman close behind.

IN THE NEXT WEEKS, TRAINING took on a more practical dimension. One afternoon Herman's class was taken out to a tree-topped hill, told to observe the valley below, and to take notes of what they saw. They concealed themselves among bushes and grass with cut foliage tied to their helmets. Propped up on their elbows, they scanned the area around them through binoculars. Herman could feel Jake take in air sharply when a platoon of German infantry marched down the road and into view.

Walter, on the other side of Herman, inched forward in the tall weeds and cocked his head toward the marching soldiers. "That's the Composite guys, Sergeant" he whispered.

Herman heard Jake slowly let out his breath.

The infantry moved toward them, followed by tanks and trucks, looking just like the German military armaments they had memorized. Walter whispered again. "I heard that some of the tanks are just cardboard."

"They look real enough to me," Jake said, his voice hushed. "It's like watching a newsreel of the invasion of the Netherlands."

Herman pushed a stalk of rough grass away from his nose. He wanted to take all this seriously, to earn good grades that would speed him into the fighting. Jake was already scribbling in his little notebook, but Walter always had one more thing to say. "Some of the tanks are real. Captured in Africa . . ."

Herman turned to Walter. "Now be quiet and pay attention. Remember what the captain told us last week. If we don't pass these classes, we'll be assigned to the Composite Group ourselves—for the duration. Do you want to spend the war in Maryland as a pretend German?"

Walter shook his head. "No, sir. No, sir, I don't," he said and clamped his lips closed. He put his binoculars up to his eyes to study the troops below.

Another platoon came into view and set up a machine gun nest beside the road. For three hours Herman's class observed the military movement they knew to be fake. When they were trucked back to the classroom, they were told to prepare a written report of all they had seen. It was due that evening before they could go to the mess hall for dinner.

Soon classroom content focused on methods of interrogation. First, and most important, they had to learn all the rules of the Geneva Conventions, the basis of legal interrogation. After they knew the rules by heart, the classes shifted emphasis to practical information on how to interrogate newly captured prisoners. One thing was made clear—all types of torture were forbidden by the Geneva laws.

Prisoners were not required to give any information beyond their name, date of birth, rank, and service number. "But your job," the instructor told the students, "is to make them want to tell you more. The most basic information they might let drop—the mention of a town they marched through the day before, what they had for supper, or the amount of sleep they had during the night, could help determine the degree of resistance to expect in an upcoming battle."

The prohibition against physical torture was clear and evident to all. "Don't touch the prisoners except to help them if they are weak or injured," the instructor told them. "A bit of physical discomfort," he said, "such as standing at attention for twenty minutes in the rain, is certainly not torture. But for a man who is hungry and battle weary, a simple cup of coffee or the offer of a meal might be enough for him to say something he considers of no consequence." The instructor cautioned that psychological pressure was a gray area that could be used, but very carefully. "There is a fine balance between the prisoner's loyalty to his code of silence and his desire to please you, his captor, without jeopardizing his honor. You must find the balance that tips him toward helpfulness."

Herman and the other students learned to be observant. "Be aware of every detail," the instructor warned them. "The type of mud on a boot or the condition of a man's uniform can tell you a lot."

After endless hours of classroom instruction, the trainees practiced on each other. They set up tents in the field, each tent furnished with a small table, two hard-backed chairs, and a few other details to give it the feel of being near the battlefront. American guards brought in men from the Composite Battalion for questioning. Herman did his best to get information from his "prisoners," but the men of the Composite, dressed in various German and Italian military uniforms, were masters at pretending to be the enemy and stubbornly refused to reveal anything of value. Some, especially the students who had been held back from previous classes, seemed to delight in portraying cold, straight-backed, disciplined, fervent Hitler lovers—almost to the point of caricature. He ended most days exhausted after hours of frustration because he had extracted so little information. In the evening, he labored over the reports of the day's interrogations, aware that a well-composed and comprehensive report was essential to passing the course. He enjoyed writing concise sentences and organized paragraphs, but as a result, was often unable to finish before dinner. Many nights he slogged out the last lines on the typewriter just before "Taps" sounded. He knew the composite guys had to write up reports on his performance as an interrogator, and he supposed this gave them a good laugh.

He figured he may as well spend his evenings on his studies because there was little recreation around camp, though officers and instructors occasionally found the time and energy to take a canoe out on the lake. Herman and his friends, forbidden to go beyond the bar just outside the main gate on class days, and too tired on their "Ban-days" to take the long bus ride anywhere, spent most of their free time going over military charts and class notes.

In mid-July, the new post exchange, the building they had noticed under construction on their first walk around camp, finally opened for business and maintained evening hours after mess call. The friends discovered they shared a common love of ice cream sodas. If their reports were done, they wandered over to the exchange. They would choose a table by the window near the soda fountain and sip their sweet foamy drinks from frosted glasses while they contemplated the gathering dusk. In the new building, there was also a sundries shop where they could buy toothpaste, candy, and stationery, as well as a barber shop and a tailor shop. There was even a tap room where beer was for sale every day except Sunday, making it possible to avoid Chocolate Park entirely if they wanted. A very un-happy Sergeant Holden raised his retirement donation fee to fifteen cents.

Satiated with vanilla ice cream soda, Herman returned to his quarters and settled on his bunk to read or write let-ters until lights out. His mother had finally received her US visa. "Idle gossip sinks ships," printed in red at the bottom of his new USO letter paper, reminded him to be careful not to say anything about his classes. In his usual way, he mingled reassurance with advice when he wrote her.

*Dear Mom,* July 20, 1943

*I hope this will be my last letter to you addressed to London. Soon I will be writing to you in Laguna Beach! The thought of that makes me very glad. I understand Bonnie is expecting a new baby soon. I know you will miss Edith's little ones, but you will love the pretty granddaughter and new baby waiting for you in California. You will be happy there. It is different from London. Even in wartime, you'll feel like you are living in paradise. I'm only sorry I won't be able to be around to see you.*

*Take as little luggage as possible with you. Whatever you need can be found in California. The trip will be rough. It is a long way to California, but you can have a break visiting your sister in New York and all the others in Chicago. I advise taking the train as the bus might be too tiring for you. Learn the latest slang from Leonora and you will begin to feel like an American.*

*There is no reason to be afraid. You will have little*

*work to do in Fred's house except pleasant housework and cuddling the new baby. I hope from now on your life will be a holiday. Maybe Fred will be able to get you a piano.*

*Hugs and kisses,*
*Your son,*
*Herman*

For Herman, the long eight-day weeks of classes seemed to go on and on, but as they added up, the rigorous training left him with the feeling he could handle whatever came his way in Europe.

In the pre-dawn dark of the first day of the eighth week of classes, they were told to report to the parade ground. There they were ordered into the back of several canvas-covered trucks. Herman and the others sat close together on the narrow benches inside and watched as the rear flap was tied closed. They bumped over the rough roads for what seemed like hours, up and down hills and around sharp curves before the truck ground to a halt. The map-reading instructor, a captain, came to the back of the truck, opened the flaps, and pointed at two men, seemingly at random. "You two. Out," he commanded. A few minutes later, the truck bounced down the road. Two more stops, and each time a team of two men was dropped off.

When it was Herman's turn, the glare of the early morning sun dazzled him. It took a moment for his eyes to adjust to the bright light. When he could see again, he realized he had been paired with Jake. This was good.

They worked well together, and his friend was smart. The instructor handed them a large map and a compass. "Your assignment is to find your way back to Camp Ritchie before twenty-four-hundred hours. Good luck, men."

The rumble of the truck driving away was followed by a silence filled only with bird song. They unrolled the map, which was entirely in German, though it seemed to cover the states of Maryland, Virginia, and Pennsylvania. Camp Ritchie was marked slightly to the left of center. The two friends looked around. They were surrounded by valleys and ridges of wooded, mountainous terrain.

Herman set the compass on a leveled piece of ground, hunkered down, and spread the map at his feet with north on the map facing the same way as the north needle on the compass. "First we have to figure out where we are," he said.

Jake squatted next to him. They both studied the map for several minutes. Slowly Jake's finger pointed to a collection of closely spaced curved lines that indicated steep terrain, then to the hills spread in front of them. "We're here, I think. See how the slopes run and the thick green growth at the bottom of that gully." He tapped on the map with his index finger. "There's a stream down there and there's a stream here on the map."

Herman pointed to the indication of a waterfall on the map, probably north and upstream of where they thought they were. "Let's see if we can find this waterfall. That should confirm our location."

The two men stood and headed to the valley below. Within an hour they heard the roar of the falling water, and when they climbed over some large boulders, the cascade came into view. In the pool at the base of the fall, they soaked their handkerchiefs and wiped the sweat and dust from their faces, pleased to have gotten off to a good start. But it was only the beginning of a long day.

Confident now that they knew their location, Herman and Jake turned and moved downstream again. As they trudged along, Herman thought he saw movement on a ridge across the river and wondered if it was one of the other teams, or possibly a wild bear, a beast made large by camp stories. The river twisted and turned, the steep banks strewn with boulders, the water boiling with rapids. Finally they were forced to leave it and make their way into the forest. For close to two hours they pushed through brambles and crawled over or under fallen trees. Still surrounded by hills, they came to a cliff they didn't expect. They slumped to the ground with a groan and spread the map out on the stony ledge, overlooking a deep gorge. Carefully they studied the squiggles showing land contours.

"Oh, God. Look here." It was Jake who located another group of closely drawn lines. "It's our river again, but it twists and turns and I think we've gone in the wrong direction. Much farther and we'd be in the next state!"

Herman peered closely at the map. "We may need to turn around," he said. "Or do you see a shortcut over the hills to get where we need to be? I don't want to fail this exercise."

"What about this?" Jake pointed to a line that indicated a small stream originating high up, near a ridgeline. "Just follow it up and over—we might still make it back before dark."

The climb was difficult, the creek filled with a jumble of rocks and rotting logs. But the water became a trickle and, before they reached the ridge, they found the spring where it began. The rest of the climb was hot and dry, the trees thick, but at the crest, the view stretched away. Wave upon wave of hills, each softer than the next, disappeared into the afternoon haze. Herman lifted the binoculars. "I see buildings. A farm, maybe. And a barn . . . there's another! Two farms. We're heading in the right direction now."

Gradually they wound their way out of the mountains and into hill and farm country. Suddenly everything became easier. Herman, never shy, walked nonchalantly up to a farmer and asked him questions about the roads, the towns, and which way it was to Camp Ritchie. Jake stood back to the side of the road and tracked their position on the map.

They knew they were almost at Ritchie when they passed the gate to Camp Louise, a girls' summer camp, and heard the squealing and laughter of teenagers as they walked toward their dining hall.

"I'm hungry. Sure would like to go with them," Herman said with a grin as they trudged down the road in the golden glow of the setting sun.

Jake grinned back. "I heard some guys tried that a few nights ago. Took the shortcut over the hill and climbed the fence." He smeared a rivulet of sweat dripping down his cheek into a muddy smudge. "They got caught, though. Did some extra time with Sergeant Dean—pushups and running up and down the hill behind the mess hall's what I heard."

Herman's laugh was low and tired. "Let's skip joining the girls for dinner this time," he said. "Not worth risking special treatment from Man Mountain Dean."

They arrived at Camp Ritchie's main gate as the street lights blinked on, silhouetting the jagged shapes of the crenellated camp wall. They were not the first team back and certainly not the last—several groups struggled in well after dark, and one final team arrived on the morning bus from Richmond—they had gone even farther in a wrong direction.

The rest of the last "Banfill week" ended with final exams, both written and oral. The results had to be evaluated before they would be issued their next assignments. When the grades were finally posted, Herman was proud to have earned the highest score in German language class. Jake had the highest overall grades with a score of 92, though Herman's scores came in a very respectable third place. Because of his excellence in German language skills, he was classified as a documents examiner. The next day, Jake, Walter, and about fifty other newly graduated students were piled into trucks and taken to Hagerstown. They came back that afternoon, newly minted citizens.

Walter jumped down from the truck with a huge grin, waving to Herman who was waiting to hear about their day. "It was great!" His excitement filled his voice. "We stood in front of a judge at the courthouse and pledged our allegiance to the Stars and Stripes and all it represents. When we filed out of the courtroom, the major gave us our citizenship papers." He waved his certificate proudly. "I'm an American now!" he said.

"It was actually quite solemn," Jake said. "I felt proud. And the judge shook each of us by the hand. 'Do a good job for us overseas, boys,' he said."

On August 17, 1943, the Ninth Class formally graduated from the Intelligence School of Camp Ritchie. After the class marched on the parade ground, Colonel Banfill delivered a rousing speech. "Graduates, what you have learned here at Camp Ritchie will help defeat the enemy. Officers in the field may not value what you do as much as they should," he said. "But don't for a minute doubt what I am telling you today. It is the knowledge you will bring them that will make it possible for the generals to win the battles."

Hearing this speech, Herman was eager to get on a ship and join the fighting troops. But when he read his orders, he saw he had been assigned to go to Fort Benning in Georgia. The army had decided he was officer material. He was pleased by the army's confidence in him, but frustrated by yet another delay to getting overseas where he could use his new skills. Jake was assigned officer training, too. Herman was glad to be assigned with his buddy, but he couldn't help feeling jealous of Walter who, along with many of the other students, was being shipped directly to England.

The officer training program in Georgia was heavily impacted by the war and had a waiting list that often took several months. Meanwhile, Herman's orders were to stay at Camp Ritchie, take a typing course to improve his speed, and help out as a teaching assistant in the documents and the German language class.

# CHAPTER 19

# ALMOST OVER THERE

THE WEEKS EASED INTO MONTHS as Herman waited at Camp Ritchie. The leaves on the trees turned from green to gold to russet, the chill evening air promised winter, and he began to doubt he would get back to Europe while there was still a war to win. Finally, when brown and gold leaves lay in piles under bare trees, he received his clearance to go to Georgia.

He left by train in late November in the company of Jake and two other men. The course of instruction at Fort Benning was condensed and intensified—all the class and field work of officer training would be completed in a little over three months. These quickly trained, wartime officers had already earned the nickname "ninety-day wonders."

At the completion of the course, after being officially terminated from the US Army as enlisted soldiers, graduating students would be reinstated as second lieutenants. This gave them the opportunity to update their personal information on the new dog tags issued with their officer's serial number.

The last evening before graduation, he and Jake lingered over shakes in the Benning clubhouse. Herman fiddled with his paper straw, stirring the melting ice cream in the tall glass in front of him. He glanced at his friend who was contemplating a wet ring on the table. "Jake, when I was drafted, I filled out my religious preference as 'none.'"

Jake looked up with an expression of mild curiosity, his finger poised above the wet circle.

Herman rushed on. "I never did like that, but it seemed natural at the time. My father was a free-thinker. He didn't tolerate talk of God in the house, and his ideas were all I knew. But now, that blank space on my tag seems like . . . well, kind of tempting fate."

Jake met his eyes and asked, "Are you thinking of putting down Jewish?"

Herman shook his head and stirred his slushy drink again. "Nothing seems right. I don't know what I am. I believe in some kind of supreme something. I think I do, anyway. . . . God, I guess. How else could I explain all that's happened in my life? Whether it's been good or bad, it's always led me forward in the right direction, as if everything had a purpose."

"Well, I wouldn't advise you to put down Jewish. The Nazis probably know that an *H* on American tags stands for Hebrew. The work we'll be doing, we might get caught behind enemy lines. Captured by the Germans." He drew a cross through the wet ring. "Honestly, I think about changing my tags to Catholic or something. In Germany an *H* could be a death sentence."

"Wow . . . I never thought you'd do that. I know some guys have, but . . ."

"I think about it, but somehow I can't bring myself to do it. My father skipped services and never kept kosher—but he'd never deny his religion, either. He might be dying in some camp somewhere because of his religion . . . or dead. I feel I have to keep faith with him."

"I never felt Jewish," Herman said, "and my father would certainly approve of the blank, or better yet, a capital A for atheist. But I don't like it. I think about dying in some muddy field somewhere with a big nothing on my chest and it scares me."

"Do you think of yourself as a Christian, a Goy?"

Herman shook his head. "Not really. I used to go to Sunday services sometimes with my Lutheran school chums and I liked the hymns, but mostly I loved watching the sun make rainbows as it streamed through the stained glass of the church windows." Herman shook his head again. "I wish I knew what I am. I'd like to be something."

"Just be whatever you want to be. Put down whatever makes you comfortable now." He looked seriously at his friend. "It's not a life commitment, you know."

Herman thought about Jake's comment. "Lutheran. Like my friends back home. That's Protestant, right?"

"Far as I know, Protestant covers lots of different churches like Lutheran, Baptist, Methodist . . . and . . . well, lots. Anything except Catholic, I guess."

"That's what I'll put on the form. Protestant. With a *P* on my tags, at least I won't be a nothing. I won't be Jewish or Catholic either. Just something."

By early March, all the paperwork filled out, his new tags issued, and his lieutenant's insignia sewn on his uniform, Herman was back at Camp Ritchie. Jake had received orders to report to some top secret intelligence center near Washington, DC—a place where, according to scuttlebutt, captured high-Nazi personnel would be brought for questioning.

But Herman had no time to miss his friend. As soon as he returned to Ritchie, he was reclassified as a prisoner of war interrogator and assigned to a team being formed called IPW 80. There was a master sergeant on the team, a buck sergeant, a technical sergeant, a corporal, and another officer besides himself, Captain Janus, the leader of the team. While they waited at Camp Ritchie to go to war, each man had an assignment, some kind of light duty. Though second officer of the team, Herman was stuck behind a desk, typing up reports, and again, impatient and frustrated.

In the evenings after dinner, Herman lingered in the mess hall, gradually getting to know the men in his group. Captain Janus organized a few meetings to discuss interrogation methods, evaluate each man's strong points, and build teamwork. They were a great group of soldiers. All they needed now was to get across the Atlantic to be part of the European Theater of Operations in time for the invasion.

Just as the men began to grumble about the days of waiting, their orders arrived and IPW 80 was moved by train to Camp Miles Standish outside Boston. They spent only three days there, being issued new equipment, and then they were transported in covered trucks to Boston Harbor. Herman looked up at the imposing black bulk of the SS *Aquitania*, a passenger ship seeing its second war as a troop carrier. Long lines of men, their bulging duffels slung over their shoulders, slowly moved toward the ship and up the sloping gangways. He was directed to the first class gangway, now being used by officers, which made him feel both proud and conspicuous.

The *Aquitania*, filled to the gunnels with nearly 3,000 soldiers, its decks laden with armaments and anti-aircraft guns, steamed out of the harbor and turned north. The afternoon wore away as the ship moved up the coast, then inexplicably turned around and headed back south to stand off Boston Harbor. At midnight, when another ship and a small cruiser escort steamed out to join them, the convoy finally turned east and headed into the dark Atlantic night.

Herman shared a minuscule cabin with another lieutenant who was assigned to a different team out of Camp Ritchie. His cabin mate, Julian Goldschmitt, was studious and quiet, but with a hard edge of skepticism that appealed to Herman immediately.

That first night, as the ship stood off Boston, they shared a bottle of wine Julian had packed in the bottom of his duffle. "The captain thinks he'll outwit the German U-boats with his fancy evasion tactics," Goldschmitt said as he sipped the ruby red Zinfandel. "But they'll find us. With this ship packed to the gunnels with soldiers, I suspect we'll leave a trail of garbage like Hansel and Gretel left crumbs. I have faith in Nazi intelligence . . . unfortunately."

Herman couldn't disagree, but he had a more positive frame of mind. "We'll turn that around. We men from Ritchie will prove their match."

Goldschmitt raised his glass. "Here's to the men from Camp Ritchie. Watch out, Nazis. Here we come!" After a long drink of the wine, he added more soberly, "We're just getting started, though. We'll be battle tested, vetted by bullets and blood. Maybe even face death. And we'll certainly have the opportunity to lock minds with our Nazi ex-comrades. It won't be a walk in the park."

Later that night, Herman tossed sleeplessly in his hard bunk. Thoughts of the reality of war and his uncertain future kept him from falling asleep. He had heard his father talk of the misery in the trenches during World War I, and he knew war was not always heroic exploits. It could also be pain and blood, injury and death, illness and disease, or simply tedium and slogging through mud. His father had been proud of his military service to his beloved Germany, and in the beginning of the Nazi years, he had hoped his contribution would help his family. It had not. Herman was thankful he was a US citizen and serving on the right side in this war. But in the darkest part of the night, as the waves slapped against the hull of the ship, he listened to the beat of his heart while the specter of a soldier's death perched on his shoulder.

He finally dozed off, but his rest was uneasy. He was unused to the movement of the ship and plagued by odd, disquieting dreams. The illuminated hands of his watch showed 5:00 a.m. when he finally gave up on sleep and left his bunk. He needed to clear his mind. It was a relief to leave the airless cabin and climb the ladder to the gun deck. He stood at the rail and gazed out to the horizon, a black-on-black line with the shimmer of waves below and the sparkle of stars above. He slammed his palm hard on the railing, the thud echoing in the stillness. It seemed ridiculous and he ought to laugh. Finally he was getting what he wanted, but he was plagued by macabre thoughts.

What good things, he wondered, could he think of to turn his mind around? There was seeing Edith again and her babies. And his mother, at long last, was safely on her way to California. And most important, he would be a part of the invasion. Soon he'd see France. French girls were said to be better than English or American girls. He'd find a French Gloria with long legs to wrap around him. This final idea perked him up considerably.

A shimmer of gray gradually delineated the horizon. As it expanded, dissipating the blackness of night, Herman's thoughts lightened. Suddenly a boom exploded around him. It shook his knees and deafened his ears. Smoke billowed above the anti-aircraft guns but no planes flew overhead. Faintly, like an echo in the back of his head, he heard a voice saying, "Practice round two. Fire!" And another explosion of gunfire rocked the deck. He turned to see a gunnery sergeant standing behind the nearest guns. The man pointed at his watch and his mouth moved, forming words that Herman heard only as if they were coming from a tunnel. "Six a.m. Artillery practice. Best to stay below decks until after six every morning, Lieutenant."

Herman went below to stand in line for chow as the ship moved him steadily toward the next chapter of his life. Finally he felt like a grown man, but he still wasn't sure what kind of a man he would be. The war pulled him forward into its embrace. It would be the crucible that tested him.

# CHAPTER 20

# INTERROGATIONS

THE SHIP TOOK THE NORTHERN route by way of Green-
land and thus successfully evaded German submarine
wolfpacks to land its cargo of soldiers and armaments safely
in Scotland. After a long train trip south, Herman and his
team arrived in the Cotswold countryside of England to
find the air electric with anticipation of the expected invasion of Europe.

Only General Dwight D. Eisenhower, the Supreme Commander of the Allied Armies, knew exactly when they would
be in France. It was mid-May and, confined to their bases, the
soldiers waited. No one was given leave. All mail was carefully
censored for the slightest hint that might aid the enemy.

Herman was assigned to the intelligence section, and
during breaks, he and the other men who worked there
talked in whispers.

"General Patton is in England," a man decoding incom-
ing messages said.

Another man joined in. "The Krauts are so afraid of old Georgie since his victories in North Africa and Sicily, they're shitting their pants trying to figure out where he'll land."

"I heard a rumor at the mess hall from a guy in transportation," the first man said. "They say that Patton's been given command of the First US Army Group and they're positioned near Kent, waiting to cross the English Channel and land at Calais." He shared a knowing look with the other men and added, "I don't think the guys who drive the trucks know anything but rumors."

Herman nodded with the others but kept quiet. He was translating documents and radio transmissions every day, and he knew that these rumors were all part of Operation Fortitude, an elaborate deception to confuse the Germans. Of course, the part about the Germans' fear of Patton was true enough. General Eisenhower wanted the enemy kept in the dark about where Patton was and where the invasion forces would land.

Herman chuckled to himself as he went back to his work station. It was a lot like the fake German tanks at Camp Ritchie, only better. The First US Army waiting near the English coast was an illusion created by theater set designers. It was made up of inflatable Sherman tanks and planes, fake radio messages, and fabricated order of battle schemes that gave false lists of the battalions positioned to strike and where they would land. All this was leaked through a double agent to the German High Command. Herman knew that Patton was not in Kent—though he was in England, waiting like everyone else.

His work was interesting, but Herman longed for real action. D-Day, the assault of Europe, finally arrived on June 6, 1944, a gray, cold lull between two storms. Ships streamed across the English Channel and their landing craft dumped American, Canadian, and British soldiers on the sandy beaches of Normandy.

Herman listened with anticipation to the reports coming back from the beachhead. There was bloody and lethal fighting for several long days as the Allies secured the beaches. The reports told of slow movement down narrow roads lined with the high, tree-topped hedgerows of the Normandy countryside. It was a labyrinth of fields and orchards subdivided by six- to ten-foot high barriers of earth and foliage. Every one of these hedgerows was a tank barrier and an enemy fortress. But the Allied armies pushed slowly and steadily forward. Herman held his breath and waited for his own orders to join the fray.

Finally, after two weeks, he and his team were transferred to the US Third Army, now under Patton's command. Assigned to the general's headquarters, Herman and the other men in his unit knew their job would be to interrogate prisoners captured as the Third Army pushed beyond Normandy, across Brittany, and to Paris, the heart of France. He was elated to find Goldschmitt and his men also among the intelligence teams assigned to Patton. The Third Army and their IPW teams bivouacked on the English coastline where they waited impatiently while the Allies established a firm foothold in France.

In late June, Patton's army finally crossed the English

Channel, though the general's arrival in France was still kept quiet. The idea was that the longer the Germans thought he would lead a second offensive against Calais, the longer Hitler might hold his extra troops away from Normandy.

As July edged toward August, Herman made the rough channel crossing with his group. He waded ashore at Omaha Beach, past the evidence of carnage—torn bits of bloody clothing, single boots, twisted wire and metal, bomb craters, and abandoned and disabled tanks, trucks, and landing craft. When he set foot on French soil, he entered the crazy world that was war.

The Third Army emerged from the veil of secrecy on the first day of August. Patton had a reputation for fast, efficient, and successful battles, and he had waited long enough. It was one of the few warm, clear days of the entire summer. The air was flooded with sunshine as the soldiers charged through a gap between high hills and the sea. The Third Army—its armored and infantry divisions, its cavalry groups, its engineer combat battalions—all moved forward, eager to fight. Herman and the intelligence team followed the fighting troops to gather up and interrogate prisoners.

Soon they had left Normandy behind, overrun Brittany, and liberated 10,000 square miles of France from the Germans. Herman felt breathless with the speed at which they headed toward Paris. In some villages, French girls lined the roadside, waving and blowing kisses, but he had little time to stop and explore their charms. The headquarters was always on the move, barely able to keep up with the army, and Patton gave it the code name "Lucky Forward."

Herman and his IPW team were in the midst of it all. From the beginning of the push, they had lots of prisoners to question at the interrogation center, which was always somewhere near, but not in, the general's mobile command center.

The prisoner holding area was run by American military police. It was a simple enclosure surrounded by barbed wire, with a spiral of concertina wire running down the middle to separate the ranks. The interrogators didn't want the German officers to intimidate or threaten their captured enlisted men before they could be questioned. The wire-bound enclosure, filled with prisoners, was nicknamed the "cage." Patton disapproved of the term because, "Prisoners are not animals," but the men still used it when they talked among themselves.

Interrogation tents were pitched near the enclosure. Under MP guard, the disarmed prisoners were marched in groups from the front lines to the holding area where the team of screeners searched them for concealed weapons, marked maps, or other hidden items. The screeners, especially Master Sergeant Lehmann, were wizards at discovering which prisoners might have important information, and even better, be willing to talk.

German soldiers did not have dog tags. Each carried a paybook with his name, rank, age, blood type, and home region. All pay allotments and assignments were entered in this precious, little book, called a soldbuch. Without it a German soldier was as good as invisible. The sergeants who did the screening of the prisoners confiscated the paybooks and checked them to help decide who might have valuable information. A prisoner's rank, how long he had been in the army, and where he had served—all these things gave valuable clues as to how much they might know that could help the Allies.

Prisoners were brought in for questioning as quickly after capture as possible. As one battle-weary German after another stood in front of Herman, he soon realized that his training at Camp Ritchie was only a beginning—nothing done in that safe haven of Maryland could come close to the actual conditions of a wartime interrogation. No fake German prisoner who walked over from peeling potatoes at the mess hall at Camp Ritchie could duplicate the fatigue, humiliation, shock, and fear of a prisoner taken on the battlefield.

Some, especially if they were officers, were stubborn and refused to reveal any information beyond their name and rank. A few would blurt out anything, true or not, to get out of the tent and back with their comrades. Most prisoners would say only enough to earn good treatment but still maintain their self-respect. A few captured soldiers were eager to help in any way they could because they no longer believed the Nazi promises and only wanted the war to be over so they could go home.

As Herman worked with more and more prisoners, he learned to read them, to sense which ones would never crack and which men, after a few minutes of tough questions or a mention of transferring them to Russian allies, would begin to chat away if offered a cup of coffee. It was all a psychological game, and within weeks of arriving in Normandy, he knew he was good at it.

Each day dozens of prisoners were escorted by an armed guard into Herman's interrogation tent, and now, on a Monday morning, one more typical prisoner stood in front of him. Covered in mud, his uniform ripped at the knee and with dark circles under his eyes, the German stood at attention. Herman looked him over carefully in order to read the soldier's personality. He could see that the short wait under the scrutiny of an American officer made the prisoner nervous. This German was little more than a boy, maybe nineteen at most. Herman remembered what it had been like at that age, frightened and unsure of what would happen next. But this soldier was fighting for the Nazi giant who had been the cause of his own fear. The memory of the terror he had felt obliterated any sympathy for the boy in front of him. He began the questioning. "Name?"

"Horst Holmbach."

"Rank?"

"Corporal, sir."

"What's your outfit?" If the prisoner responded to this question, one step beyond what was required by the Geneva Conventions, he knew he would be able to get more if he was careful.

The young soldier looked up and his eyes pleaded for understanding. "Eighty-ninth Infantry, sir."

Herman still felt no sympathy. His mission was to get information. "How many men in your unit were wounded yesterday?"

"Ten."

"How many replacements did you get for those ten?"

"Six. And two of them were Poles. They don't even speak German properly, and they keep to themselves."

Herman pointed to the big map of France that hung from the tent wall. "Here is the city of Rouen, here Mantes. And here is the Loire River." He moved his finger, slowly tracing the blue line on the map, and gazed with feigned concern into the eyes of the haggard soldier. "Where did you sleep last night?" he asked, his voice low and gentle.

"I wouldn't call it sleep, sir. But we spent the night in a muddy foxhole about here." The prisoner hesitantly lifted his eyes and touched the map to indicate a spot outside a nearby village.

Now Herman knew he had the makings of a successful interrogation. If the boy knew anything of value he could pull it out of him, bit by bit. He hoped that even one small part of the story might prove to be significant. One could never tell what little detail, when patched together with the variety of different answers given by other prisoners to other interrogators, might complete the overall picture of enemy strength that General Patton needed. Herman searched his memory for the order of battle details he had learned at Camp Ritchie. He knew this soldier's unit, therefore now he knew which regiment was in the area. He knew they hadn't slept well for several days and that their replacements were thin and inadequate. He needed to plan his next questions carefully—at this point everything and anything could be important. He looked at the soldier again. His shoulders slumped forward and his knees seemed about to buckle. If he passed out, the questioning would have to stop.

Herman walked over to the tent flap and called out to the guard. "Sergeant, I need a cup of coffee in here. Hot and black with lots of sugar." Then he turned to the waiting prisoner. "At ease, Corporal."

Slowly Herman pulled a hard chair over in front of his work table, sat down behind it, and shuffled a few papers into neat stacks. "Sit down, Corporal. Let's talk more about your unit. Who was your commanding officer?" The boy sat heavily in the chair, looked at Herman, to him simply a kind, German-speaking American, and began to talk.

Later that day, Herman had a report to take to his superior officer, Captain Janus. It confirmed that German troops were on the run and getting tired.


AS THE RETAKING OF FRANCE progressed, the Third Army moved fast, and the command post with its interrogation teams had to move with the army. But sometimes there were days of waiting, with everyone hunkered down in their foxholes—days when no prisoners were brought in to question. Once, when the army's progress was stalled like this, Captain Janus called Herman into his tent.

"Lang, we need to get a prisoner who knows something!" he said. "Form a team, the best men you can find, and go out and get a German. Drag one in if you have to. General Patton wants information, and it's our job to get it for him."

Immediately, Herman formed a patrol from the men he trusted most—Goldschmitt as second officer, Master Sergeant Ernie Lehman because he was good with a knife, and Corporal Marcus Gross who was light on his feet and a quick thinker. The patrol would sneak behind enemy lines and capture a German for their general.

They moved out at dusk. Each with only a sidearm and a knife tucked in his boot, the four-man patrol stole across the front lines and crawled on their bellies to a tangled patch of bushes and fallen trees within a hundred yards of a string of German foxholes. Herman motioned his group to stop and stay low.

The pale light of the full moon revealed the rims of fifteen protective foxholes curved along the edge of a stand of trees, an open meadow beyond. Herman inched up to rest his binoculars on a fallen log, Goldschmitt beside him. They inspected the enemy carefully from one end of the line of entrenchments to the other. Everything seemed quiet. Outlines of helmets showed occasionally above the piled earth. Slowly Herman moved his binoculars to search the shadowy shapes of the line of trees, looking for a perimeter guard or a man who had left his foxhole to take a leak. Nothing moved. He put down his binoculars and rubbed his eyes. Then he saw the telltale glow of a cigarette among the trees and lifted the binoculars again to look more closely. The dark form of a man took shape, his hand, cupped to cover the glow of the cigarette that dangled from his lips. He had a rifle in his other hand, a guard, but not a vigilant one.

Herman silently pointed in the direction of the German. Goldschmitt nodded and nudged Lehman in turn.

As they watched, the man by the trees snuffed out the glowing ash of the cigarette under his boot, walked up to the far end of the trees, turned, and came back toward the Americans. When he was about sixty feet away from the hidden Americans, he sat down on an old stump of a tree, rested his rifle across his knees, rubbed his eyes, and kneaded his temples. Within minutes the German's head wobbled and the hand on his rifle slid downward, the fingers loose. Finally Herman saw the distinctive head-jerk of a man falling asleep on the job.

With a few hand signs, Herman indicated that Lehman and Goldschmitt should move around behind and make the capture. They melted silently into the trees. Herman inched closer to Corporal Gross and gestured for him to follow. They crawled forward, avoiding branches that might snap and came to a halt behind a low bush thirty feet from the dozing German. They settled in the grass, their concentration on the prize and the moving shadows behind the guard.

It was agonizing to wait and watch the slow progress of Goldschmitt and Lehman as they moved into position, paused to study the situation, and then stepped out of the trees. First the guard's head tipped back as Lehman grabbed his hair with one hand and with the other, encircled his neck. Goldschmitt held his pistol to the guard's temple, then swiftly pulled him into the woods. At the edge of the trees they pushed the German down into a tangle of underbrush just as a volley of fire burst overhead from the American artillery line, shells exploding in the field in front of the foxholes.

Herman kept his eyes on the tangle where his men lay hidden. "Wait," he mouthed to Gross. All the Germans in the foxholes were now wide awake, their helmets and rifles cresting the protective rim of the entrenchments. In the flashing light of random gunfire, he saw the German prisoner surge upward amid the trees and try to break free of his captors. A singular flash of gunfire burst amid the shadows, the sound of it drowned in the clamor of explosions from the artillery barrage, and the German leaned to clutch his thigh. Herman saw Goldschmitt deliver a sharp pistol blow behind the man's ear as he fell backward.

"Let's go," Herman commanded. He and Gross lunged forward and ducked into the tree cover toward their buddies.

It was a good catch. They dragged their unconscious prize a safe distance into the forest. Corporal Gross quickly bound the flesh wound in the man's leg, tied his hands behind his back, and searched him for hidden weapons.

The prisoner stirred and groaned. When the man opened his eyes, Herman's left hand held the German's shoulder down to the ground, the knife in his right hand against the prisoner's throat, the sharp blade drawing a thin trickle of blood. "Quiet down or I'll slit your throat," Herman hissed in German. The man didn't move. "Not a sound. If you cooperate, next month you'll be in Texas picking tomatoes. If you try to run, I'll shoot you in your good leg and turn you over to our Russian allies. Want to spend the rest of the war in Siberia?"

The prisoner, his eyes wide with fear, shook his head in tiny jerks and clamped his lips together as Herman eased the knife away from his throat.

Herman stood and motioned to his patrol. "Let's get this man back to camp." He took the lead while Goldschmitt and Lehman supported the limping prisoner as they shuffle-marched him over the line into American-held territory. Gross walked behind, his rifle trained on the German's back all the way to headquarters.

Before dawn, the prisoner stood at attention in Herman's interrogation tent. Peppered with questions and standing on the wrong side of the front lines with blood oozing through the thin bandage on his leg, the German was eager to talk. Before breakfast, Herman delivered new information to Captain Janus who would bring it to Colonel Allen. The general would have it at the morning meeting. By then the prisoner would be at the medical station, his leg wound clean, sleeping in a cot for a few hours before being sent to a holding camp, far better than the cages at headquarters.


AS THE THIRD ARMY ADVANCED, a steady stream of trucks filled the roads of France. They moved out from the Normandy beachhead and carried food, ammunition, and gasoline to the front. In the other direction, trucks transported wounded American soldiers back to the beaches where doctors had set up a mobile medical unit and boats waited to transport the injured back to hospitals in England. Worst of all were the trucks which moved the dead, each body wrapped in a clean mattress cover. When Herman watched these trucks rumble down the road past headquarters, the precious cargo jostled on their final trip, he was filled with anger. These American boys would never go home again—they would rest forever on a hill overlooking the English Channel.

One morning, as he walked the short distance between Lucky Forward and the interrogation center, he saw a truck off to one side, tipped precariously, half in, half out of the roadside ditch, its axle broken. Its canvas cover was stenciled with a large red cross and the driver and two medics struggled to unload the wounded. Because of the unsteady pitch of the truck, the three men had a difficult time balancing a heavy stretcher. The wounded soldier they carried screamed in terror and pain.

Without hesitation, Herman sprinted to the ambulance. "Let me help." He reached up to steady the stretcher and helped ease it to the ground by the side of the road.

The stretcher hit the soft, uneven dirt with a thud. The wounded man shifted at the jolt, screamed again. Herman saw that both his legs were covered in blood, one mangled and crushed, the other gone below the knee. His stretcher and his uniform blouse were soaked with blood, too. Rough tourniquets were wrapped around both thighs.

"Where's my leg?" the soldier moaned. "Did you find my leg?" He grabbed Herman's hand and squeezed it so tight his dirty fingernails dug into his rescuer's soft palm. "Lieutenant, have you seen my leg?"

Herman returned the soldier's grip and saw he wore a wedding ring. He seemed barely more than twenty, a young man with a bride waiting for him at home—maybe even a baby on the way. His broad forehead and freckled nose were pale and clammy, his hands cold. His hair was clotted with blood.

"Shhh," Herman whispered. "Don't worry, Private. Soon you'll be safe in England." He turned his head and looked for a medic. The man was helping another soldier who could still walk, but who wore a bloody bandage wrapped around his head and down over his eyes.

Herman felt the grip on his hand tighten and heard the moan of pain as it escalated and rolled out of the young soldier's throat. He turned back and saw the man's eyes wild with fear, the pupils dilated.

"Medic!" Herman yelled. "Medic!" He yelled a second time and realized the man was beside him.

"He needs more morphine," the medic said and pulled a syringe from his pack. He jabbed the needle into the soldier's bloody thigh and after a few moments, the boy's eyes calmed.

Herman turned to the medic. "Did he step on a mine?"

"No. Run over by a tank. The Nazi bastards just kept coming."

Herman looked down at the young soldier again. He seemed quieter, but still awake and lucid for a moment. He slid his arm under the man's head and gently lifted him, still holding his hand tightly. "Private, what kind of tanks? What kind of tank ran over you?"

The soldier's eyes fluttered open and he tried to focus. "Panzers. SS Panzers." The words slid out with his labored breathing. Then his eyes glazed over and Herman felt his grip loosen. He lowered the man's head to the stretcher.

"Doc?"

The medic put two fingers to the side of the young soldier's throat and felt for his pulse. He shook his head and closed the man's eyelids with a gentle stroke of two fingers.

"Dead," he said. Slowly the medic stood up. His eyes were tired and his face streaked with dirt and blood. "There's still more wounded in the truck, sir. Can you get us help?"

Herman stood and brushed the mud from his knees. "I can help you." And he moved toward the tipping ambulance.

Within ten minutes another truck arrived with two more medics and room in back for the injured Herman had helped. His own work was waiting. He looked one last time at the young soldier with the lost leg, quiet now, a handkerchief covering his freckled nose and lifeless eyes. The medic stood nearby, waiting with the body for a truck to transport the dead.

As Herman turned away and headed toward the gate of the interrogation center, a line of German prisoners marched inside. Soon he would be questioning these men. Perhaps there would be SS Panzer soldiers among them.

Late that afternoon, after interrogating a constant stream of prisoners, a military police sergeant entered Herman's tent.

"Excuse me, sir. There's one more prisoner. The guys up front just brought him in and the screeners say he could be important."

Herman saw his chance for a hot meal in the near future rapidly evaporate. "Okay, Sergeant. Bring him in." He swallowed the last dregs of his cold coffee as the Waffen-SS Captain came through the tent flap. He was escorted by another MP who handed over the man's soldbuch and left the tent. The German gave Herman a smart Nazi salute and stood ramrod straight in his mud and blood-smeared black uniform.

The hated stiff-armed salute sent a chill up Herman's neck. "If I see that disgusting salute again, you son of a bitch, I'll turn you over to the Russians. Their center is right next door and they'd happily put a bullet in your head for that kind of disrespect. Salute only as your grandfather did in the Weimar Republic or you'll be in Russian hands before your arm comes down."

"Yes, sir." The old-style salute that followed was accompanied by a smirk.

Herman glanced through the soldbuch and at the officer's uniform insignia. He was from a tank battalion. Panzers. Herman began his interrogation. "Name? Rank?" to which the correct answers were given.

"Captain, what regiment are you from?"

"I do not have to answer that question. Geneva Conventions. Article Number Five."

"Ah, but it would be better for you to answer. Some simple answers and you can go to the cages and get something to eat." Herman cleared his throat. "I repeat. What regiment are you from?"

"I will not answer. Geneva Conventions, Article Number Five."

"Who is your commanding officer?"

"I refuse to answer according to Article Five."

Herman's anger rose. He had been warned at Ritchie not to allow personal feelings into the interrogation tent, but he was having a hard time with this German. The sight of the SS insignia on the man's collar brought back memories of the fear he felt that day in the Meiningen police station when he had been startled by the two SS officers. It was a man like this who had probably tormented his beloved Uncle Martin until he died at Dachau. It could have been this same officer who had ordered his tanks to roll over American infantry, leaving a young, freckle-faced soldier without legs as he faced death by the side of a dusty road.

"I don't want to hear any more about the Geneva Conventions, you son of a bitch. I know it as well as you do, and I may choose to ignore it."

"Sir, if you ignore it, I have the right to lodge a complaint with your military authorities. That's Article Twelve."

Of course he was right. Herman could not ignore the Geneva rules. An hour later, after a constant barrage of questions, the Nazi still stood at attention, never flinching. He was unwounded and the blood on his trouser leg could have been American or German, but in Herman's imagination, the red stain represented the blood of his great-uncle and his cousin. It was a vivid reminder of the young American soldier who had died in his arms that morning and was now a body wrapped in a cold mattress cover. This SS officer stood and spouted the articles of the Geneva Conventions by number like they were Bible verses, while others lay dying in the mud. In a voice that thinly covered his escalating anger, Herman said, "I assume you know Article Twenty-seven."

"Yes, sir." The German stood up straighter than before. "It allows for prisoners to be asked to do labor as long as they are physically fit." He actually smiled. "The work can be nothing that has to do with the operations of war. But that is in Article Thirty-one."

Herman ignored the last bit of information. "And are you physically fit?" he asked.

"Absolutely. It is my duty as an SS officer and a representative of the master race to remain fit and healthy."

The mention of the master race pushed Herman over the edge. He needed to break this captain and make him talk. He hoped the threat of some unpleasant labor would do the trick. "Do you agree that you could be asked to do some work? According to Article Number Twenty-seven?"

"Yes, sir. As an officer, I would need to volunteer."

"You better volunteer, because otherwise I'm going to keep you standing at attention all night without food or water or a place to piss, while I ask questions you refuse to answer."

"I volunteer to do any labor you can find. You'll see how strong we Aryans are . . . you little man who speaks German. I see you for what you are—a Jew who got away."

Herman turned his back to the man without a word, lifted the flap of the tent, and called one of the MP guards over. "Sergeant, come. We are going to escort this prisoner to where he can do some sanitary work to improve the conditions of the prisoners' enclosure." Herman had forgotten his own hunger. He was feeding on anger and frustration. He led the way to the back side of the cages. The prisoner followed and the MP brought up the rear, his weapon trained on the German's straight back. The disgusting smell of the latrine filled the air. In the evening cool, the flies had turned sluggish and sat on the piles of human waste and bits of crumbled newspaper that filled the long trench.

Herman pointed down into the smelly ditch. "We've

been getting complaints from your friends. It really is disgusting, don't you think?"

"Ya, sir." The German captain's haughty expression melted away.

"Get in there and clean up all that unsightly paper trash," Herman ordered. "I want you to pick up every single piece of shit paper and put it in the refuse barrel."

"Article Thirty-three demands hygienic conditions—"

"Shut up about the articles!" Herman took a deep breath to steady himself. "You can wash your hands with disinfectant when you're finished. Of course, if you don't like this work, I'll be happy to take you back to the tent where you can talk to me. What do you say?"

Herman watched as the SS man stepped down into the latrine and gingerly bent to pick up a soiled wad of newspaper. "Don't let him stop until he's picked up every last crap-covered scrap of paper out of there," Herman told the guard. "When he's finished, give him hot water and soap and some cold dinner—assuming he still has enough stomach to eat." He turned and headed for the mess hall. He had lost his appetite, but he would have loved a strong drink.

Later that night, he tossed on his narrow cot. Nightmares swarmed through his brain. A Panzer tank rolled over his legs, and he tried to walk on the bloody stumps. He slipped and fell in the mud because his legs were uneven and tumbled down in a ditch. He choked and retched in his dream because the ditch was full of human legs and feces, all mixed together.

Suddenly Herman sat up, wide awake. He struggled to the door of his tent and vomited in the mud outside.

CHAPTER 21

# PATTON'S MAN

A FTER THE SUCCESSFUL DRIVE TO Paris, Patton's army
headed for the Rhine. Slower forward movement
brought fewer prisoners to headquarters, so Herman often
went to the front lines where there were sometimes a few
recently captured Germans he could interrogate.

One midsummer day in northern France, he spent a
fruitless afternoon at the front. The only prisoners there
were Poles forced into the German army. They knew nothing. They spoke German so badly they probably had trouble
understanding orders, let alone making sense of whispered
gossip between the other men. They were happy to be on their
way to a POW camp in England, and when Herman tried to
talk to them, they grinned and spoke in halting German mingled with streams of Polish as they tried to convince Herman
that they hated Germans and loved the Americans.

Discouraged, he decided to return to Lucky Forward
where he hoped he'd have time for a shower while the pond

used as a water source still held some of the warmth from the afternoon sun. He walked out to the highway where a monument of the crucified Jesus guarded the crossroads. He hardly noticed the common sight of radio communication wire strung across Christ's shoulders as he sat on the stone footing. His helmet chafed his skull, and he took it off to let the breeze ruffle his hair and cool his scalp. He looked down the road, hoping to see a supply truck rumbling his way.

The speed and dependability of the supply trucks had earned them the nickname Red Ball Express, and Herman liked to hitch a ride with them. Their drivers, all members of the segregated transportation division, were usually upbeat and a bit rowdy. They reminded Herman of Negroes he had known in Los Angeles, mainly porters and musicians. As truck drivers, they found the task of navigating the byways of France an exciting change from their circumscribed lives in the States. It was the chance of a lifetime to see something of the world. The drivers were always looking for Nazi souvenirs—a helmet or an Iron Cross medal—items easy for an interrogator to find among the personal gear abandoned by the prisoners. In return for these treasures, the drivers had a way of seeing that a bottle of wine or extra cigarettes "fell from the load" where an interrogator could find them.

Herman looked down the road in time to see a jeep crest the hill, three large red stars emblazoned on its hood. He stood up and brushed the seat of his pants when he recognized the straight figure of General Patton in the front seat. Quickly he checked to make sure the tan tie of his uniform wasn't crooked and slapped his helmet back on his head. The general was particular about proper uniform for all officers in his army, and Herman wasn't in the mood to get chewed out by the commander himself. He rubbed the top of each boot against his pants legs to bring up a shine as the jeep pulled to a stop.

"Where you headed, Lieutenant?" Patton's voice, as usual, was high and animated.

"Sir, I'm on my way back to Lucky Forward, sir."

"I'm going that way myself. Hop in."

"Thank you, sir." Herman couldn't believe his luck. He settled into the rear passenger seat next to the mounted machine gun, though there was no gunner in the jeep, only the general and his driver, and on the other side of the weapon, the white panting dog that always accompanied Patton. The vehicle started up with a jerk, and they soon bumped along the highway, swerving to avoid potholes created by the passage of heavy tanks and countless trucks.

Patton turned in his seat, nudged his helmet up a bit, and peered at Herman. "Lieutenant Lang, isn't it?"

"Yes, sir."

"I've noticed you at headquarters. Heard good things about you from Colonel Allen."

"Thank you, sir."

"Good to see you out at the front, Lieutenant. I expect all my officers to come here to see what it's like for the guys who do the real fighting." He paused. "See anything of note today?"

"I talked to a few prisoners, sir. Things have been a bit slow in that department for the last few days."

"I'll get it to pick up again soon. Don't doubt that for a minute." Patton shook his head and rubbed the back of his neck. "We're a bit stalled right now because Supreme Headquarters is diverting our gasoline up north to Montgomery. Those Brits are having a slow go. Brave bastards and damn good fighters, too. But there's lots of hard-fighting Jerrys farther north. Supreme says they need more gas so they can come up parallel to us."

"Tough luck for us though, sir. The men can use a rest, I guess, but they'd much rather keep going and hit the enemy in their own backyard. Kick Hitler in the butt and end the war, sir."

"I agree, Lang. Too bad Supreme doesn't realize that the Third could practically do this job by themselves." A smile spread across Patton's face and he chuckled. "I could be in Berlin by November if they'd let me go." He turned to gaze at the green countryside for a moment, then turned back to Herman. "This your first time in France?"

"Yes, sir. I spent some time in England in '39. But I missed France."

"Too bad. It's a damn beautiful country in regular times. Lots of history here, too. If you get a chance, hitch your way to Chartres and see the cathedral there. It's a gem. All spires and stone as light as lace."

"I'd love to see it, sir. When we were near Paris, I went into the city for a day and visited Notre Dame. The stained glass there was the best I've seen. All those colors with the light pouring through. I didn't even care what the pictures were—I simply liked the way the light shone down like a rainbow."

"If you like stained glass, you damn well better not miss Chartres. It'll make you forget Notre Dame." He turned to the undulating fields that bordered the road and swept his arm in a gesture that encompassed it all. "This countryside right here was used as an encampment by the Crusaders under Richard the Lionheart on their way to Jerusalem. And it's seen a fight or two since then. Napoleon came through here more than once in his battles with the British."

Herman had heard that Patton was a history buff and here he was riding with the general as he talked about his favorite subject.

They were coming up to another crossroads. Patton waved to the driver to stop at the junction. He stood up to look over the windshield and down the side road that twisted and turned before it disappeared over a rise. In the distance there was a higher hill crowned by trees and what looked like a jumble of stones.

"See that, Lieutenant?" Patton pointed to the hill. "There's an old crusader castle up there. I've been wanting to check it out. Are you interested in a small detour?"

"I'd love it, sir." So what if he missed his shower, he thought. It wasn't every day a lowly lieutenant could get a personal history tour with the great general.

When they got to the top of the hill, Patton stood up in the jeep, took a deep audible breath, and spread his arms wide. "What a beautiful vista!" He continued to stand as the driver smoothly brought the vehicle to a stop. The general hopped down. "Come on, Willie," he said, and the white dog jumped to the ground beside his master.

Herman climbed out of the jeep and looked around. Fields of wheat and vineyards heavy with grapes stretched away from the base of the hill. Herman could see the twisted road they had recently traveled disappear into the distant haze. Behind them, jumbled rocks and the remnants of an old stone stairway led up to the ruin of an ancient tower, its crenellated parapet mostly intact. He heard a musical jingle and looked down to see Patton's dog sniffing his pant leg.

Herman crouched and scratched behind Willie's ears. "Hey, boy. Hey, Willie," he said, his voice a low croon in the dog's ear. "You got yourself a fine collar with bells and your very own dog tag." He fingered the metal nameplate on the animal's collar. The dog rubbed against his arm, left a string of drool on the sleeve of his uniform, then trotted back to his master. Herman stood and wiped his sleeve with his khaki handkerchief.

"If Willie likes you, that's a good sign," Patton said. He turned and started to climb the rough stairs, the dog following close behind, the bells on his collar jingling. "Come on, Lang. Let's look at the view from the tower. Do you know much about the crusades?"


THE NEXT MORNING AFTER THE briefings, Colonel Allen came up to Herman. "Well, Lang, looks like you've captured the confidence of Georgie." There was a twinkle in Allen's blue eyes. "He wants someone to go over the lines into German territory and watch the traffic on the main road to Metz. He says you'll know where to go. Something about four or five kilometers past some old crusader's castle." The assistant G2's eyes were steady and serious now. "Can you handle this mission on your own, Lieutenant? I could send Master Sergeant Lehman with you, but Georgie suggested a one-man reconnaissance effort. And he asked for you."

"Yes, sir. I'll be fine with this." Herman loosened his tie. "At least I won't have to wear this thing if I'm off spying on the Germans." He carefully rolled the tie into a spiral and tucked it into his shirt pocket. "I can be ready to head out in an hour. Can you requisition a good map of the area or at least a copy of an aerial photo? And a ride as far as the castle would be great. It's not far off the main road on our side."

By late morning, Herman was slipping from tree to bush down the backside of the hill where he and General Patton had inspected the ruins the day before. Going behind enemy lines was dangerous, but it was an adrenaline rush too. He had left his tie, his rank insignia, and his helmet on his cot back at camp. He wore his khaki fatigues, an old regulation bomber jacket, and a brown, army-issue, knitted cap pulled down over his ears. The only weapons he carried were his .45 caliber pistol in a holster under his jacket and a knife stuck into the high top of his boot. It was a balancing act. He needed to be inconspicuous in case he was seen by a farmer, but he still had to wear enough of an American uniform so that, if captured, he would be taken as a soldier gone astray, not a spy. The Germans shot spies without a trial.

Not far into German-held territory, he found an abandoned farmhouse on a hill near the main road to Metz.

It was a ruin obviously hit by heavy artillery not too long before. A few chickens still pecked about the yard in search of food. The barn was a pile of rubble, but much of the ground floor of the house remained, a gaping hole in one wall, the front door off its hinges, and the window shutters hanging in splinters. Half a wall with a glassless window, braced by a corner fragment of the adjoining wall, was all that remained of the second story.

He climbed up the stone stairs to the upper floor, which was open to the sky. The empty window looked toward the Metz road. It was a perfect lookout location. He settled in to count the heavy traffic on the road. With a stub of pencil and a tiny notebook that fit into a hidden pouch under his waistband, he recorded the number and type of vehicles as they rumbled past.

Herman knew to stay low and perfectly still—movement could be quickly detected by an observant spotter. After several hours of counting traffic, his legs cramped and he shifted his position in the dust and rubble on the floor. He rolled away from the wall, then rolled back to below the blasted out window and positioned himself again. Only his eyes and the top of his head peeked above the wooden window frame.

Dusk approached and the cold air settled in hard. Herman wrapped his arms around his chest. He knew the night would be uncomfortable, but he didn't want to be in the open after dark. Besides, it would be good to do more observation in the morning. The road was unusually busy, and if the traffic continued, that was a sign of important troop movement. His corner in the abandoned farmhouse was probably as safe a place as any other he could find. A blanket would be great, but his jacket would have to do.

The trucks and tanks inched forward without headlights. As the dusk deepened, it became almost impossible to see the road. Herman stuffed his notebook in his pocket and took a swig of water from the canteen on his belt. He was hungry. He had brought a can of pork and beans and a chocolate bar, but he wondered if it might be worth a check of the basement or the kitchen for some food. He hoped he could find a few bits of dried fruit or a wedge of cheese left by the farmer in his rush to leave.

Suddenly he was alert, every muscle tense. Faint noises came from below. He held his breath. He heard the scrunch of boots on the rubble-strewn floor, cupboard doors being slammed. Then voices. German words echoed up the stairwell.

"No one here, Sergeant."

"No food either, sir. The cupboards are bare."

"Another cold dinner. Ah . . . for a bowl of soup. Or a sausage."

It sounded like there were two, maybe three of them. They must have come up from behind the farmhouse, Herman thought. He'd been too busy contemplating food himself to hear any warning clucks from the chickens.

"Private, did you check upstairs?"

"No, sir. Right now."

Herman's skin prickled as he heard the soft scrape of boots on the stairs.

He looked out the window. It was maybe twelve feet down to the ground and there was no welcoming pile of hay below. But it had to be done. He scrambled as quietly as possible to the window ledge and lowered himself over the edge. The sill was sturdy, but he clung to it for only long enough to check where he would land. His feet hung about six feet above uneven ground. He let go. A sharp pain stabbed through his knee as he landed, and he rolled toward the protection of the wall. It was a bad landing, and he had twisted his leg badly. He lay close against the building and listened to the sounds of the German soldier as he inspected the upstairs room where he had been only moments before.

"All clear here, sir."

After he heard the soldier's footsteps retreat down the stairs, Herman stood and sprinted to the crumbled remains of the barn. With each stride, a searing pain pierced his left knee. In the shelter of the broken walls of the barn, he rubbed his leg and hoped he could make it to some safe spot to spend the night. He slithered through a gap in the fallen stones and into the adjoining field.

Herman stood again and tried a crouching run up the sloping field and toward a small clump of trees. The pain in his knee came with every step and almost threw him to the ground. When he was out of view from the farmhouse, he fell prostrate in the fallow rows of churned dirt. Gingerly he felt his knee. It was tender and beginning to swell.

He lay in the dirt and looked around. A large old tree stood nearby and he crawled toward it on his belly. At its base, close enough to expose the tree's tangled roots, he found a hole blasted open by artillery fire and he slithered down into it. With his hands he dug out a comfortable place to curl up and wait.

The night stretched into an eternity. Herman opened the can of beans with his knife and ate them cold. His knee throbbed and he wrapped his handkerchief around it, hoping that would help. He was constantly aware of how little cover he had in his hole open to the sky and visible to any observant night patrol. The bite of the chill night air pierced his bones. His sleep was broken and uneasy. He dreamed of being captured by Germans who yanked off his dog tag and threw it in a ditch. They held a gun to his head and yelled, "Jude! Dirty Jew!" The dream turned, and he was captured by Americans who made him stand at attention and asked for his paybook. He scrambled about in the dirt, searching for his dog tag, but it was gone. One of the GI's kicked him in the knee and the pain of it woke him up. Still half in the dream, he fumbled in terror around his neck, relieved to feel the cold metal of his dog tag against his chest.

For the rest of the night, he stared at the sky and watched the stars fade into the gray beginnings of dawn. He nibbled slowly on the chocolate, and when it was gone, he lifted his canteen, drank the last two swallows of water he had carefully saved for morning and crept out of the hole. His knee throbbed and he loosened the handkerchief. He wondered if he would be able to make it back to the American lines. Even with the pain, he knew he wanted to check out the traffic on the road one last time. Patton depended on him.

Herman crawled to the crest of the hill and scanned the distant highway. The string of vehicles had slowed compared to the day before. Troops moved along the road, but not as many, and they were far enough away that it was difficult to make out their units, even with his binoculars. But Allen had been clear. He was to make the sortie short and quick, no more than twenty-four hours. It was time to return to Lucky Forward and see what could be made of the information in his notebook.

His progress was slow. He more or less slithered his way back down the hill and hobbled westward, resting at whatever cover he could find. Finally, about midmorning, he found a sturdy branch that could be used as a walking stick. It was late afternoon when he reached the old crusader castle and limped down the road to the highway.

The wonderful sight of a truck of the Red Ball Express rolled into view almost immediately. Herman waved his arms in the air to flag the driver. He would have run up and kissed the fender of the truck if he had been able to run.

The burly driver stuck his dark face out the window and looked down at Herman with the concern of a father. "What you doing out here all alone, Lieutenant Lang? You look a bit beat up, sir."

"Out for a night with the Jerrys." He tried to keep his tone light to show he was okay. "Sure could use a lift back to Lucky Forward, though." He laughed to make it sound like a joke.

Back at headquarters, Herman went straight to report to Colonel Allen. He stood at attention and saluted his superior.

"Lang, I was starting to get concerned. At ease, Lieuten-ant." He looked closely at Herman and pulled a chair over to his desk. "Sit. You look like you need it. And tell me what happened."

Herman gratefully dropped into the chair and stretched out his left leg with a groan. "No problem, sir. A bit of a near scrape with a few Germans—nothing serious." He pulled the notebook out. "I took a good count of traffic on the Metz road. There's a lot, sir. Not enough to indicate a major offensive, though. But certainly heavy replacements determined to hold the city."

Allen looked eager. "Good work, Lang. I'll report directly to Patton and tell him you made it back." He stood and walked around his desk to put a hand on Herman's shoulder. "I'll be putting in for a promotion for you to first lieutenant," he said. "But for now, get to the medic's tent and have some-one check out your leg. And get yourself some chow. Then type up a report before you fall asleep on your feet."

Herman saluted. "Yes, sir!" He stood up slowly and limped outside. He looked around Lucky Forward at the neat rows of sturdy canvas tents, at the men in their smart uniforms busy with their duties, and at the Stars and Stripes flapping on its pole. It was good to be home.

CHAPTER 22

# METZ AND MUD

THAT SUMMER, AS THE THIRD ARMY progressed further and further into France, the Lucky command post, home to more than one hundred officers and staff, moved by truck and jeep several times a week. At each location, be it an apple orchard, the edge of a wheat field, near a liberated village, or a clearing in a forest, a virtual village mushroomed within hours.

Early every morning, the planning staff met with Patton in the war room tent. They looked over casualty figures, indications of enemy losses, and Allied movement from the day before, and used all the information available, including reports gathered by the intelligence teams, to plan that day's advances. Colonel Robert S. Allen and his superior, the head of G2 Intelligence, Colonel Koch, were important members of this inner group.

At 8:30 a.m. every day, Herman and the other officers joined the planning staff for a daily briefing. The atmosphere of Patton's War Room was always charged with excitement as the men faced the huge map of the western front and awaited their orders. With the general in charge and everyone present, the briefings followed a set order. First, the operations section gave an overview of the Allied situation, which concentrated on their movement of the day before. Then the breezy manner and slow New Mexican drawl of Lieutenant Colonel Pat Murray kept everyone awake during his report on the flying weather expected and the success of the past night's bombing missions.

During the intelligence report that followed, Herman listened carefully for information he had contributed with his own hard work. The entire briefing usually took less than twenty minutes. Well before 9:00 a.m., everyone at headquarters had begun the work of the new day.

The members of the prisoner of war interrogation teams were mostly, like Herman, refugees who had fled Europe because of Hitler, though one or two were American born with an aptitude for languages. Now the Ritchie-trained refugees found themselves in France, each with his own personal reasons to defeat the Nazi Reich. Brotherhood came naturally to these men. They shared their German heritage and understood the struggle to bury personal hatreds and sorrows during daily encounters with German soldiers.

Friends since they had shared a cabin for the Atlantic crossing, Herman and Julian Goldschmitt often found themselves together in the officers' mess tent. Over dinner, their talk turned to books, missed family, the latest news, or the day's activities. The summer had been wet, and now, in late September, as the two men shared a table in the dank mess tent, rain pounded on the canvas roof. Herman wished the War Department's prophecy that the fighting would be over by fall had come true. The warm soup from lunch had filled him with lassitude, and he sipped his coffee slowly. If the brew was good, he preferred it black but with plenty of sugar, but today he had added an ample swirl of powdered milk to smother the bitter taste. The earthy smell of the sodden ground below the duckboard floor mingled with the lingering aroma of beef that clung to his empty bowl. His toes inside his boots had begun to throb and wiggling them didn't help. Finally he bent down, pulled off one boot, and rubbed his icy toes back to life.

Julian Goldschmitt wrinkled his nose, waved his spoon, and grunted. "Please get that boot back on, Lang. You're going to spoil my lunch."

"Sorry. I haven't had a chance to wash my socks in four days." Herman rolled his sock back on and tied the laces of his boot. He pulled up his trouser leg and adjusted the elastic bandage he now continually wore on his left knee to ease the ache. "At least we can keep our socks dry most of the time and don't have to worry about our feet turning black like the poor guys in the foxholes. I saw a soldier on one of the transports yesterday who had both feet amputated because of gangrene from a bad case of trench foot. But he was smiling. 'I'm on my way home,' is what he said. He laughed and told me his wife wouldn't care about his feet."

Julian grunted again, the last remnants of soup forgotten. He rubbed his forehead. "I heard Georgie gave hell to

Ol' God Almighty General Lee at Com Z last week about the lack of supplies getting to the front lines."

Herman straightened his trouser and flexed his leg to ease the stiffness.

"Allen says Patton is constantly fighting to get more gasoline, and only about half of what he asks for is delivered. The rest goes to the British."

"God! If only Montgomery would use the gasoline to catch up with us." Julian grinned. He took another spoon of his now cold soup, made a face, and pushed the bowl away. "What I wouldn't give for some of my *grossmutti's* chicken matzo soup," he said.

"Myself, I long for the roast beef they served at the Zebra Room in California!" Herman stood up and refilled his cup from the huge metal dispenser the mess staff kept constantly hot. He came back to the table and cradled the cup between his palms, savoring its warmth and the bitter aroma of the coffee. "Patton is pushing to get those bridgeheads on the Moselle River. Maybe we'll be enjoying sauerkraut and bratwurst soon." He scratched his chin. "I can't wait to set my feet on German soil again. I feel a kind of excitement about it. What about you, Goldschmitt?"

Julian looked up. "I don't know. I was only a kid when I was last in Germany. My family moved to Belgium in '33. Then on to the States in '35." He stood up, tucked his book into his jacket pocket, and pulled on a pair of woolen gloves. "But you're right. I want to get back there. To fix it or punish it . . . or I don't know. And the sooner we get there the better. I have a cousin and his family who never left Germany as far as I know. My uncle was a rabbi and he wouldn't leave his people. I think they went into hiding . . . in Berlin. I don't know."

Herman put his hand on Julian's shoulder. "I'm sorry, Goldschmitt. Maybe they got out."

Julian shook his head and blinked before turning toward the door. "Come on, Lang. Back to work extracting truth and lies from the prisoners. And trying to tell the difference."

Herman zipped his battle jacket, stood, and followed Julian outside. They stood for a moment in the shelter of the tent overhang, then each dashed through the mud to his interrogation tent.

At the end of September, the Third Army's steady advance ground to a halt on the orders of Supreme Headquarters. They were told to dig into defensive positions and the Lucky staff—from Allen to Herman to the cook in the mess hall—was upset. But the orders came directly from General Eisenhower who insisted the Allied lines must be evened up and consolidated to prepare for a coordinated push across the Rhine River. Herman counted the passage of the days of October as they sat in the Moselle Valley astride the river, while the temperature continued to dip and the rain turned to sleet. When he went out to the front, he saw soldiers hunkered down in their foxholes in a quagmire of mud, without the warmth of woolen blankets, winter boots, or overcoats, but there were no prisoners to interrogate.

At the morning briefings, Patton could barely contain his anger about the lack of supply support. He had ranted that, even with "sit down" orders, the troops needed to stay vigilant to hold the lines. They couldn't do their best without proper food and clothing.

In spite of there being few prisoners for Herman and his team to interrogate, G2 was busy. One of the other teams infiltrated behind the lines to gather information and brought back two prisoners who told of thousands of slave laborers being used to install guns and build additional defenses on the German border. When the weather cleared enough for the planes of Air Tactical Division to fly, they brought back aerial photos for intelligence to analyze. The photos confirmed that the Germans were regrouping and reinforcing.

Patton was finally given the order to move forward and take the fortified city of Metz, a major concern with its heavy artillery, mine fields, and thirty-five surrounding forts. The taking of the city had been an important goal ever since early planning in England, yet it still remained the center of a pocket of German-held territory.

One morning in the last week of October, the general spoke to Colonel Allen after the daily briefing. "I have a job for you and Lang's team," he said. "Meet me in the planning room in fifteen minutes." Herman and Colonel Allen found Patton seated comfortably, puffing on a cigar, with Willie at his feet. The thrum of a generator in the background was accompanied by an old Victrola playing a piano concerto. Herman recognized the music as a piece his mother used to play. Willie trotted over to Herman and sniffed his leg, then rubbed up against him in recognition before returning to his spot by Patton's chair.

"Gentlemen, we need to know more about the situation in Metz." Patton stood and slapped his thigh in frustration. "Goddamn that place. It hasn't been taken by assault since 451 AD. But we're going to do it." The general's voice rose even higher than usual. "The Germans have been there for four years and they aren't going to see five!" He paced once across the room, then cleared his throat. "We've got Metz pretty well bottlenecked, but as you know, we've had a hard time with the fort at Driant." Patton's gaze seemed to look into the distance as he continued. "Heavy fighting. Our boys are valiant, but they can't seem to take that damned place. I've had to order the troops to withdraw and only half the men I sent out returned." He wiped his eyes with a clean handkerchief and looked down at his dog. Willie looked up at his master, and Patton stooped down to scratch behind the dog's ears before continuing. "I'm not used to withdrawal, and I won't accept it," he said, his voice raising. Suddenly he slapped his fist against his chest. "Vengeance, that's what I want! We'll take Metz, with or without that bloody, damn Fort Driant." Patton took a deep breath and seemed unable to go on.

"What are your orders, sir?" Allen asked.

"We need more information! We need to plan better next time, and to do that, we need to know how many men are garrisoned in the city. We need to know everything." Patton paced back and forth again. "How much ammunition do they have? How much food and water? What is their morale like?" He stopped his pacing and locked his gaze on Herman. "I want you to talk to a prisoner, Lieutenant. Someone who has recently come from Metz."

Herman stood as tall as he could. "Yes, sir! But that won't be easy, sir. Nobody is coming out." He saw Patton's face cloud over and his jaw tighten. "We'll go in and get someone ourselves, if we have to, sir," Herman said, but he hoped it wouldn't come to that. If it did, he would have to send someone else because his lame knee still slowed him down.

"Good. Lieutenant, I know you're one of the best. I'm depending on you."

For the next two days, Herman rechecked all the information on the few prisoners brought in. None had been in Metz. He gathered a four-man patrol, designating Master Sergeant Lehman to head it up and infiltrate the city the next evening. But before they left, luck fell into his hands. In the dark of the frigid, moonless night, a prisoner was taken about two miles outside the city wall. He had left Metz, and judging by his heavy clothing and full pack, was setting off on a long, winter journey. The MPs brought him directly to the interrogation center.

Herman had not gone to bed that night, but sometime halfway between midnight and dawn he had dozed off, his head cushioned by his arm and a stack of papers on his desk. It was still dark outside when Lehman burst into his tent to announce the arrival of the new prisoner. "You'll want to talk to this one, sir," he said with unconcealed excitement. "He's only hours out of Metz, sir."

Herman was instantly awake. "Give me five minutes. Keep the man standing at attention." Lehman stepped outside the tent and his barked orders could be heard through the flap. With the slowdown of forward movement, the tents of the interrogation center were more substantial, with a wooden floor, and a ridge pole high enough for a tall man to stand. Quickly Herman straightened his desk and threw several large pieces of wood onto the low embers in his battlefield stove made entirely of tin pipes. The fire chamber blazed, turning wood to cinders and the whole stove, pipe and all, became red hot in minutes. Heat radiated to fill the tent. Herman took off his jacket, draped it over the back of his chair, and called out to the MP standing guard to bring in the prisoner, then sat down at his desk, waiting and ready.

The German was forty-five or fifty years old, with a grizzled, day's growth of beard. He wasn't an inexperienced schoolboy like so many other enemy prisoners. Herman glanced through the man's paybook. *Stabsfeldwebel* Erich Schroeder, the equivalent of a master sergeant. He had fought in North Africa and Italy, in Russia after that. He was obviously a professional soldier, and Herman knew this man would not easily give up information.

He looked up from the paybook and examined Schroeder. He was dressed for the cold weather and though the MPs had taken his weapons, he still wore his full pack with a bedroll tied to it. He had on a thick, woolen greatcoat, boots, and winter weight woolen trousers. Herman figured that under the coat he wore a jacket, a warm shirt and at least one layer of woolen underwear. As the prisoner stood at attention in the warm tent, perspiration already beaded his forehead.

"*Stabsfeldwebel* Schroeder," Herman began, "you've already had a long night. Let's make this as painless as possible. I need information about Metz. How are things there?"

"Schroeder, Erik. *Stabsfeldwebel.*" The man stood rigid, his arms at his sides. A trickle of sweat rolled down his cheek and dripped into the collar of his coat.

For almost an hour Herman continued to try to get something from the man, but the interrogation was going nowhere.

Finally he stood and pointed to the spot to the right of his desk. "*Stabsfeldwebel.* Stand over here. I want to get a closer view of what a stubborn man looks like."

The soldier did as he was told, but in his new position, Schroeder stood even closer to the hot stove. Herman waited. He tapped his foot and stared at the prisoner. The light of dawn leaked under the flaps of the tent entrance. The prisoner began to sway and sweat poured in rivulets down his forehead and cheeks.

Herman remained calm. "I have all day, Sergeant. I am not tired. I have been resting all night, not traveling like you. I am willing to spend all day with you, if I need to. You will stand here until you tell me about Metz." In a firm, even voice, he began his string of questions again. "How many men are in the city now?"

"Schroeder. Sir. *Stabsfeldwebel.*"

"How much ammunition is left?"

"Schroeder . . . *Stabsfeldwebel.*"

"We know you are not getting replacements. No shipments mean no supplies. You must be low on food. On ammunition, too. Is that why you left, Sergeant? Are you a deserter?"

Schroeder's face contorted with a flicker of anger, and he blinked several times as the salty sweat rolled into his eyes. He said nothing.

"We can stand like this for hours if you want," Herman said. "But you've left the city for some reason. Not with a division or a patrol, but on your own. I'm inclined to think you are a deserter. Why don't you talk? I want to know what you've left behind. We'll be taking Metz in the next few weeks whether you talk or not."

"Schr . . . d'r." The words were beginning to slur. "St . . . b . . . feld . . . w'le." The prisoner's face had turned grayish, sweat no longer beaded his forehead, and he was unsteady on his feet.

"Tell me what's in Metz, Master Sergeant. You can make it easier on yourself. General Patton wants Metz and he'll take it. Give us the information we need and you'll make it easier on everyone. You might even save some German lives." Herman watched Schroeder closely. He swayed dangerously. If he fell against the burning stove, it would all be over. It would all be over soon anyway. Herman could see the man was about to faint. "Schroeder! Talk to me," he shouted, unable to keep the tone of concern out of his command.

"*Bitte.*" Please. Schroeder's words whispered from his lips and his knees buckled under him.

Herman reached out and pushed the falling body away from the stove. He pulled the German by the collar of his coat toward the door, opened the flap of the tent, and called to the waiting MP. "Get me some water, Corporal."

Within minutes, the sergeant opened his eyes and his color began to return, but all the fight had gone out of him. "*Bitte,* Lieutenant. I'm taking a letter from my commander to his wife. The garrison is low on food, but there are still potatoes."

The words flowed as he sipped the water Herman offered.

The information the German sergeant gave was exactly what Patton had asked for. Herman quickly typed up a report and hand carried it to Allen. At the bottom of the document, he wrote a note regarding the prisoner.

> *Stabsfeldwebel Schroeder is a career soldier who is nearing retirement age. He was on a personal errand for his commanding officer. He cooperated with the interrogator. Recommend expeditious transfer to location in Britain or US and a light work assignment.*

ON NOVEMBER 4, AT THE daily briefing, Patton personally addressed his staff for the first time since mid-August. They would restart their assault eastward within the next four days.

"In spite of the difficulties we face," Patton told the assembled staff, "and notwithstanding my considerable talents as a bullshit artist, I can assure you that we will succeed in breaking through the Siegfried Line, penetrate into the heart of Germany, and win the war."

This was typical Patton bravado, and Herman loved it. He would follow this general to hell and back.

Patton finished by saying, "I want to kill as many Germans as possible between here and the Rhine, so we won't be annoyed by the sons of bitches after we cross the river. Always keep in mind that the Rhine is our objective."

Everyone focused their attention on the daily weather reports, hoping for clear weather the day of the scheduled assault, but it continued to rain steadily, with low, gray clouds that made it impossible for planes to fly. Bombing raids were part of the plan to soften German resistance and thus save American lives, but the planes couldn't go up in such bad weather.

On November 5, thick, low-hanging, black clouds again kept the bombers grounded in the morning, but in the afternoon, the sky cleared and the planes took off to bombard Metz and its surrounding forts. November 6 and 7, the skies were again rain drenched, forcing the planes to stay on the runways. At the morning briefing on November 7, Patton stepped forward. "Tomorrow, damn it! We attack!"

Imagining the bad weather protected them, the Germans were caught by surprise. The American forces moved forward, taking one stronghold after another. On November 11, the first snow of winter fell during the night, and Patton's soldiers slogged through ice and mud to gradually close the lines around the pocket of resistance at Metz. Within two weeks, the fortress city was in Patton's hands, and he turned the troops eastward toward the Siegfried Line and the Rhine.

Herman was elated. He had helped make it possible. The weather cleared and the planes resumed regular bombing runs. Prisoners flooded through the interrogation center again, hundreds of them every day, and the teams could hardly keep up. Four thousand prisoners were taken at the city of Metz alone.

With the huge influx of prisoners, all team members had to act as screeners. Herman knew that the observation of the smallest detail could result in vital information to the

Third Army. A lifetime of observing German character and culture, plus the last months of observing and interrogating German prisoners, had enabled Herman, and many of the other Ritchie Boys, to develop secret and crafty ways to identify prisoners. When they came in by the hundreds and thousands, it was impossible to interrogate them all, but they needed to be divided into groups according to their units. If the intelligence team knew how many prisoners had been taken from a specific division, they could calculate how much strength the enemy maintained in various sectors. After that, Herman and his men needed to interrogate only a selected few from each unit in hopes of getting other important information. Camp Ritchie had trained them well and experience had honed their skills.

Herman had been promoted to captain after his success at Metz and was assigned a jeep, a driver, and two military police to assist him. On a morning like many others, he arrived at the cages where the prisoners milled about and had his driver pull up in front of the bedraggled and muddy crowd of men. He climbed onto the jeep's hood, which put him well above and in a superior position over the prisoners. The MPs stood on each side of the vehicle, rifles at the ready. Herman surveyed the hundreds of uncertain prisoners. All he needed was to recognize the uniform or insignia of only a few. Sometimes, if he knew the area well, and knew where units were positioned, like in a particular area of swamp, or in hills where there were clay deposits, he only had to see the mud on their boots to know what unit they belonged to. He lifted a large, battery-powered loudspeaker and shouted orders in German.

"Prisoners, get into lines. Now!"

German prisoners were good at this—regimentation was part of their training—but even in rows they were still mixed up together. Herman looked for a man with an insignia he recognized and quickly saw one—in the second row stood a man from a tank unit.

He pointed straight at the man. "All you from the 2nd Panzer Division, fall out and form to the right." The man he pointed at led the way and others followed him without thinking. They wanted to stay with their friends. They were captured together and now they didn't want to be left behind.

Herman pointed to another man, one who was older—a father type the younger men would respect. "You. Take your unit to the left. Step quickly."

And they moved.

Another target was selected. He pointed to a man whose boots were caked with the telltale black mud of the Hürtgen Forest where Herman knew a particular infantry unit was fighting. "Fall out, 275th Infantry Division. Step front and center!"

Soon there were a few stragglers left. Herman's arm swept to indicate the men standing lonely and scattered in the mud. "You men, fall in according to your units."

Once the initial divisions were made, the prisoners would stay together. Herman knew that Germans found comfort in staying with their unit and following orders. After they were counted, a few from each group were selected to be interrogated. Later they were all trucked off to the rear together. Within twenty-four hours their usefulness would evaporate, and any information they had was probably old news. Only a selected few, those who seemed to have special knowledge or expertise, might be kept longer.

The compiled information gathered from prisoner interrogations had the men of G2 Intelligence worried. There seemed to be a buildup of German troops to the north and east of Luxemburg City, where Lucky Main, Patton's more permanent headquarters, was now located. The buildup was confirmed by air tactical reconnaissance, and Colonel Koch sent word to Supreme Headquarters. Herman and the others of G2 were surprised when no move was made by the Allied Command to break up this growing pocket of German forces.

The men at the front had other worries, and it seemed the generals at the top did, too. Winter was starting in earnest, and cold weather uniforms had still not arrived. Brutal fighting in November had left the Third Army 9,000 men short with no replacements on the way. A call for volunteers for the front lines went out to staff on all levels. Cooks, truck drivers, and clerks were transferred to infantry units, but interrogators in G2 were told to stay where they were. Their special training and skills made them indispensable.

Herman felt proud that his work was considered vital to the war effort. General Patton knew he and his team would make a difference.

CHAPTER 23

# THE BULGE OR "I'M NOT GERMAN!"

B Y THE MIDDLE OF DECEMBER, snow fell steadily over France and Germany. The Siegfried Line, its pillboxes and gun emplacements, softened by crusted snow, stood only a few miles in front of Patton's army. Extra air cover had been promised. Finally Patton received clearance to begin the attack on December 19.

But three days before the battle was to start, strange news trickled in about unexpected troop movement to the north. Herman sought out Colonel Allen. The two men had come to trust and respect each other in spite of the rank difference, and sometimes they shared confidences not strictly in the line of duty. That evening after dinner, he stopped Allen near the door of the officers' mess tent, far enough from the other men that they wouldn't be overheard, but still inside, away from the bitter winter wind.

"What's going on, Colonel?" Herman asked. "We hear whispers, but nothing we can trust."

"It's bad. The Germans have launched an offensive attack. Don't know how bad it is, but it's serious enough that Bradley has ordered Patton to rush the 10th Armored Division to the vicinity of Luxemburg City."

Herman feared the worst. "Georgie won't want to do that. It'll upset his plans for the nineteenth."

"That's what he told Bradley." Allen sighed and leaned closer to speak in a tense whisper. "But Bradley told him that it was urgent and he should get the division moving at once."

The next morning, the staff briefing was abuzz. The Germans had launched an immense, well-planned, last-ditch offensive, and they were pushing the First Army backward at an alarming rate. The next day, at the Lucky briefing on December 19, Patton was visibly shaken as he spoke to his staff. "Our plans have changed. We're going to fight, but not where we thought we would." Their help was needed, he explained, to aid the First Army. "After we save their hides," he promised, "we'll come back and finish the job down here."

Within twenty-four hours, one armored and two infantry divisions of the Third Army were turned north and within range of the Germans near the breakthrough in the Ardennes. There they found four SS Panzer and five German Infantry divisions pushing north and west into American-held territory. The Germans had already overrun the command post of the First Army in Spa, a luxurious resort where the American troops had been soaking in hot mineral baths and drinking champagne a few days before. Individual combat units now fought for their lives as the Germans pushed them back. But the American troops would not give up. They stood and fought. And they died.

Herman was ordered to the area of the fighting with three other men from G2 Intelligence. Rumors were rampant, and the general needed to know what was happening. They took two jeeps, each with an MP escort, and followed the Third Army forces heading north toward Luxemburg City.

What they found was chaos. A severe winter blizzard limited driving visibility and covered everything in a thick blanket of white. Herman was in the lead jeep, Master Sergeant Lehman at the wheel, and the MP riding shotgun. They huddled against the wind and blowing snow as they inched forward. The roads were clogged with trucks, tanks, and infantry.

A main road junction emerged from the swirling snow. The confusion at the crossroads was out of control. A tank attempting to make a u-turn had backed up traffic in both directions. Two ammunition trucks were pulled off to one side. Their drivers stood outside in the snow, puffs of hot breath rising into the frigid air as they talked. A single MP vainly tried to direct traffic.

Lehman idled the jeep behind the trucks and the MP jumped out, ready to take whatever action was necessary.

"Sergeant, see what you can find out about this mess. And Whitmore, go help that poor bastard trying to direct traffic by himself," Herman ordered. As soon as Lehman swung out of the jeep, Herman moved over into the driver's seat and jiggled the accelerator to keep the engine running.

The jeep's canvas cover gave little protection from the cold, but at least there was some warmth coming across his feet from the motor.

Within three minutes, Lehman reappeared through the windblown snow with information. "Sometime this morning the main road sign here was switched. Looks like an infantry regiment followed the misplaced sign and marched the wrong way. No one knows where they are. There's word that some Germans in American uniforms have been caught not far from here."

"How far?" Herman wanted to know more. "Anyone know where?"

"I think about five kilometers ahead. They said there's a village that's being used as a temporary command post."

Herman made a snap decision. It was too cold to sit still anyway. "Lehman, we need to split up our efforts. You stay here with MP Whitmore and see what you can find out from some of these truckers standing around. They always know the scuttlebutt." Herman gestured toward the men up ahead. "Looks like the Red Ball Express guys have been pressed into service to move stuff up toward the battle in Bastogne." He revved the engine again. "Keep your eye open for Goldschmitt and Neumann in our other jeep. They should be only fifteen to twenty minutes behind us. If you miss them, catch a ride up with a Red Ball."

Sergeant Lehman looked doubtful. "Captain, are you sure that's a good idea? You going off alone, without a driver, I mean. You know the rules. And besides, it's bound to be crazy up there."

Herman, as usual, itched for action. "I'll be fine, Sergeant. You stay here. That's an order."

Ernie reached into the rear of the jeep for his rolled-up blanket bundle. "Yes, sir. I'll be on the lookout for the other jeep." He looked at Herman quizzically. "What shall I tell Goldschmitt you're doing, Captain?"

Herman put the jeep into gear. "I'll see if I can make some headway up the road and locate where they're holding the German spies. You follow ASAP with Goldschmitt when he gets here. I won't go past this village you heard about. It's probably the best place for us to hole up for the night, anyway." He eased the jeep forward, past the traffic snarl, and down the road.

Herman was alone when he came to the roadblock outside the village.

It was late afternoon and drifts of snow heaped against the makeshift blockade that had been set up by a unit of three MPs who checked every person and vehicle coming down the road. He tried to swing around the blocked traffic, but one of the MPs jumped in front of his jeep with his M1 carbine aimed and ready.

"Sir! Identity check is ordered for all personnel." The MP, who was only a corporal, looked uncertain about how to handle the situation.

"Easy, soldier." Herman handed over his identity card. "Captain Herman Lang, like it says."

The MP inspected the card as if it might hide a secret code. Finally he handed it back. "Sorry, sir. Where are you going, sir?"

Herman looked carefully at the man. His months of interrogation had made him a good judge of a man's emotional state, and he could see this MP was nervous. "I've come from Patton's headquarters. On the orders of Colonel Koch. I intend to find a warm corner here for the night. Maybe interrogate some prisoners, if you have any. Then move on in the morning."

The MP had been listening with a special intensity to Herman's explanation. His clasp on the firearm seemed to tense. "You are going to have to get out of the jeep, sir."

Very carefully Herman eased out of the vehicle. He had been warned about situations like this at Camp Ritchie, and the lesson suddenly came back. "I am Captain Lang," he said calmly. "Assigned to G2 at Lucky Forward. You know what that is, right, Corporal?"

"Yes, sir. I apologize, sir, if you are who you say you are. But you do have a German accent. I can hear it."

Herman took a deep breath. "Yes, I do. I was born in Germany, but now I'm an American citizen. I remember everything I had to memorize to become a citizen like, 'We take these truths to be self-evident, all men are . . .'"

"Anyone, even a German, could memorize that! It doesn't prove anything. There are German commandos all over the area. They're dressed in American uniforms, talking perfect English, and flashing fake ID cards and dog tags—just like you. You could be one of those spies lying to save your skin."

"Well, I'm not. And I need to get up into the village to interrogate these very men you're talking about. I heard they were being held here. Is that true, Corporal?"

"I can't disclose that. Maybe you're here to rescue them. We have orders not to let anyone through without confirming they're true Americans." The corporal seemed to think for a moment, then his eyes lit up. "Who pitched for the Chicago Cubs last season?" he asked.

This is getting ridiculous, Herman thought as the memory of the border crossing at Tijuana flashed into his head. "How long have you been in Europe, soldier?"

"Since October, sir."

"Well, I've been over here since last May, first in England and then in France since right after D-Day. While you were stateside finishing your training and listening to the World Series on the radio, I was here slogging around the French countryside and making my skills with the German language useful to the US Army. I've been much too busy to follow baseball." The MP continued to keep his carbine ready to fire and pointed directly at Herman's chest, but he shifted his feet nervously. "Yes, sir. But I can't release you, sir. Not without some kind of proof or—"

"There's another jeep from Lucky Forward that will be coming along soon. They can confirm who I am. Two of them also have German accents. But the other, Sergeant Neumann, was born in Milwaukee. He can vouch for us all. And there should be two of your fellow MPs with them. They're as American as apple pie."

"That's good, sir." He glanced at the backed up traffic then turned to Herman again. "I need you to surrender your weapon, sir."

Reluctantly Herman eased his sidearm out of its holster,

set it on the front seat of the jeep, and stepped away from the vehicle.

"Stand over there near the building and out of the wind," the young MP commanded as he made a slight motion with his carbine to indicate the place. "Flag down the men that can identify you when you see them." He seemed to be uncertain what to do next. "I'm sorry about this, but we can't be too careful, sir. You understand."

Herman did understand, but he didn't like it. He was wasting time while the actual spies were somewhere else, maybe under interrogation by an amateur. He hoped that the others weren't held up in the traffic jam down the road.

The MP guard followed him over to the protection of the building near the roadblock. "You stand here and don't move, sir. If you see your friends, shout out and wave. But I warn you. If you leave this wall and go near your jeep, you will be shot." He returned to the jeep, transferred Herman's revolver from the driver's seat to the floor under the seat, and moved the vehicle to the side of the road, allowing the long line of traffic to inch forward. He glanced over at Herman again, then turned to question the driver of a truck next in line.

Herman huddled close to the stone wall and scanned the long line of jeeps and trucks stretching down the road. His knee was stiff and sore. Ever since twisting it the night he jumped out of the farmhouse window, it bothered him if he stood on it too long. Without the support bandage, it sometimes flared up and made him limp.

The temperature dipped rapidly as night approached. He feared the MP would move him inside to some holding room, and he would miss the other jeep altogether. He could see the three MPs at the roadblock glance his way every few minutes. They were probably discussing what to do with him next. After about half an hour, the oldest of the three MPs, a lieutenant this time, walked toward him. Those guys better come soon, Herman thought.

The MP lieutenant approached, his gun ready to swing into action. "Sir, we need to ask you to step inside the building. I want to ask you some questions, sir."

"Wait, please. My men should be here any minute." Herman squinted into the dim light and swirling snow. The situation could get worse any moment. He peered down the road, one last time. He could make out the dim outline of a jeep with two MPs clinging to it. Yes, it was them! He recognized the bulk of Sergeant Whitmore. He waved and called out their names. "Lehman! Whitmore! Neumann! Over here!" He was almost gleeful as he turned to the MP. "See, it's the others—right there."

As soon as the jeep pulled close, the MP officer shouted, "Any of you know this man? He claims to be an American."

Whitmore jumped down and smothered Herman with a hug. "This is Captain Lang. He's a bit cocky sometimes and takes risks, but we love him." Then he turned serious and saluted. "Sir, I know this man and I can vouch for him. He is indeed an American citizen, and he's on General Patton's special interrogation team, sir."

The officer motioned to the others still working at the roadblock and one of them came over. He trained his rifle on the group. "All of you, one at a time, step into the shed out of the wind. I need to check everyone's papers." The MP lieutenant was all efficiency. "If everything is in order, you will be on your way in a matter of minutes."

Two hours later, they were all eating K-rations in the relatively warm corner of the cellar below a greengrocer's store. The grocer and his family were gone, but they had left behind a bag of onions. Only a few slices of raw onion greatly improved the tinned pork.

"You were lucky," Whitmore said. "These guys were willing to believe another MP. You and Goldschmitt and Lehman, together with your Kraut accents, it could have been a night in jail for you and the firing squad in the morning."

"Come on, you always exaggerate." Herman chuckled and took another bite of raw onion with the greasy, canned meat of his K-ration. "Though I'll admit I was happy to see your ugly face, not to mention Neumann. I've never been so glad to be a verified American!" He sighed and continued. "Too bad the German spies had been moved from this village an hour before you rescued me. At least we know for sure that there are Germans masquerading as Americans. They'll be shot as spies, that's for sure—after some kind of short tribunal, no doubt."

"First a quick trial with witnesses and recorded minutes before a shot to the head." Whitmore pointed his finger toward the wall of the cellar and pulled an imaginary trigger. "Bang!" He blew the end of his finger like it was a smoking revolver in a western movie. "We are Americans, after all."

The nervousness of the troops about imposters in their midst lasted for several weeks, and after he returned to

Lucky Forward, Herman and the other interrogators with German accents were ordered to stay at headquarters. Only the men born in the United States were sent out to question captured prisoners.

FOR THE REMAINDER OF DECEMBER and into January, the focus was on relieving Bastogne. Surrounded by German troops since December 19, the city was valiantly defended by a combination of American paratroopers, a tank battalion, and other assorted units, including a segregated field artillery battalion. These defenders had little food and no medical supplies, but they refused to surrender.

One day of clear skies on December 23 allowed American transport planes to drop medicine, food, blankets, ammunition, and artillery shells into Bastogne. Just in time. On Christmas Day, the Germans launched a massive assault against the city. Simultaneously, Patton's troops attacked from the south and pushed toward Bastogne, creating a vicious and bloody tug-of-war battle that raged around the town for more than a week until the German Panzer units began to withdraw and the enemy infantry followed.

Herman watched the whole thing on the situation maps at Lucky Forward. He counted the days as the Germans were pushed back. Finally, Herman was allowed to go out to where German prisoners were being kept, sometimes miles from headquarters during the retaking of lost territory. Travel was dangerous and grueling. The roads were icy, the skies hung with black clouds, snowstorms whistled through the night, and the temperatures dipped well below zero almost every day.

Back at Lucky Forward, wrapped in a woolen blanket and huddled over his typewriter, Herman composed a single-spaced, typed message to his mother on the tiny page of a V-mail letter.

01/12/1945 Dear Mutti, Thanks for the letter from Dec.14. Thank Bonnie for the wonderful postcard too. I really haven't the time to write often; our lives are hectic these days and we seldom have a chance to relax our weary bones. The weather makes it tough on us. The snow is deep and gets deeper every day. The roads are slippery and dangerous. I haven't been in bed for a couple of days because I've been on the road, driving in blackout over the most dangerous routes they have. But I like the excitement. I'd rather stay busy and without sleep than sit in a warm room and wait. The Germans are pretty well stopped after a lot of excitement the last few weeks. Nobody knows how long it will take to finish this war. Everything is hanging in the air. I guess the side with the most guts will win. No one has more guts than "old blood and guts Patton." I sure wish I was back in California now. I'd lie on a couch and read till I fell asleep. After a nap, I'd eat and eat, go to a movie or dance with a girl, like in the good old days. We boys always talk about what we want to do when we get home. It is the miserable living conditions now that make us imagine the most wonderful fantasies. I don't need

```
anything   except   maybe   razors.
Don't send food. Either it arrives
spoiled, or all the guys look sad
when you eat it. Give my love to
everybody. Herman.
```

It wasn't until the end of January that all the territory
lost in December had been regained. The Battle of the Bulge
was over, and they were again poised to assault the Siegfried Line and push across the Rhine River into Germany.

## CHAPTER 24

# THE FATHERLAND

GENERAL PATTON DID NOT WASTE any time. One day after the Third Army regained all the ground lost to the German offensive, they were on the move eastward. Though he had no clear orders to do so, Patton launched a chain of assaults that would break the Nazi war machine in less than two months.

One morning in early February, Herman arrived at a daily briefing to find the air electric with the latest directives from Supreme Headquarters. Patton had been given a limited time to assault the Siegfried Line. After February 10, his job would be to protect the British and Canadian forces in the north as they launched the main assault into the German fatherland.

After the briefing, Herman approached Colonel Allen. "What is Supreme thinking?" he asked. "Patton and the Third are the best and the fastest. We could clean up this mess before the snow melts, if they'd let us."

"Seems the Joint Chiefs of Staff, sitting comfortably in their heated offices in Washington, DC, want to make all the decisions." Allen shrugged in disgust. "They have no idea of the reality of the situation on the ground. It's all political to them." He looked up at Herman and gave him a wink. "Our Georgie," he said in a low voice, "will find a way to do what he wants and explain it later. There's nothing like success to soften the punishment."

Herman watched the Third Army push hard to be the first to reach the Rhine River, swollen and angry due to an early thaw and heavy rains. At the Siegfried Line, well-fortified with pillboxes, bunkers, trenches, and gun emplacements, Georgie's troops were motivated and pushed through. One morning at the staff briefing, Colonel Allen proudly announced that the 90th Division had destroyed 153 fortified pillboxes in one day.

Herman nudged Goldschmitt, who stood next to him as they listened to the report. "Our troops keep pushing forward with no regard to the calendar," he said. "We'll be in Germany before the deadline. Our fighting general will see to that. Not even Eisenhower can keep him down."

Herman's faith in Patton grew every day. By the end of March, at a location now in the heartland of Germany, Herman and the rest of the staff at Lucky Forward studied the map of Allied movements set up in the War Room. Though the Brits and Americans moved forward each day, Patton was always in the lead, the French tagged along, and to the east, the Russians converged on Berlin. But Herman couldn't linger long studying the maps.

The prisoner of war cages overflowed with close to 81,600 men who had been captured during the campaign since they crossed the Rhine River. The interrogators had an impossible job. There was no way they could question even ten percent of the prisoners. They learned to grab the ones who looked intelligent and hope they had chosen men who had information.

One afternoon, standing on the hood of his jeep in front of more than 5,000 prisoners, Herman was startled to hear a voice calling his boyhood name.

"Hermanle! Hermanle! *Bitte*, Hermanle!"

He searched the crowd for the man who had the nerve to call out to an American officer. An old man pushed through the lines of soldiers, waving his arms. With a start of recognition Herman realized the man was Herr Raeder, a close family friend, who had lived nearby and often been a guest in their home, his pockets filled with peppermints for the children. He had continued to visit their family long after the Nazi takeover. Now, the old man took off his hat and waved it frantically, the skin of his partially balding head the only thing clean in the entire crowd of muddy Germans.

Herman knew his authority and status as a conquering American would be shattered if the man received recognition. At Camp Ritchie, they had been warned about giving special notice to any former German friends they might run into. He leaned down and whispered to the MP. "Stop that man. Make him be quiet." The MP moved forward and blocked Raeder as he came to the front of the rows. Herman saw the old friend hesitate, lower his hand, and stand still.

Without any change in his expression, Herman continued directing the groups of prisoners to move forward and into the barbed wire enclosure. Occasionally he pulled aside a man who looked reasonably intelligent, but also frightened enough to be a good subject for interrogation. He made sure that Raeder was directed into the enclosure—the old man probably didn't know anything important anyway, and Herman was afraid his composure would crack if they were alone together in an interrogation tent. His glance did not waver as the man who had once given him sweets passed through the gate and into the cages.

Later that night, Herman worried about Herr Raeder. Was he hungry? Was he well? He must be at least in his late fifties. He might be ill. Recently it seemed that the foot soldiers of the German infantry were mainly old men and young boys. The next morning he tried to find the man who had stayed a friend to his family until Hugo's death, but there were thousands in the enclosure and they were transported by the truckload every hour to be taken west to the holding camps in Belgium. It had been impossible, but he couldn't help feeling bad about doing nothing to help the old man.

The deeper they advanced into Germany, the more prisoners were gathered. One private Herman interrogated told him the German army had orders directly from Hitler to fight to the last man. The soldier had cracked easily, something Herman counted on when he saw the prisoner's youth.

"I only want to go home," the frightened boy said. "I've been in the army for three months, and all we keep doing is retreating. Once in all the confusion, a buddy and I decided to simply walk away. We were only about twenty miles from my home, and I figured we could easily disappear."

Tears rolled down the soldier's beardless face, and Herman handed him a clean handkerchief.

"What happened?" he asked.

"They found us. We were walking on a farm road and feeling pretty good because I recognized the country. An SS unit sent to gather up stragglers and enforce order found us. They were at the crossroads, waiting. My friend tried to run into the trees, and they shot him in the back. I was too scared to do anything but stand with my hands in the air. I thought they'd shoot me too or take me to prison for desertion. But they didn't." The boy shuddered. For a moment he seemed unable to go on.

Herman waited patiently for a minute, then prompted him again. "What did they do to you—these SS?"

"Sir, they took me back to my unit. Told my commanding officer to keep a better eye on me and to put me in the front of any engagement with the enemy. 'Let him fight and die like a man,' the SS told my captain."

The boy was sobbing now. "The other men wouldn't talk to me much after that, and I had to shoot and shoot whenever we met the enemy. Sorry, sir. I had no choice. I was happy to throw down my gun." He turned his red and swollen eyes up to Herman. "Please, sir. I don't care what you do to me. I'm not a coward. I'm not cut out to be a soldier. I wanted to be a teacher, but not this . . . this killing . . . sir."

Herman turned away. He couldn't allow the boy to see the empathy he felt. He went to the tent opening and called the MP over. "Sergeant, this man is suffering from nervous fatigue. Get him a hot meal and a bed in the prisoners' infirmary. Tomorrow is soon enough for him to be sent to join his comrades in the cages." He hoped the boy would be on the next transport to the coast and a ship to the United States. Maybe he would be picking cotton stateside by summer.

By the end of March, Patton's army was moving easily through central Germany. Spring burst forth in the country as they fanned across the green hills. The skies were blue most days, and wildflowers blossomed among the rubble of the roadside. Away from the cities, there was little destruction in the villages. Only where pockets of snipers lingered to resist, did the towns become targets of American artillery. Herman felt a strange ache as they neared his hometown.

In the first days of April, General Bradley came from the Allied Command Headquarters to visit Patton at Lucky Forward. An hour after the meeting of the two generals, Herman saw Colonel Allen in the mess hall getting coffee. "How did it go with Georgie and Bradley?" he asked. "Same old stalemate?"

Allen grinned. "Well, poor Bradley brought a message from Supreme Headquarters that they want us to slow down and let the First and the Ninth catch up. He wasn't convincing in his arguments, and Georgie pretty much ignored him." Allen stirred his coffee and continued. "Patton told Bradley to relax and enjoy the show. His exact words were, 'In only a matter of weeks, it'll all be over.'"

Herman laughed out loud. "That's our general!"

At that moment, Goldschmitt entered the tent and walked over to the table where the two men sat. He saluted Allen, then turned toward Herman. "Aren't you from around here? I heard that Meiningen has been captured. Do you know it?"

Herman jumped up, spilling his coffee. "That's my hometown!" He sat down again and shook his head. "I can't believe it. It's been six years. Do you know anything more?"

"I think we did blast it a bit, but not much." Goldschmitt sighed. "The Germans blew up the main bridge across the Werra River themselves in a last futile attempt to slow us down. What a waste."

Colonel Allen stood up and put his hand on Herman's shoulder. "Take some time tomorrow, Captain. Get a jeep and a driver and check it out."


SERGEANT ERNIE LEHMAN WAS AT the wheel of the jeep as they drove through the streets of Meiningen the next morning. Herman recognized a few familiar faces, though everyone seemed hunched and older than he remembered. Heavy artillery rockets had fallen on the railroad station and several had missed their mark to destroy nearby buildings. The old school, where he had been given low grades for good work, was a pile of rubble. Herman hoped the children had not been in class. Up the hill from the station, the town cemetery was in ruins. He wandered among the jumble of gravestones and uprooted trees but could find no remnant of his father's headstone. It was just as well. Hugo would have hated where the gravestone had been. The family had no choice but to bury him in the Jewish section way at the back, when years before he had paid for a plot with a lovely view overlooking the town.

Discouraged by the destruction on the hill, Herman pointed the way to the center of town, directing Lehman down the main street, past the theater, to his childhood home. "Stop here, for a moment. I need to look." The catch in his voice surprised him, and he cleared his throat.

Lehman turned the engine off and sat quietly, waiting. "Don't you want to go to the door?" he finally asked. "Confront the bastard Nazi who took your house for his own."

Herman shook his head, surprised to find that the idea of a confrontation over his old home turned his stomach. "They weren't as bad as some," he said, but he climbed out of the jeep and looked across the street to the entrance gate. "They were friends of my father. They gave my mother a fair price and a place to live upstairs." He pointed to the round windows of the tower room. "See up there, Sergeant. My mother lived there under their protection until late in '39." Herman had his camera with him and took a few shots of the house, sorry to see it was in need of paint and a corner of the roof was blown off.

As he climbed back in the jeep, he turned to Lehman. "How about you, Sergeant? Where did you call home?"

"Austria, sir. I lived near Salzburg. We lost practically everything. It was different in Austria."

Herman was interested in the man's comment. "Different? How?"

"Well, we thought we were safe, not being part of Germany. But with the *Anschluss*, the Nazis took control overnight. I was fourteen and belonged to a bicycle club. We used to go riding every weekend, and we had lots of fun together. I thought the fellows were my friends. But the day after the Germans marched into Austria, one of my buddies, a guy from the bicycle club, came with a policeman to our street. I stood at the window of our living room and watched as he pointed up toward our apartment. Then he went into the building vestibule with the policeman. I was still looking out the window, when he walked out with my bicycle and rode away on it. I'll never forget the sense of betrayal I felt. A few minutes later the policeman knocked on the door. 'Jews must work,' he said. And he pulled my father and me out and made us clean the fire hydrants with our toothbrushes until after dark."

"But you were able to get to America?"

"Yes. I was the oldest—the only son. My parents sent me alone to an uncle in New Jersey."

"What about the rest of your family? Did they follow you?"

"Yes, sir. My mutti was born near Prague and had to wait for a place on the Czech quota. My sister was still a baby and my mother wouldn't be parted from her. Of course, Papa wouldn't leave them. They emigrated soon after I left, but they had to go to Cuba first. They arrived in the US four months ago, when I was already over here. I haven't seen them in a long time. But we were lucky."

"Yes . . . lucky," Herman said. "My mother was in London during the blitz waiting, but now she's in California."

As they talked, he began to wonder if his childhood friends had been as fortunate. From what he had seen and heard in the last weeks, life in Germany had not been easy. The idea of talking to someone from his childhood engulfed him. "I want to go somewhere down past the main square," he told Lehman. "I'll show you the way."

He was unsure of the route, but after a few false turns, he located the building, and he stood in front of the home of a favorite school teacher. Dr. Geiselhardt had been especially close to his older brother, but he had also taken Herman under his wing. It had been a difficult time for both teacher and student. Geiselhardt had refused to join the Nazi Party, and as a result, in 1936 he had lost his teaching position. Herman wondered if this old man, with his open heart and democratic ideals, had survived the war.

"Wait here, Sergeant. I might be only a few minutes. But if I find what I hope, don't worry if I'm not back right away. There's no danger here with the Americans in town. Don't let anyone siphon off the gasoline from the jeep. That'll be the biggest temptation, I should think."

He climbed the stairs and he rapped on the wood of the front door he remembered well. Would he find an empty apartment, he wondered, or an unknown face? Slowly the door opened a crack and an old man peered out.

"Yes?"

Geiselhardt seemed puzzled and a little frightened. He had aged tremendously and was barely recognizable, his straight back and neat classroom presence gone, his chin covered with gray, unshaven stubble and one lens of his thick glasses cracked. He stood in the darkened square of his doorway, his thin stooped shoulders wrapped in a threadbare blanket.

"Can I help you?" His voice was gravelly and confused, but a moment later his eyes lit up. "Is it you, Friedel? Is it really you?" And he opened the door wide to pull Herman inside.

"Sir. It's Herman Lang. His younger brother. Do you remember me?"

"Yes. Yes . . . Hermanle. I remember how you worked hard to do well in school. But always under the shadow of your older brother." He turned toward the kitchen. "Gerda! See who has come to visit. It's Hermanle. All grown up and an American officer."

Frau Geiselhardt came from the kitchen. She hobbled up and peered at him. One eye was clouded, but the other was clear and bright. In an instant of recognition, she flung her arms around his neck and covered him with kisses.

"Gerda. Take care. You'll frighten the dear boy." Geiselhardt gently pulled his wife away. "Do we have tea for our guest?"

"Yes. Some hot water and a few leaves of mint." She returned to the kitchen. "I'll put on the kettle." Her feet and ankles were swollen and her every step appeared painful. She wore heavy woolen socks and a pair of loose men's house slippers that flapped as she walked.

"Be comfortable. Please sit down." But Geiselhardt himself couldn't sit still. He walked over to a desk covered with papers. "Look." He swept his hand over the clutter.

"I've kept up with all the news for the entire war. Even when it was forbidden, I listened to the BBC. Every word from the BBC, I wrote down. But I've been careful. All my notes, I hid in a space behind the wardrobe in our bedroom. Until today. I've brought my treasures out of hiding this morning." He sighed. "It's harder to listen to the radio now. We get little electricity these last days."

Gerda returned and set down a tray on the tiny living room table. A faint aroma of mint rose when she poured the pale, hot liquid from the teapot into three cups. There was no sugar or milk, but she had found an apple, which she had cut into thin wedges and laid out on a saucer. She looked at her old husband lovingly. Her soft voice seemed to caress him as she spoke. "We have had some letters from your brother Friedel over the years. They also we hid. But today they are returned to the daylight." She lifted up a pile of letters from the desk. "We have read them all again this morning. Your visit is like a miracle."

The next morning, less than twenty miles from Meiningen, Herman screened prisoners as they entered a POW enclosure. He watched the line of thousands of prisoners closely for any likely men to interrogate. Suddenly his eye caught the gaze of a soldier who stared at him. A glimmer of recognition flickered before the man turned his head away. But in that short instant, he had recognized his classmate Otto Warner. Once he had thought they were best friends forever. But when Otto had joined the *Hitlerjugend*, drawn by the uniforms and the outdoor activities, everything had changed. Now the man never looked back—he just walked past the guards, into the cages, and melted into the crowd.

Herman still felt badly about his earlier denial of the old man Raeder. He wanted to do better this time. It was his habit to walk through the enclosures in the evenings. It was a good way to discover a prisoner with a look of importance—a man who might be an SS officer trying to pass himself off as an infantry private. That evening, when he walked among the dejected Germans, his MP escort at his side, Herman kept his eye open for Otto Warner. He wasn't sure if he would speak to him if he found him, but he wanted to make sure his old friend was okay.

The moon was full with only wisps of clouds passing over it. Near the back of the enclosure, he saw Otto. He stood alone near the fence. Herman motioned for the MP to stop and asked him to go over to a group of men clustered under a tree to check that they weren't hatching a plan. When the MP was gone, Herman stood quietly in the shadow of an old farm outbuilding that provided some shelter under its eaves. He watched Otto study the fence. It was a hastily erected enclosure, and Otto had found a weak point. He knelt down, and as a cloud drifted over the moon, he slithered under the barbed wire. Herman stood motionless and silent as the man's silhouette slipped away into the night. He knew Otto would be with his family by morning and he wondered if the precious motorcycle that had once been his waited for the escaping prisoner.

Besides prisoners, the hilly country around Meiningen yielded buried treasure. Locals, eager to help the Americans, led the way to the deep caverns of a salt mine. Goldschmitt had seen the stash himself as it was being brought up from 2,000 feet below.

"You wouldn't believe what was found," he told Herman. "There was a hoard of four thousand five hundred solid gold bars and assorted Allied currency stashed away in case the top Nazis needed to make a fast escape."

"In case they lost the war?" Herman wondered what Hitler would have thought of such defeatist attitudes. "I guess Patton's speed caught them by surprise," he said.

"Maybe only the guys in Berlin knew about the stash," Goldschmitt said. "There was a collection of fine art work, too. Paintings stolen from France and the Netherlands, all carefully wrapped. But worst of all were the stacks of suit-cases. At least thirty of them filled with watches, jewelry, even wedding rings, and silverware. And two cases over-flowed with gold dental fillings. Where else could all this have come from but the Jews who died in the Polish camps? Maybe it's not all Russian propaganda."

Herman shook his head. "I hate to think," he said. "I hate to think of it."

The war would be over soon. Herman knew, from his interrogations of prisoners, that most German soldiers wanted to go home. But Hitler had demanded a fight to the death. For some time, Herman and his G2 team had heard tales from prisoners that the Nazis planned a last-ditch stand in the Alpine regions of southern Germany. The rumor was that even when the rest of the nation had fallen to the Allies, the upper echelon—Hitler, Goebbels, and Himmler, with their elite SS troops—would shelter in the mountains and fight a guerrilla war. At least now they wouldn't have all their gold.

Fighting an enemy forbidden to surrender, the American and British armies continued to push across Germany. The Third Army was told to swing south and make contact with the Soviet forces near the Danube River. Eisenhower wanted them in a position to inflict a mortal blow to any attempt by SS units to make a break for the Alps for a fight to the death in the mountains.

As Patton's army barreled into Bavaria, the casualty count diminished every day and the prisoners continued to pour in. On one day in mid-April, only three Americans were killed and thirty-seven were wounded, but 15,000 German prisoners were taken. Rear Headquarters ordered no more prisoners were to be transported to the overflowing camps in Belgium. There would be no more convoys of ships to take prisoners to the stateside camps and the relatively easy life of farm laborer in the South or the Midwest. From now on, all POWs were to be held where they were captured, while Supreme Headquarters decided what to do with them at the end of the war.

## CHAPTER 25

# IT CANNOT BE EXAGGERATED

A T OHRDRUF, THE THIRD ARMY troops liberated their first Nazi concentration camp. It was a grisly place, populated by the dead and dying victims of slave labor. Smoke from an open burial pit where the cremation of corpses was in progress hung over the area.

This was not the first evidence of the Nazi policy of systematic genocide. Nine months before, the Russians had discovered Majdanec, the abandoned Polish death camp where only 500 inmates remained alive. Auschwitz and the nearby camps of Birkenau and Monowitz were liberated by the Russians in late January, 1945. But the reports coming from the East were so horrible that Herman, along with many others, thought the stories must be exaggerated rumors—Russian-hate propaganda against the Nazis. How could he believe that the boys he had known in school, average German boys, could have turned into men who could commit such atrocities?

Now the Americans and the British, in their sweep across Germany, had begun to discover horror camps too—Ohrdruf, Buchenwald, Nordhausen, BergenBelsen. General Patton, with Eisenhower and Bradley, visited the concentration camp at Ohrdruf shortly after its liberation. Herman was in the staff tent when Patton confirmed that the inhumanity of the concentration camps could not be exaggerated. It was all true and worse. Herman trembled to think of what might have happened to him—to his family—if they had remained.

News of the horrors of the Nazi concentration camps continued to accumulate. On April 29, just outside Munich, the Seventh Army discovered Dachau, the oldest concentration camp and its surrounding satellite camps. These camps were not killing factories, like Auschwitz where huge gas chambers were built to murder and incinerate trainloads of humanity, yet they were no less terrifying. Dachau was mainly a political prison where constant labor, exposure, starvation, and disease could be relied on to kill the inmates. The gas chamber there and the accompanying crematoriums were used to expedite the death of the weak and the ill, and to cleanly and quickly dispose of the bodies of the dead. In the end, they had not been able to keep up.

General Eisenhower issued an order that all officers and GIs able to go were to visit Dachau in order to bear witness to the unthinkable.

Herman was haunted by the knowledge that both his cousin and his great-uncle had died at Dachau. He ignored the rule against officers driving on their own and took a jeep to drive the back roads toward Munich. He arrived at the Dachau camp two days after Eisenhower's visit. He found himself with a group of reporters and news photographers who were led toward the gate by Lieutenant Johnston, a member of the Combat Engineer Regiment assigned to deal with the aftermath of liberation.

The first sight they saw was a line of fifty flatcars filled with haphazard piles of skeleton-like bodies. The train was parked on a siding near the camp entrance, and the corpses were being removed, one by one. Men, some dressed in suits, others in overalls, moved the lifeless bodies to waiting carts while other men and women labored to push the carts onto the road. A long line of carts, some pulled by horses, others by people, moved steadily off toward the nearby town.

"Where are they going?" one of the newsmen asked the engineer guide.

Johnston's answer was slow and matter of fact. "They're going to a burial ground called Leitenberg on the other side of town. The colonel has ordered that the bodies be taken directly through town forcing the citizens to see for themselves the atrocities that happened right under their noses."

"Are those town civilians loading the bodies?" another newsman asked.

"Yes, they're citizens of Dachau and farmers from the surrounding area." Johnston waved his hand in the direction of the awful scene. "Our C.O. ordered them to dress in their best, out of respect for the dead. We have men stationed at both the loading and unloading areas to make sure it is done as gently as possible." He cleared his throat. "Unfortunately, because of the numbers and the degree of decomposition of most of the bodies, we must resort to mass burial. We wish we could give each body its own plot, but it's impossible. We had to use a bulldozer to dig a trench as a burial place, and we may have to create several more trenches before it's all over."

"So many dead?" Herman's voice was a croak of despair.

"Yes, Captain. And they continue to die by the hundreds each day."

Herman gasped. "Why? Aren't we giving them food and medicine?"

"Of course!" Johnston was obviously offended. "But you must understand the enormity of the situation. We have thousands of fragile and starving men, women, and children to deal with. An epidemic of typhus is raging through the camp. The inmates were previously not allowed personal hygiene of any kind, and they are infested with body lice that spread the typhus. We dust them with DDT, but sometimes it's already too late."

The newsmen looked around nervously. "You needn't worry for yourselves," Johnston said with a note of disdain. "These people are weak and they succumb easily to the disease. You will see the survivors are just bones covered with skin. They suffer from severe starvation and their digestive systems are so dysfunctional that they must be fed solid food in small amounts, as carefully as if it were strong medicine. Many of these survivors became violently ill from overeating on the first day of liberation when our GIs gave them C-rations."

The newsmen stood in stunned silence. Finally one man spoke up. "We need to see all this ourselves. And we need to show the world or no one will believe the stories." He seemed embarrassed by what he said next. "Can we take pictures?"

Johnston grunted his assent. "But have some care for the feelings of the people. If they are still alive, ask their permission."

The group entered the main compound and a spectacle of unspeakable human misery assaulted their senses. Naked and partially clothed bodies were stacked like firewood in various places around the camp. One mountain of bodies stood over five feet high and almost twenty feet wide, the hundreds of emaciated corpses half-covered by a brown tarpaulin. The stench of death and rot was everywhere. Herman held a handkerchief over his nose and felt the tears run down his cheeks. Groups of emaciated men sat huddled in the sun, motionless, with glassy stares. Others hobbled on swollen feet, two by two, supporting each other. Their filthy, striped uniforms hung from skeletal bodies. Their eyes were sunken black holes staring from a shaved head, the thin skin stretched tight across bony skulls. Arms, legs, heads, and faces were covered with sores and bruises. Herman could distinguish a variety of languages—Polish, Russian, Yiddish, and German. The mix of languages reminded him of Camp Ritchie, but these were the ones who hadn't made it out of Germany. These were the unlucky.

His group was taken to the barracks, now hospitals where medics and GIs ministered to the survivors. They walked to the gas chambers and the crematorium where more bodies were stacked. At the dog kennels, the guard dogs lay dead, shot by angry GIs who had discovered them.

The group walked along the electrified fences with the empty guard towers looming above. A moat ran parallel to the fences, and in the murky water below, Herman could see the floating corpse of an SS guard. Most telling of the numbers of souls who had passed through this camp of death was the huge warehouse overflowing with suitcases, shoes, clothing, shorn hair, and eyeglasses.

Toward the end of the tour, the group passed a gathering of young male prisoners. They were only teenagers and seemed to have some energy left. With the resiliency of youth, they waved and smiled at the visitors. "*Ami, Ami,*" they cried out. "Americans."

Herman would have liked to close his eyes and have it all disappear, but he was unable to stuff his thoughts into a dark corner and ignore them. His emotions raged from fury to horror to disbelief to guilt. First, there was the fury at all Germans, especially all SS, at anyone who could have committed or condoned the deliberate murder and torture of millions. But Herman's mind also filled with questions. Was it possible that his school chums, men like Otto Warner, could have contributed to this inhumanity? Did they know about it and ignore it? If he had remained in Germany, would he have been one of these starving survivors? Surely not, for he would have been dead long ago. As he stood in front of the crematorium, he thought of his cousin, who had been a young man of twenty, filled with political enthusiasm for the Communist cause, when he died in this same camp back in 1934. He remembered his dear Uncle Martin who, after Kristallnacht, had last been seen alive in Dachau.

Where were their bones buried? Or were they reduced to ash blowing on the wind? Grief and guilt for his own survival when so many had died for no other crime than being Jewish or Communist or gay overcame him, and for several long minutes, he trembled, unable to move.

He remembered how the Nazi media in the 1930s had dehumanized the Jews, the Gypsies, the Poles, even the mentally disturbed and beautiful simple souls like Gracie. If he had not been so detached, so determined not to let all that was happening affect him, could he have saved even one life? The chief of police in Meiningen had done more than he had. In his quiet way, this man had saved Herman's life. He remembered the story his mother told him of her friend, the policeman's wife, who one morning had walked near her on the market plaza and spoken as if to the wind or the trees. "I am still your friend in my heart," she had whispered and dropped her lifesaving note in his mother's shopping basket. If this woman had not taken a risk, would his own mother have ended her days at a place like Dachau? Or worse—been sent to one of the death factories in the East. The small bravery of his mother's friend had saved a life, for the next morning Clara was on the train to England.

That night, unable to sleep, Herman was haunted by what he had seen at Dachau. How could this have happened in the country of his birth. Germany was the country his father believed was the epitome of civilization. Taught by his father, he had loved his homeland. He had been proud of its music, art, philosophers, and poets. He had been proud to be a German—but then suddenly he wasn't. He wasn't

German anymore, and he wasn't proud. He had fled and started a new life. But he hadn't known where he belonged. He had seen racial prejudice and hatred in America, especially in Georgia and Maryland. He had seen it in the American army too, where black soldiers fought in separate units, mainly relegated to driving trucks. Perhaps no place was without hatred. The darkness of these ideas overpowered him, and his sleep was tormented by nightmares.

The next morning he awoke as dawn drained the darkness from the sky. He wrapped his rough blanket around his shoulders and walked out into the gray mist that hung low against the tents. He gazed past the gates of Lucky Forward and watched the spring sunshine slowly evaporate the fog. In the distance, the hills, scarred with the ruts of convoys, were covered in new green, and the gnarled branches of trees burst with buds. He knew he would never forget the sights and smells of Dachau. After what he had seen there, how could he not hate the Germans who allowed such things to happen? But was it every German? What had they actually known? Certainly the men and women of the village of Dachau must have suspected something evil was happening right next door. And the SS . . . the guards, how could he not hate them? He closed his eyes and pushed these depressing thoughts to the back of his mind. Hate was what had destroyed Germany. He would not allow it to be part of him. He was a man of action now, and in his small way he would try to make the world better.

He returned to his tent, took out his kit bag, and lathered his face. He looked in his small shaving mirror and said out loud, "I am not a Jew. I am not a German. I am an American now." He would be the best man he could be. If he must work with evil in the line of duty, he would try to put his hatred aside. He hoped he could do that.

## CHAPTER 26

# REGENSBURG

FIGHTING PERSISTED BUT MOSTLY IN isolated bursts from die-hard Nazi troops. Everyone else knew the end was near. News came over the headquarters' radio of Hitler's death by his own hand and of the fall of Berlin to the Russians on May 2. Still, there were pockets of small fanatical groups of SS fighting in southern Bavaria. On May 6, the rumors at Lucky Forward buzzed. The new leader, Grand Admiral Karl Doenitz, was trying to negotiate a final surrender of Germany to the Allies.

That same evening, Herman received a new assignment and a new billet. He was to help bring some order to the chaos at the huge POW camp near Regensburg. Only a mile from Patton's command post, the camp was a completely different world.

Early the first morning of his new assignment, Herman approached Regensburg camp. A steady rain fell, shrouding everything in a veil of gray. On the road from his farmhouse quarters to the site, his driver struggled to keep the jeep from fishtailing on the muddy and slippery track. An MP escort sat in the rear of the jeep, swaying with every lurch, but he managed to keep the mounted machine gun steady. As they entered the enclosure, Herman was horrified to see the conditions at the camp. The area was large, close to 200 acres, but it was packed with 70,000 Germans and Hungarians. Every day their number increased. Herman looked over his reports while the driver negotiated the difficult terrain. The day before, nearly 2,000 men had been marched into Regensburg every hour.

Rain had been falling for a week. The camp was a morass of mud and men, surrounded by hastily installed strings of barbed wire and guarded by nervous MPs with submachine guns. No one had anticipated the numbers of prisoners who would suddenly become the responsibility of the US Army, and there was not enough shelter or food ready for so many. As he drove through the camp, Herman saw prisoners forced to lie, stand, and sit in mud. They huddled together in close-packed groups for warmth. It was obvious to him that when night came, they would wrap themselves in their coats, share a few tattered blankets, and sleep in the mud.

Water dripped off the prisoners and stood in brown, murky puddles, but there was not enough clean water fit to drink. Once a day, a water truck moved through the camp. The prisoners rushed to stand in line for hours to fill their canteens. Food was scarce everywhere in Germany, but at Regensburg there was nothing for the prisoners but K-rations—

one a day per man. Herman knew this diet would keep them alive, but in the long term, it was not enough to prevent malnutrition. These conditions would soon lead to disease and slow death. Such deprivation could also lead to riots and mass prisoner escapes. He had heard of the high death rate in the overflowing camps in the Rhine River area, and he was determined that the same would not happen here.

The prisoners were frightened, and rumors ran like wildfire from man to man. They whispered that they would surely all be put before firing squads and killed. The officers, especially the SS, feared that if they escaped death, they would get twenty years hard labor whether they were guilty of atrocities or not.

As in all camps, the officers were separated from the enlisted men, but the situation in both sections of the camp was the same quagmire of mud and fear. In fact, so many officers were now surrendering to the Americans, that the smaller officer area of the camp was, if anything, more crowded than the main compound.

This first morning, Herman observed the conditions and made mental notes. He did not allow the driver to stop and he did not get out and talk to anyone. He knew he had to come up with a plan—fast. There would be no time for trial and error.

In the afternoon, after consulting with the camp commandant who gave him free rein, Herman sat at the dining table in his farmhouse billet, paperwork spread around him. Until late that night, he studied the accounting of the prisoners to see what kind of men he would be working with. Among the many prisoners—the worn-out old timers, the scared teenagers, the battle-hardened career soldiers—were many Waffen-SS, many of them officers.

He knew that this branch of the SS was a different breed from the SS-*Totenkopfverbände*, or Death's Head SS, who were responsible for the concentration camps and the deaths of millions of Jews. The Waffen-SS was an elite, frontline, combat organization. Its members had been at the forefront of most of the crucial battles of the war, especially active during the Battle of the Bulge. They were still SS and most were fervent Nazis, but he hoped they were, first of all, soldiers. Herman thought these men with their background in honor and military discipline could be an asset. He needed to find one who had not lost his soul.

He went through the paybooks of the captured officers and made a list of those who came from privileged backgrounds or old German military families. There was a chance that these officers might be in the army because of their love of Germany, rather than because they were fervent Nazis. He looked for men who had a higher level of education, especially the few who had attended university in the United States or Britain and had been exposed to democratic ideas before the war.

Early the next morning, Herman again drove around the camp. He studied the short list and observed the selected officers. He tried to detect in their bearing, in the way the other officers spoke to them or ignored them, which man might be the one he needed to make his plan work. One officer caught his attention. SS *Obersturmbannführe* Richard

Schulze stood six feet, two inches tall, head and shoulders above the other prisoners. He also had the background Herman wanted. He was only thirty years old, from an old military family, and, though he had not been to school overseas, he had served as aide to some of the top Nazis, including Ribbentrop and the evil Theodor Eicke. For a year he had even been an adjutant to Hitler himself. This would give him authority with the other prisoners.

However, Schulze's last official assignment was of a different sort. He had been commander of the SS Junkerschule, the officer training academy in nearby Bad Tölz. He was captured in southern Bavaria, not far from the school, at the head of a regiment of cadets, most barely over eighteen years old. It was said that the surrender was on Schulze's orders and that none of the young soldiers had been injured during the two weeks he had marched them around the countryside, avoiding conflict with the Americans as much as possible. Schulze told the GIs who took his group to the cages that their unit was called the Nibelungen after the heroic dwarfs in Richard Wagner's famous Siegfried saga operas. But one of the guards spoke German, and he began calling the youthful regiment the *nie gelungen*, meaning "the ones who never succeeded." The nickname stuck. In spite of his rank and his association with Hitler, Richard Schulze seemed to have maintained a core of humanity that would set him apart from many diehard Nazis.

Herman went back to the farmhouse to finalize his plans.

On the morning of May 9, news arrived that the unconditional surrender of Germany had been signed. The war was over in Europe, and the guards who surrounded the cages at Regensburg went crazy with joy. They began to shoot their weapons into the air, laughing, shouting, and hugging each other. The loud gunfire and crazy behavior of the Americans terrified the prisoners. They imagined that at the next moment the American guards would turn their rifles in toward the camp.

Just as the confusion began to settle down, Herman drove into the officers' cages. This time he was alone—no driver and no intimidating MP escort armed with a machine gun. When he was in the center of the officer section, he told one of the camp guards to bring him Richard Schulze.

The SS officer appeared, covered in mud, but he snapped to attention in front of Herman. Even the grime could not disguise his movie star good looks. He was the picture of Hitler's ideal Germanic type, tall and straight and blond—a poster boy for racial purity. Herman knew this added to his stature among the other POWs in camp.

"Get in the jeep," Herman ordered. Schulze hesitated only a moment before he climbed into the passenger seat. Though the prisoner surely had no idea what to expect, Herman liked the way he sat tall and straight as they proceeded out of the compound. Neither Herman nor the prisoner spoke a word as they rode down the rutted road between fields of once prosperous farms. Several times, when he had to slow for a truck at a crossing or navigate around a pothole, Herman glanced at his companion and willed him not to jump out of the vehicle and run. If the German bolted, Herman would have to pull his side gun and shoot. But the SS officer didn't run, and they arrived at the large stucco farmhouse without incident. Herman pulled the jeep up to the front door and jumped out.

"*Folgen Sie mir!* Follow me!" His order was terse. He turned and walked into the house. He held his breath until he heard the sound of Richard Schulze's boots follow him into the building. In the vestibule, he turned abruptly and faced his puzzled prisoner. The man towered above him, a full twelve inches taller. Herman looked up only enough to focus on the German's chin, testing to see how the tall man would handle the situation. "The war is over. And we are no longer enemies," he said.

Schulze relaxed his posture a bit and lowered his eyes to speak man to man. "Yes, Captain." His gaze was steady.

So far Herman was pleased. "We should have a drink to celebrate. Come." He walked into the dining room and over to the glass-fronted cabinet where he kept a bottle of French cognac recently liberated from a German general. He poured two glasses of the amber liquid and handed one to Schulze who had followed him. If the German was bewildered, he managed not to show it. Herman raised his glass. "To the end of the fighting in Europe. And to peace."

Schulze silently raised his glass to acknowledge the toast and downed the brandy.

"I'm sure you would appreciate a bath and a shave."

The German's eyes widened in surprise. "Yes, Captain."

"There is a bathing room upstairs, and we have plenty of hot water here. I've laid out some clean clothing. Thankfully they are not my castoffs, thus there is a chance they will fit you." Herman grinned and continued. "Go upstairs. Take your time. Wash up. Shave. Even rest a bit, if you want. We will have dinner in an hour."

Schulze hesitated. His eyes turned longingly up the stairway to the second floor.

"Yes, I mean it.," Herman said. "I'll see you in an hour."

"Thank you. Captain . . . I . . . ." He turned on his heel and went up the stairs.

Exactly an hour later, the German descended. He sparkled—now clean-shaven, his skin ruddy from hot water and scrubbing, his blond hair slicked back, the borrowed pants riding only two or three inches above the tops of the house slippers that had been provided to replace his muddy boots. Herman led him to the dining room where the table was set for dinner with a linen tablecloth, wine glasses, silverware, and place settings of good china. A small vase of flowers graced the center of the table, and next to it sat a plate with thick slabs of black bread and a butter dish heaped with rare, fresh butter. An open bottle of red wine breathed on the sideboard.

Herman motioned with his hand to one of the chairs. "Sit and be comfortable. I think you will enjoy dinner, though it is meager by pre-war standards." He picked up the bottle of wine and poured two glasses before he sat. "I've been lucky enough to find an excellent chef. Wolf used to be the head chef at the best hotel in Heidelberg until two years ago when he was inducted into your army. I found him among some prisoners taken in last month. It's truly amazing what he can do with powdered eggs." He sipped his wine. "But tonight, I think he has something better prepared. I was able to claim the hind quarter of a pig that fell victim to a mortar round less than a week ago. I imagine that we will have a dinner fit for the Kaiser."

Schulze did not flinch at Herman's reference to the old, pre-Nazi, emperor of Germany. He sat quietly, holding the stem of the wine glass delicately between two fingers, waiting to see what would happen next.

Burly, gray-haired Wolf entered the room, a platter held in front of him to reveal its display of a shoulder roast of pork, the skin crisp and golden and the meat falling off the bone, surrounded by boiled potatoes and sautéed cabbage. He placed it in the center of the table but avoided meeting the gaze of the SS officer. The aroma of roasted meat filled the room as Herman carved, pulling large chunks of meat from the pork. He piled a plate with food, passed it across to his guest, and then prepared another plate for himself. He raised his wine glass. "To health and the happiness only peace can bring," he said.

Schulze raised his glass, too. "To peace," he echoed, and took a deep swallow of the wine. But he could not ignore the food any longer. Herman knew that as a prisoner he had eaten nothing but C-rations for more than a week. Still the man ate slowly, with the natural good manners of a gentleman. Herman allowed him the luxury of the meal without conversation. Schulze cleaned his plate with a slab of the bread slathered in butter but would not accept more. "I dare not," he said. After he swallowed the last bite of bread, Schulze wiped his mouth with the linen napkin. "Thank you, Captain. It was delicious."

"Have some more wine." Herman reached across the table, refilled Schulze's glass, and gently led his guest into conversation. First some small talk—the heavy rains, the hope of spring, the need to get the farms operational again. Finally he asked questions about Schulze's background—questions he knew the answers to and would allow him to judge the man's truthfulness.

The SS officer seemed to be relaxed. Warmed by the good food and the wine, he willingly began to talk about himself—where he was born, how his brother and father had both died on the Russian front, and how he had no idea where his mother was. He had joined the SS right after his twentieth birthday, he said, and became a member of the Nazi party three years later. He explained that he had done so only in order to keep his job with *Obergruppenführer* Theodor Eicke. Herman surmised that this was only a half-truth but acceptable under the circumstances.

As they talked, the afternoon gradually turned into dusk. Wolf came in to take the plates away and leave a dish of baked apples. The chef bent to light the candles at the center of the table and returned to the kitchen without a word.

Herman shrugged. "I'm sorry. We're trying to conserve our generated power."

"Very understandable." Schulze's eyes lit up with humor. "I have been used to candles and firelight for some time now."

The bottle of wine stood empty. Herman retrieved the French cognac from the sideboard and poured some into fresh glasses. "There is nothing like a good cognac to warm a man on a cold night."

"I was fighting on the Russian Front in the winter of '41. I still believed in Hitler's dream of a thousand-year Reich at that point. The Russian cold goes deep in your bones." Schulze cleared his throat and took a sip. "Not even cognac can reach it. But vodka . . . well, maybe."

"Is that where you earned the Iron Cross?" Herman was pleased to see the man was completely relaxed but not drunk.

"Yes. And later the Cross of Gold, too." He set down his glass and pushed up his sleeves. "That summer, I was wounded. Both arms." He stretched his arms out on the tablecloth, revealing a labyrinth of scars, some deep and disfiguring. In a dreamlike way he traced the worst area of shiny white scar tissue on one forearm with the fingers of the other hand. "It was a lucky wound, as it turned out. Hitler was told of my injury when I was in the hospital. My older brother had been Hitler's adjutant, a member of the inner circle and a favorite of the Führer. So, when I recovered, he took me also as his adjutant. My brother was killed in battle the year before and the Führer said he meant to save my family name. He promised to keep me away from the fighting."

Herman stretched and tried to show only moderate, friendly interest. Most of this he had already known. "Were you happy to work close to Hitler?" he asked.

Schulze looked across the table and held Herman's gaze. "Yes, certainly." For a moment the silence held multiple meanings. "The Führer could be unpredictable, it's true. Yes, sometimes even difficult. But he had loved my brother. For me, it was a good career move."

"And did he keep his promise to you?"

"I never saw fighting again—not until these last two weeks. When he sent me to Bad Tölz, to be commander of the Junkerschule, I was even farther from the action, but still I was doing something useful. The students were enthusiastic. Fresh and young but also terribly indoctrinated." Schulze took a deep breath and seemed to shudder as he let it out again. "I saw the way the war was going. My friends at the Berlin bunker began to hint at their growing doubts. I wanted to somehow protect the young men under my command. Keep them from the fighting the same way Hitler had protected me. It was obvious we were losing, though one was not allowed to say this out loud." The German seemed to look inward and did not say more.

Herman waited. Here was his opportunity to ask an important question Patton and the other generals still wanted to know. "It's rumored some SS and Hitler's inner circle won't admit the war is over. There's talk that they have run to the mountains and will fight to the death." Schulze looked up and Herman met his gaze directly.

"Is there any truth to these rumors? Do we need to worry about months of guerrilla fighting with fanatics?"

"Ah, the Bund Werwolf." Schulze shook his head. "They are a few fanatics. Very disorganized and motivated by talk and pipe dreams." He rubbed his hand over his face. "Some plans were made for a few disruptive actions on the eastern front, but the leadership was never in agreement. All fell into chaos. No supplies were stockpiled. No plan for where to go or how to coordinate. There may be a few eccentrics who will hole up on their own in the Alps. But they'll be no threat." The German sighed. "Tell Patton not to worry. Nothing will come of it. You have my word that it's only a rumor with no substance."

"Thank you, Schulze. I'll let the general know." Herman saw that the man's eyes drooped toward sleep. He wondered when the prisoner had last enjoyed a dry bed. He stood up and walked around the table. "It's late, and tomorrow we must discuss what we can do to help the men at the camp. But for now, I think it's time to sleep."

Schulze rose slowly and put his hand out in a gesture of thanks and friendship. "Thank you, Captain, for a most enjoyable evening."

Herman clasped the offered hand, shook it, and led the prisoner to the bottom of the stairs. "You are my guest tonight. The room is ready for you. Enjoy a good sleep, and we will talk some more over breakfast." The prisoner's eyes widened with surprise. He turned, grasped the bannister, and with his back straight, he slowly and unsteadily climbed the stairs.

Herman served himself one of the untouched baked apples and took a bite, the sweet taste on his tongue a happy ending to a day of calculated risk. He had been right and he was elated. This man was not just a Nazi and a member of the SS—treating him as a human being, with respect, had yielded more important information than straight interrogation could have. Herman went to the living room, taking the dessert and his unfinished brandy with him, and typed his report.

In the morning, over a breakfast of reconstituted powdered eggs mixed with onions, cheese, and mushrooms, the
two men settled down to business. They worked for a common purpose. Thousands of prisoners needed better shelter
and nutrition while they waited for Allied supplies to catch up
with the demand. The German officer knew the Nazi army
had many hidden storage facilities, most left undiscovered
during the rapid advance of the American troops. Schulze
knew there must be plenty of blankets, canvas for shelters,
even tents and food hoarded by officers, stashed around
Bavaria. All they needed to do was locate them. He would
return to camp and talk to the other officers. They would
know where much of these German army supplies were hidden. Herman would wait to hear from Schulze and be ready
to send trucks to gather up what could be found. Herman
would work from the outside. Schulze would work on the
inside of the camp to gather information about stashed supplies. Together they would improve the conditions for the
prisoners and turn the camp into a safe environment.

In less than a week, the POW camp at Regensburg was
a model of German efficiency. Canvas tents and shelters
stood in neat rows. Most of the men had blankets or at least
a winter greatcoat to wrap up in at night. Some even had
cots. New latrines were dug on the high, dryer side of camp.
A canvas-covered mess hall served hot meals prepared from
recovered Polish tinned meats, hoarded potatoes, and stolen wheels of cheese, all cooked by trained chefs from some
of the best German pre-war restaurants. Late in the week,
a generator was delivered by Allied command. Light posts

rose up, some prisoners happily brushing them with white-wash, while others strung electric wires and installed lighting fixtures made from a crate of German flashlights.

Under Herman and Schulze's direction, happy prisoners worked for a fortnight to get the camp in order. Sometimes the two men rode into the countryside together to gather up tinned goods or blankets hidden in a barn or cellar. Schulze spoke to the farmers and village caretakers in a gentle voice, avoiding any hint of SS coercion. On the rides back to Regensburg, followed by a truck filled with supplies, the two men talked of their pre-war childhoods, laughing over their mutual fear of the boogeymen of the *Struwwelpeter* stories. Tentatively they shared their concern for the German people and how they would manage to overcome the devastation and mistakes of the war. Herman saw Schulze as one of those conflicted men like Herr Mueller, the police chief, torn between his Nazi membership and his humanity.

When life at camp finally ran smoothly, Herman wanted to show his appreciation to the SS officer. One evening, as he typed a report, he remembered what Richard had told him about his mother that first evening after dinner. During the war, she had remained in their home in Spandau. But in her last letter, she had written that the next morning she would flee their home. She was afraid of the Soviet Army, which was getting closer every day. Hopefully she had made it safely into an American- or British-held area, but her son had received no news for more than a month. She might be with a sister who lived near Munich or an uncle who had owned a factory outside Nuremberg.

Perhaps, Herman thought, he could locate the officer's mother. But it wouldn't be easy. First of all, Schulze was a common name. And the roads of Germany were clogged with refugees of all kinds, going all directions. Released slave laborers who had the strength struggled to return to their homes in Poland or Czechoslovakia. City dwellers from Dresden, Nuremberg, and other bomb-destroyed cities searched for shelter in the countryside. Thousands of Germans had fled from Berlin and its vicinity, ahead of the Russians who had a reputation for brutality and rape. Herman knew that it would take luck to find one woman among these constantly moving masses of displaced people.

But he had contacts. He telephoned Goldschmitt, newly assigned to USFET headquarters, the US post-victory organizing body. After he told Julian what he wanted, he waited but his friend said nothing. "Are you there?" Herman asked, thinking they might have been disconnected.

Finally Julian's voice came over the line, low, almost whispering. "Are you sure you want to do that? It could cause you trouble."

"Schulze's gone way beyond to help get the camp functioning," Herman answered. "I'd like to do something for him."

"I understand he's been a good boy now that we've won." Julian seemed a bit terse. "But after all, he is SS. He knew Germany was losing. That's the only reason he saved those boys just before they were captured. To make himself look good. And you fell for it."

Herman felt his back stiffen. "Look, Julian. I know the Nazis committed countless atrocities. But Schulze didn't do any of that stuff. He was on the front lines, he got injured, he was doing office work for some big-wigs, and then he ran a school. And now he's the most cooperative of prisoners." He took a breath. The silence at the other end of the line made him feel like he talked to a wall. "Julian?" He said his friend's name with affection.

"Well, I'm sure every SS has an excuse. Every German has a reason they did whatever they did or an excuse for why they did nothing. But we can't just let them forget it all. They have to pay the price."

"Julian, the old lady's his mother. Many families on both sides are separated. You know that. I just want to help a son find his mother."

Herman heard a long sigh through the line and the shuffling of papers. "Look, buddy, some of the guys here, fellows like us who have lost their loved ones to this mess . . . some of them would happily send every SS to the gallows. You need to be careful." Another sigh echoed down the line. "I'll see what I can do," his friend said. "I wonder, though, if things were turned around, if some Nazi would have helped me find my mother. But for you, Herman. I'll see what I can find out."

Amazingly, three days later, Julian called back. He had located Schulze's mother. She was at a camp for displaced persons in a town near the Austrian border. Herman made arrangements to have her brought to Tegernsee, a village only an hour south of Regensburg.

Early the next morning, he went to the camp and pulled Schulze away from his work with the excuse that they must check out a recently discovered stash of food and wine meant for German officers. During the drive, they chatted easily about the need to set up a prisoner committee that could deal with minor problems and complaints.

When they arrived in Tegernsee, Herman directed his driver to pull the jeep into the yard of a small pension. "We are to meet someone here who will direct us to the supply depot I told you about," he told Richard. "Go inside and check if the contact is there yet. The code word is 'mother.'" He watched Schulze's tall figure walk into the entrance.

If all his efforts had succeeded, Richard's mother waited expectantly in the foyer. Herman sat in the jeep for ten minutes to give his companion the time and space to properly greet his mother. Finally he went into the adjoining bar and asked the barman to deliver a message to "the tall man in the lobby." He stood at the counter and sipped the foam off the top of his beer until Schulze came into the bar with a stately, white-haired lady on his arm. They both beamed with joy as they came toward Herman.

Only a short visit was possible before mother and son had to part, each to return to the camps that were their current homes. But now each knew the other was safe and they would write.

The next afternoon, a general from Supreme Headquarters came to inspect the camp at Regensburg, and Herman took him on a tour. The general was amazed. "I was here three weeks ago and the place was unspeakable. Now, I'm told you're responsible for this change. How did you do it?"

Herman grinned. "I couldn't have done it without Richard Schulze," he said. "He made it happen. Not me."

"Regardless. Your name will be submitted for a commendation." The general turned and waved his arm over the bustling camp. "We can't give credit for this to an SS officer, but we can use his expertise. The new SS officer detention camp could use some serious help. Supplies from Central are beginning to arrive. That'll make his work easier than it was here."

"I'd rather not lose him. The men listen to him and a system of self-government is just being established among the prisoners."

"Make the most of the next few days," the general said. "Schulze will be going to Auerbach as soon as I can get the paperwork approved."

All too soon, Herman said good-bye to the German officer who waited his turn to climb into a transport truck that would take a group of German officers to the new camp.

Herman shook the hand of the SS officer with a true sense of regret. "I'll miss your help. It's been a great experience." He felt a kinship with the man that he hadn't expected and a strong desire to continue their friendship. It was unimaginable that only last month they would have been enemies.

"I won't forget your kindness," Schulze answered. "If you need me for anything, you'll be able to find me, I'm sure." Then he hoisted himself into the back of the open truck.

Herman could see him standing head and shoulders above the other men as the transport rumbled away.

CHAPTER 27

# GOOD-BYE POWS

B Y THE END OF MAY 1945, with peace only a few weeks old, the Third Army headquarters was disbanded and Patton was made Military Proconsul of Bavaria. The tents came down, the trailers were moved away, and Lucky Forward was no more.

In June, with Regensburg under control, Herman was reassigned to the general's support staff. He soon found himself living in the spa town of Bad Tölz at the Waffen— SS Junkerschule, the same place where Richard Schulze had been the last commander.

The new headquarters of US Military Government for Bavaria, only weeks before an elite military academy to train officers for the Third Reich, boasted a gymnasium, a swimming pool, an athletic field, and a riding hall, as well as a theater and a chapel. There were more than nine hundred offices and rooms in the main building, which surrounded an immense parade ground. Nearby, on a hill overlooking the town, there was a residential neighborhood of elegant villas, until recently the homes of some of the most powerful men in Nazi Germany. One of these estates was requisitioned for Patton.

The general renamed the school Flint Barracks, in memory of a comrade who had fallen during the Battle of Normandy. But he was there only two weeks, just long enough to get his office set up, before he left for a conquering hero's tour of the United States. While the general was gone, Herman and the rest of the staff began the difficult job of bringing order to their corner of Germany. Herman, with his language and interrogation skills, became involved with one of the most pressing problems, the release of the prisoners of war.

The gates of the cages could not simply be thrown open. Public horror at the atrocities committed in the concentration camps demanded that prisoners be screened. Since March, all members of the Gestapo, SS intelligence and SS officers, as well as concentration camp guards and Nazi Party and *Hitlerjugend* officials, had been immediately arrested when captured. They were held in special camps until each case could be investigated for crimes against humanity and if appropriate, brought to trial.

At the end of the fighting, more than one-and-a-half million German prisoners of war were in the hands of US troops, either in Belgium or in cages scattered across the devastated countryside of Germany. By law they were entitled to the same rations and quarters as American troops of the same rank, but in reality, this was impossible. Herman and all the G2 staff knew the prisoners had to be released quickly before the food ran out.

Immediately after the surrender was signed, orders came to release prisoners who had been agricultural workers, coal miners, and transportation workers, as well as men over fifty and women. Nationals from Poland, Hungary, France, Italy, Belgium, or the Netherlands, many of whom had been forced to fight for the German army and captured with German troops, were sent to their own governments.

This still left tens of thousands of prisoners to process and release. To carefully check each one before he could be sent home was the slow and tedious endeavor that occupied Herman. First, a medical officer needed to give a physical examination. Besides looking for contagious illness, the doctors examined the underarm area of each man for evidence of the blood-type tattoo common to all members of the SS—a tattoo that resulted in automatic arrest. Seriously ill prisoners unable to travel were held and given treatment.

Once a prisoner had a clean health certificate, he was required to fill out a counterintelligence questionnaire and undergo a brief interview. Herman and other interrogators spent all day questioning men, one at a time, about their political affiliations and their assignments during the war while a long line of more prisoners waited for their few minutes of interrogation.

If Herman, or one of the other interviewers, determined that the man was safe to release, he was asked to fill in a card with his name, the names of his relatives, and where he lived. Given the final okay, the ex-soldier received an official discharge slip from the German army. If he would be traveling far to reach his home, he might be given a half loaf of black bread and a packet of lard to serve as rations for his trip.

By the first week of June, the Third Army had discharged more than half a million enemy troops.

At the end of a long day of interviews, Herman was glad to be able to return to his room in the Flint Barracks. It was a luxury to have his own space—clean, dry, and with hot water in the shower—though not as nice as that farmhouse he had enjoyed while he worked at Regensburg. In the mess hall at Flint, the food was carefully rationed, though well prepared, and he was certain that they were eating better than any German in the entire country.

Toward the end of June, Herman lingered over after-dinner coffee with Julian Goldschmitt, who had stopped for a visit after an assignment in Nuremberg. "The heart of the city is totally flattened," he told Herman. "Sometimes the stench of the unburied dead is unbearable. Rats and feral dogs run everywhere without fear. The rubble is littered with fragments of ancient stonework and sculpture from medieval buildings. It's a sad thing to see such destruction."

"Hitler's insanity infected Germany like rot on a peach," Herman said. "Even good men lost their reason and blindly kept fighting, even when all was lost. If they had only surrendered, the bombing would have stopped sooner." Herman lit one of the plentiful American cigarettes supplied by the US Army and leaned back in his chair. "What have you heard about the organization of the Zones?"

This was something everyone talked about. Germany would be divided into four administrative zones, one for each of the big powers, but the areas held on VE day did not match the plan formulated at the conference tables. Thanks in large part to the aggressive battle tactics of Patton's army, American forces held much of the territory that was designated for Britain and Russia. The French held some areas that were to be in the US zone. Julian shrugged and sighed. "Not much. I've heard the French want to take everything with them that isn't nailed down when they leave Karlsruhe. They've even asked for our help with transportation."

"The French have the smallest area in the end and I guess they're feeling the pinch," Herman said. "What about Berlin?"

"There's a big meeting planned at Potsdam next week. I expect the generals will sort out the details." Julian shook his head and wiped his forehead with a handkerchief. "A jointly held capital city surrounded by Russian occupied territory. Whose bright idea was that?"

"Berlin is bound to be nothing but problems in the future," Herman agreed. "But we couldn't just let the Russians have it all to themselves."

"I suppose not. But from what I hear, there's not much left. Berlin is probably flatter than Nuremberg."

Herman had a concern of his own, more important to him than Berlin. "How long before the zoning will be complete, I wonder. Have you heard anything about the schedule for the US moving out of Thüringen and turning it over to the Russians?"

Julian knew what Herman was talking about. "It won't be long. July tenth is the deadline for all readjustments. If you want one last visit to Meiningen, you better go soon."

Herman stubbed out his cigarette. "I'd like to visit my old teacher again, if I could. But it's impossible to get time off now. We're processing prisoners nonstop. Got to get them heading home. And there are thousands of homeless labor-camp inmates. They're overflowing the American run camps, but most have nowhere else to go. Tomorrow we have to screen men from a labor camp north of Munich. Seems a lot of them are *mischlinge* who were in the army, some as late as the early forties, but in the end they were all drummed out. Can you imagine that? Half-Jews in the Wehrmacht. Some of them were even officers, but were they Nazis? I can't imagine what that's all about, but . . . well, there are problems everywhere."

He shook his head, stood up, and walked over to the big urn to get a fresh cup of coffee, then returned and picked up the conversation where he had left off. "Finding German men to take over the civil government is an impossible task. You know, if a man didn't join the Nazi party, he couldn't work or feed his family. But he could still be drafted into the army and sent to die on the Russian front. And we're supposed to find men who were never affiliated with the Nazis to take over the local governments. Where will we find these hidden ghosts?" Herman had seldom felt this discouraged. "All this makes it impossible to go to Meiningen now. I no longer have any ties to the town, except for Gieselhardt. I recommended him to the officer in charge of the American military occupation. But however that might have helped, it'll all be a new ball game when the Russians move in." Herman turned with concern to Julian. "How about your cousin and his family? Any word of them?"

His friend closed his eyes for a minute before he answered. "Nothing really. I went to their home outside Nuremberg and talked to some of the neighbors. They thought my cousin may have made it to Palestine—escaped with a Zionist youth group. But his parents, my aunt and uncle—no one has heard from them since they were rounded up and transported to a camp in Poland about two years ago. The German friend they left in charge of their flat seems to have disappeared too, and the neighbors, those who would talk to me at all, didn't want to say more than that." He cleared his throat and rubbed his hand over his face. "I keep checking the records of the registered DP's, but it seems almost hopeless."

Herman placed his hand on his friend's shoulder. "Give me their names and anything else that might help. Sometimes I'm near one of the DP camps. I can put up a notice and ask some questions at registration."

Julian looked up. "Thanks," he said. "I suppose, considering what we know about the camps now, I shouldn't hope. But, there's always a chance. Some did survive."

"Yes, some did. Many are in hospitals and not yet documented. Don't give up." In an effort to get Julian's thoughts away from his personal sorrows, Herman changed the subject. "At least Patton will be back soon. Next week. Maybe we'll see some action when Georgie returns."

"I don't know." Julian said. "Patton was great in the heat of battle, but I don't think he has his heart into being Proconsul of Bavaria."

Herman was always ready to defend his hero. "When the assignment came down, he didn't yell and swear like he usually does, though anyone could see he was angry that he couldn't go to fight in the Pacific. But I'm sure he'll step up to it when he gets back. Like he always said, 'Do more than is required of you.'"

"Herman, don't be naive." Julian, as usual, took a skeptical view. "Our hero, Patton, is about to fall off his pedestal. Have you been reading the papers from the States? It looks like he may be in trouble if he means half of what he's saying over there. He needs to be careful or the press will crucify him."

By the next morning, Herman had forgotten Julian's warning. When he arrived at the interrogation center, he was told that about fifty men had been brought down from the German Labor Camp he had mentioned to Julian the evening before. The prisoners all needed to be questioned. It would be a long day for the team of interrogators.

Herman lowered himself into the desk chair in his small office and had the first man brought in. He was thin, though not emaciated, his jaw shadowed by stubble, his hands calloused and bruised. He was wearing a kind of crudely made uniform, dark brown with lapels and, strangest of all, he wore a German Iron Cross high on his chest. He stood at attention like a soldier and saluted, not the stiff Nazi salute, but still a salute.

"Name and rank?"

"*Unteroffizier* Helmut Fischer. Wehrmacht, sir."

The man was a noncommissioned officer or had been. Probably a corporal. Possibly a lance sergeant. Herman was puzzled by his appearance and the way he identified himself. "Are you active in the military, Fischer? I understood your group was brought from a labor camp."

The man seemed to slump into himself. "Yes, sir. I was at the camp. We built a factory first, but lately we mostly worked clearing up the bombed-out sections of Munich. Stacking rubble and burying bodies." He collected himself and straightened his shoulders. "Before that I was in the army. I was drafted in 1939 and fought in France and at the Eastern Front. That's where I earned the Iron Cross for bravery. I should have been promoted too, but it wasn't allowed."

"Why was that, Fisher?"

"I was designated a *mischling*, first degree. Do you know what that is, sir?"

"Yes, I do," Herman said. "How is it that a half-Jew could be in the Wehrmacht? Are you a Nazi?"

Fischer shook his head vigorously to emphasize his words. "Oh no, sir. I never was a party member. We half-Jews were drafted like everyone else. At least until 1940. After that we were all supposed to sign a declaration of ancestry. I avoided it for a while and my commander covered for me, too, because I was a good soldier. I was proud to serve my country. But in 1942 it caught up with me, and I was discharged for racial reasons. I was told to go home. With no leave, no pay, nothing." He reached into his pocket and pulled out a tattered paybook. "Look, sir, you can see the discharge in my soldbuch. I still have it."

Herman took the book like so many he had seen and turned to the final pages. Handwritten across the top were the numbers 8.4.1940 and 20.4.1940 and below that three letters. Herman turned the book toward Fischer and pointed to the letters. "What does this mean—n.z.v.?"

"Stands for *nicht zu verwenden*. And above that are the dates the law was passed. The one excluding half-Jews from serving in the military."

*Nicht zu verwenden*. Not to be used. They certainly hadn't learned any of this at Camp Ritchie. Fischer seemed willing to talk, and Herman wanted to hear more. He pulled a straight-backed chair closer to his desk. "Sit down, Corporal." The man didn't object to this rank and Herman continued. "Please help me understand how a Jew could serve the Reich."

Fischer sat on the edge of the chair and clenched his hands in his lap. "I didn't think of it as serving the Reich. Not the way you mean. I was raised a Christian by my father and German by both parents. They taught me to be proud of my country. My father served in World War I. And my mother's brothers served, too. One of them died in the trenches, and the other was awarded an Iron Cross for bravery in battle."

Herman thought of his own father, a veteran of World War I, and of his grandfather, Kohn, who had served in the Franco-Prussian War. "But why did you try to stay and avoid signing the ancestry paperwork?"

Fischer lifted his head and looked Herman in the eye. "The men in my unit accepted me. They didn't seem to care about what I was besides being a good soldier. It was different from being a civilian where everything was terribly difficult. And I thought I could help my mother and my younger sister," he said. "My mutti is the one who is full Jewish, and my being in the army would help her. And it did for a while. I was able to get her a regular ration card, not a Jewish one. With it, she could get meat and eggs. And once when some SS came to take her away, she showed them my picture in uniform and they let her stay in her apartment."

"Where is she now, Fischer?"

"I don't know, sir. I haven't heard from her since I was sent to the labor camp. My sister was sent to a camp in France, and I haven't heard from her, either. And my grandmother was deported to Theresienstadt. I heard it was better than some of the other places, but she was old. I worry a lot about them all. That's why I need to get home."

"Your father? What about him?"

Fischer made an ugly noise with his lips. "He divorced my mother in '36. Three months later he married a Lutheran. We didn't see him much after that. Though he wrote once in '39 to say he was proud of me being in the army."

Herman stood and Fischer rose, too. "I'll sign a clearance for you, verifying you're no Nazi," Herman said. "Good luck, Fischer. I hope you find your mother safely at home."

The rest of the day was filled with a string of men with similar stories to tell. Their mother or their father had been of Jewish heritage. Some had been raised as Christians but that made no difference. Most had been drafted, but one had volunteered. They had served out of patriotism or because they had no choice. Or they hoped military service would protect themselves or their loved ones. They often volunteered for extra assignments to prove their worthiness. Many had hidden their ancestry as long as possible, but in the end, they had been discharged and sent home. Then they were drafted into forced labor. They told of brothers who went into hiding rather than going to the labor camps and of comrades-in-arms who remained friends. Several believed that if they had not been excluded from the military, they would have died at the Russian front. Herman had no doubt that if Hitler had won the war, they would have followed their Jewish grandparents, aunts, uncles, and cousins to places like Dachau and Auschwitz.

In the late afternoon, yet another man walked into his office. Herman didn't look up from his paperwork at first. He waved his hand toward the chair across his desk and said, "Sit down. I'll be with you in a minute." Then he heard a deep voice quietly breathe his name.

"Hermanle . . . is it you?"

His head jerked up. Tall and straight with long blond hair that hung rakishly over his eyes, the man in front of him was his cousin. "Max! My God . . . are you here?" He was around the desk and the strong hand clasp turned into an embrace. Herman pulled away. "Wait a minute," he said. He stuck his head into the waiting area and motioned to the MP in the hall. "Don't send me anymore. This is my last man for today." He turned back to his cousin. "Max. Are you okay? Your mother? Everyone else?"

His cousin's story was not much different from the ones he had heard all day, but now it was his family—Max's family. Max's grandfather and grandmother both dead at Theresienstadt. His sister and mother in hiding for the last two years. His father also in a labor camp because he was married to a Jew and wouldn't divorce her. His time in the army had been short. He hadn't been drafted until late 1939, and when the new laws were passed that excluded half-Jews from the military, he had immediately informed his commander of his heritage. He had even been able to attend some pre-law classes at the university until he was sent to the labor battalion. There he and his fellow *mischlinge* were given the most dangerous work—they cleared away bomb-torn rubble, searched the ruins for unexploded bombs to defuse them, and buried the dead.

Max was exhausted. He took a deep breath and asked Herman about his family. A smile lightened his face when he heard they were all safely in England and the United States.

"And you, my Hermanle. A captain in the American army."

Herman nodded in assent.

"Will you stay in Germany? Come back to help us rebuild?" Max asked. "We need men like you who remember our better days. Before the Nazis, we were a great people. A people of culture."

Herman wanted to answer this question honestly. It had been in the back of his mind for a long time, and now he needed to articulate his thoughts so his cousin would understand. Max sounded too much like Hugo, always loving

Germany. When Herman spoke, his words were slow and considered. "No, I don't want to live in the past. I can't be a German again. This country has been on an evil road, and I'd always be looking over my shoulder. I'm an American now. I'm proud to be a citizen and a soldier of the United States." He thought a moment about his future. "I want to make my life in America. I don't know yet exactly what that life will be, but I know America is the best place for me."

## CHAPTER 28

# WORKING WITH GEORGIE

IN SOME WAYS, MEETING WITH his cousin confused
Herman. He had no idea what he should do next. The eas-
iest course was to do his job as Patton's head translator and
one of his adjutants. The truth was he liked working under
the general and being in the army. For now, it gave him a
sense of purpose.

The general came back to Bavaria with some fanfare
and settled into his lakeside villa. When Herman was sum-
moned by Patton, he often found the Proconsul of Bavaria
agitated and discontented, not at all the confident man he
had been when leading troops into battle. In spite of the
tranquil setting of the mansion, the general seemed more
at ease in his offices at the Flint Barracks, where he worked
in the room that, only months before, had been the domain
of SS Officer Schulze. Even so, Patton seldom sat at the
big desk he claimed had belonged to Field Marshal Rom-
mel, his adversary in North Africa. More often, he stood

at the window, a cigar clenched in his teeth, and gazed toward the distant mountains. Willie always sat obediently at his feet. Patton seemed to care little for meetings with German civilians and less for overseeing how Bavaria was being governed. Herman realized his hero was not a diplomat and there had been a lot of truth in Julian's warning words. What little enthusiasm Patton could muster was directed toward patching the infrastructure in Bavaria. He didn't much care how it was done or who did it, as long as his district ran smoothly.

Most of Herman's assignments involved travel to nearby villages or towns, even as far as Berlin, to investigate possible civil appointees. Every person who hoped for a position in the new democratic Germany had to first go through a denazification process. Herman's job was to investigate any possible ties the applicant might have had with the Nazi Party during the Hitler years. All civil appointees were required to fill out the dreaded questionnaire known in German as the *Fragebogen,* and Herman traveled all over the country to investigate the truth of their answers.

It was up to the military government, which in Bavaria meant Patton and his staff, to decide who was sufficiently Nazi-free to be given a job, and the constantly changing guidelines were open to interpretation. No man or woman with more than minor Nazi party participation was allowed to take any kind of public position in occupied Germany— nothing—not postal worker, teacher, city clerk, bus conductor, and certainly not lawyer or court judge. Former Nazis were only allowed to work as common laborers.

Because of his frequent travel, Herman again had a jeep and his own personal driver. On his fact-finding trips, he talked to Germans of all kinds. Some were as kindly and democratic as Dr. Geiselhardt. Many others had simply spent the war trying to go unnoticed and stay out of trouble. Now they declared themselves to be "little men who knew nothing." Others were sleazy or even outright criminals. Most had something in their past they wanted to keep quiet, especially if they had been involved in business with Nazis or had been Party members. In order to ensure their safety, get a job, or collect extra ration cards, they would eagerly disclose secrets about the crimes of others. They were happy to make deals with Herman in hopes of winning his favor, and sometimes their tales led to discoveries of confiscated art or stolen Jewish property.

One afternoon, in a town only an hour from Bad Tölz, Herman and his driver, Frank, sat in a local café quietly finishing their meal of black bread and salami, all that was available to eat in the countryside. Two civilians approached their table, and the taller of the two men bowed slightly to Herman.

"May we sit?" he asked, his tone low and secretive. "I hear your general likes horses and we have something interesting to tell you."

Herman did not invite the man to sit, but he slid into the vacant chair anyway. His younger, shorter companion stood behind him. The older man took off his cap and laid it on the table. "Is it true General Patton is a man who loves to ride?"

Herman maintained a look of disinterest. "And what's that to you?"

"I think he will like what I have to show you. Will you take the time to see something exceedingly special at a nearby farm?"

Herman explained the proposal to Frank who, as the driver, had a good sense of the roads and their safety. The sergeant's lopsided Texas grin spread across his face. "Why the hell not?" he said. His loud American voice made the older man wince.

The man told Herman to go out of town and wait at the first crossroads. "We'll meet you there and direct you the rest of the way."

Thirty minutes later the four men stood in a huge barn. The smell of fresh hay tickled Herman's nostrils and reminded him of his days in the barn in Suhl. An old farmer held two horses by their halters. The animals stomped their hooves and tossed their heads, barely containing pent-up energy. They were the most beautiful horses he had ever seen, and it was obvious they needed exercise.

Herman walked over to the animals and slowly stroked the sleek neck of first one and then the other. They calmed at his touch. He looked quickly at their teeth and their bright eyes. It was difficult to contain his excitement, and he shook his head at Frank, a rancher's son who had been riding since he was in knee breeches, to stop him from grinning. Herman didn't want the farmer and his friends to see his enthusiasm and ask an unreasonably large reward. "I'll let Chief of Staff, General Gay, know about these animals," he said. "Will you be available late this afternoon to show them to the general, if he is able to return with me?"

"*Ja. Ja.*" The three men nodded happily. "*Ja, natürlich.*"

Back in the jeep, Herman's enthusiasm almost bubbled over. He turned to Frank and kept his voice steady and low. "Frank, drive away slowly . . . as soon as we are around the bend, hit the gas."

Finally allowed to smile, Frank's grin was as broad as his face. "Those are fine horses. Patton will want to have them, no doubt about that!"

As they sped down the road, Herman laughed into the wind. "We may get a medal for this."

Frank waved his cap in the air and drove faster.

In the last warm light of the afternoon, they returned on the same road, back toward the farm. This time General Patton sat in the front seat and his friend, General Gay, sat behind. Herman, also in the rear seat, leaned forward to talk to Patton just before the farm came into view. "General, sir, I think you are going to enjoy what you see. I know horses, sir. And these are truly fine specimens."

The jeep pulled to a stop, the barn doors opened, and the farmer stepped out, leading the two horses into the open yard. His friends remained behind in the shadows of the barn.

Patton and Gay climbed out of the vehicle and walked around the animals. Patton approached the dark, russet-colored mare, took its halter in his hand, and stroked its twitching, velvet nose. General Gay was beside him and took the reins of the black gelding. With an imperious hand Patton waved off the farmer.

Herman touched the farmer on the sleeve. "*Bitte, gehen Sie ein paar Schritte zuruck,* Herr Grotz. Step back, please."

But he stayed just close enough himself to hear his two superiors' conversation.

"What do you think, Hap?" Patton's eyes sparkled. "These are the finest horses I ever hope to see. Prettier than those dandified Lippizaner stallions we liberated back in May." He reached up and stroked the mare's neck. "Steady, girl." His voice was soft and tender. "You're not some silly prancing horse, are you? You're a lady who loves to run, I'll wager."

General Gay agreed. "I think we should liberate these animals from their sedentary life." He turned to Herman. "What does the farmer say about how he happened to be boarding such horses?"

"The story is that they were left for safe keeping by an important German officer. For the time being, the old man has conveniently forgotten the officer's name and rank. But he seems sure they are race horses, probably brought from France. He says he can't feed them properly anymore and would we please take them?"

"Tell him we will take them off his hands," Patton said, "as a favor. Let him know my aide, Master Sergeant Dittleman, will come tomorrow morning with a trailer to take them away. The farmer will be amply compensated for their upkeep over the last months."

"Yes, sir." Herman turned to the old man and spoke to him in German.

"How much compensation?" Herr Grotz asked hesitantly. "I have had to feed and board these animals for four months without pay. They eat a lot, sir. I had to give them even oats from my wife's cupboard." He gestured toward the barn. "My friends will want a cut too, sir. For finding you."

"*Macht nichts.* Don't worry. Your compensation will be generous." Herman felt a bit impatient with the man's begging. "It'll be a lot more than you'd get from the Nazis for your trouble."

General Patton stroked the velvety nose of the mare one last time and put his lips to her ear. "Tomorrow you are mine," he whispered, handing the reins reluctantly to the farmer. He gave a crisp nod of his head, "*Danke*, Herr Grotz." Then he turned and strode toward the jeep.

As they drove off, Herman looked back to see the farmer who remained in the yard, the two horses by his side. The man saluted an old-style salute and turned to lead the animals into the barn. Patton was fairly bouncing in his seat, his happiness evident. He turned to his friend sitting in the back with Herman. "See the man beside you, General Gay? Captain Lang is a miracle. He keeps revealing one talent after another. Getting prisoners to help set up their own camp. Now, horses. What next?"

Herman could feel his chest expand. It was more praise than he had ever heard from his father, Hugo.

By noon the next day, the French horses were installed in the deluxe stables at Patton's villa. He and General Gay took the afternoon off to test the horses, and Herman could not resist a visit to the estate to welcome them back at the stables. The two men galloped in, both exhilarated.

When he had dismounted, Patton strode over and clapped Herman on the back. "You are a treasure, Captain.

You will never be able to top this. What an afternoon we have had. Down to the lakeshore and all over the hills. These horses have needed to run as much as I needed to ride. Such fine animals!" He contained his enthusiasm and spoke more seriously. "Captain, these special horses deserve the best care. They need a topnotch groom—the best. Not just a soldier raised on a ranch in Wyoming like Dittleman. I heard Baron von Wangenheim is in one of our prisons. Find him for me." He saw the doubtful look on Herman's face. "That's an order, Captain. Offer the baron the job of stable hand and groom. He'll take it if you tell him about the animals."

Herman knew better than to object to Patton's command, though he worried about the repercussions. Wangenheim, who had been the captain of the gold medal-winning German equestrian team at the 1936 Olympics, had also been a diehard Nazi and a colonel in the SS cavalry. Herman was concerned that a Nazi in Patton's stables might cause problems, but with the general's written orders, the prisoner was located and released "for a special assignment." Baron von Wangenheim would be a stable boy, a common laborer, and as such, he did not need to be denazified. For Patton the long morning rides became a daily ritual, the dark, russet mare his favorite mount.

It became increasingly obvious that Patton did not care about the rules set by the joint military government. Though he always came to the central mess hall to have early breakfast with his staff, he usually did not go upstairs to his office at the Flint Barracks until later in the day or not at all. If he made appointments, they were scheduled around his morning ride, something he would not miss now that he had his new horses. He went on frequent junkets to visit friends or he went hunting. He spent most evenings at his temporary home, where he smoked his cigars, drank a glass of brandy, and read until late at night.

Occasionally he invited staff officers to dinner at the villa. Herman enjoyed the glow he felt eating at Patton's home with other officers. Liquor was ample and conversation flowed freely. The general held court until late at night, totally candid, if not always careful, in his opinions and pronouncements when he was surrounded by loyal and devoted staff.

Herman was mesmerized by the man's intellect and dominating personality. He would have been happy to work as his adjutant for a long time. But things were changing in Germany, and Patton wasn't adjusting to the peacetime activities. Herman wondered how long his job would last.

# CHAPTER 29

## GISELA

WHILE THE VARIED CHALLENGES OF his job reinforced Herman's belief in his own creativity and resourcefulness, there was something important missing in his life—girls. He was having too many dreams of Molly and not a few of Gloria. When he started dreaming of the French prostitute he had visited, a woman in a tight skirt, lips lacquered with scarlet, and hair stained coal black, he knew it was time to find a girl who would give him the warm comfort that only a woman could offer.

Gradually, as Patton began to care less and less for his work, Herman's duties as translator dwindled. He had more free time, which would make a social life possible, but there was a big problem. The US Army had a rule against fraternization with Germans. Everyone from privates to generals disliked the rule. It was, at the least, difficult to enforce, but Central Command felt it was important for maintaining order and discipline.

Herman found the non-fraternization rule almost impossible to keep. His ability to speak German made talking to the locals natural and easy—besides, his job required it. He could not resist the little children who flocked around asking for chocolate and chewing gum. The young ones who had been born just before or during the war had probably never seen these childhood treats until the Americans arrived. Their happy faces reminded him of his own childhood, and he wondered if his friends from school now had children this age who ran ragged in the streets and begged candies from the American conquerors.

His love of America had made Herman an apostle for democracy. Still, he was a young man, and, like most soldiers, his strongest desire was to have a female companion his own age. The German girls seemed eager enough, but he felt constrained, partly because of the rules against fraternization, but also because of his memories of how the *Hitlerjugend* girls had snubbed him in his youth. That anti-Semitic attitude he associated with German girls was too much like the three letters in Corporal Fischer's soldbuch—*n.z.v.*—not to be used.

Fines were imposed on soldiers caught in violation of the non-fraternization rules. Just a friendly conversation with a German could lead to a ten-dollar fine. A penalty of sixty-five dollars was imposed for physical intimacy with a German woman, a fine equal to a month's pay for a private. Of course, in his line of work, Herman talked to many Germans in an official capacity, but they were almost always old men, matronly older women, or the tainted mistresses of Nazi officers.

Herman and Frank were determined to find a way to get past the non-fraternization rule and find themselves young, attractive girlfriends.

Not far from Bad Tölz, in Bad Aibling, there was a large camp for displaced refugees and released prisoners who had no place to go. In the protective enclosure, close to a thousand former prisoners of war and an equal number of displaced persons, called DPs, awaited repatriation. The DPs consisted of Jewish survivors of the concentration camps, as well as nationals from Eastern Europe who had been pressed into service by the German army or forced into slave labor. Most of these were from the Ukraine, Russia, Poland, Hungary, and Czechoslovakia. If they returned home, they feared they would be considered traitors by the occupying Russian troops. They were stuck in Germany with nowhere else to go until the fervor of Russian reprisals against Germans and their collaborators, however unwilling, died down.

Herman soon realized that many of the DPs were attractive young women, and he easily found an excuse several times a week to swing by the camp at Bad Aibling. He told the sentries that he needed to question inmates who might know something of importance for one of his investigations.

Frank was pleased to be part of the excursions. "These babes are mostly not Germans, you know," he said in his slow drawl. "They're Czechs or Russian—our allies. I say the non-frat rule doesn't apply. We can talk to them about anything we want."

"Exactly right," Herman said. "We can certainly talk to our allies. I have my eye on a Russian beauty. Did you see that cute blonde I spoke to last week?" He moved his hands in the curving shape of an hourglass. "Ooh . . . la la! What beautiful boobs, so perky under her dress, and . . ." He closed his eyes and allowed himself to imagine the girl's body.

Frank shifted gears as they entered the camp gate and turned to wink at Herman. "How could I miss her? She had her baby blues glued to you." He slapped the wheel and laughed. "But I prefer my girls tall. I saw a delicious long-legged, fiery-haired Polish damsel out by the laundry lines. I helped her pin up some sheets and gave her my most winning smile. No sign of a wedding ring, but not much English either." He rolled his eyes and smacked his lips. "She knew some German and after two months as your driver, I understand enough German to get her drift. Maybe I'll learn a bit of Polish, too." He puckered his lips. "My lips can speak in many ways," he said.

The jeep screeched to a stop in front of the camp commissary building.

Herman swung himself out of the front passenger seat. "I'm going in to see if I can find my curvy little blonde again. How about we meet back here in thirty minutes?"

Herman walked into the building and looked around. The pretty Russian girl was stocking shelves with stationery, pencils, and inexpensive pens, popular items with the camp residents. She turned from her work as he approached, and her eyes smiled, but her lips remained solemn.

"Hello, do you remember me?" he asked, speaking in German.

"Yes, Captain. You are the American who questioned me about the Russian woman who worked for the German general. I told you I didn't know that woman."

Herman smiled. "No problem. This week I'm looking for another woman." He held his hand at a height even with the top of her head. "She's about this tall. She has blond curls and delicious blue eyes. I think she's your twin. Do you know her name?"

The girl giggled. "I don't have a twin, Captain."

"I will settle for your name then."

She looked at the floor, hesitating. When she raised her eyes to meet his, she said, "I am Gisela." Her voice was so soft he almost couldn't hear her.

"Will you come and sit with me a bit?"

She shook her head and indicated the shelves and the box at her feet still filled with envelopes and pencils.

"Allow me to help you," he said, and he moved to lift the box from the floor.

"No. No . . . that's not good," she said quickly. "Wait for me over at the canteen. When I am finished, I can bring you some coffee."

Herman did as he was told. He waited, perched on the high stool near the bar counter where residents could buy beer and coffee. It wasn't long before she joined him. She set a heavy white mug of steaming coffee on the counter and stood quietly a few feet away. He saw she had taken off her work apron and tucked some stray strands of hair behind her ears.

"Do you take powdered milk and sugar, Captain?"

"Just sugar would be nice." When she returned, he spoke as he stirred the crystal lumps into his coffee. "Please call me Herman. I'd like to be a friend, not a captain to you."

"Herman. That's a German name and you speak such good German?"

He could see she was wary and skittish again. "I am an American. I lived in California before the war."

"California. What is that?"

It was the beginning of a pleasant conversation about sunshine, movie stars, his work at the Zebra Room, how he had learned English, and how she had learned to speak German. She relaxed as they talked. Finally she looked up at him through long lashes and almost flirted as she asked, "Will you teach me some English words? I think it will be a good language to know."

"Absolutely! It will be my pleasure." His longing overcame him and impulsively he reached out and touched her hand. As if she had been shocked by a jolt of electricity, Gisela jumped away, her eyes wide with fear. He looked at her in puzzlement. "I only wanted to hold your hand. I'm sorry."

She lowered her eyes and whispered, "I thought you were going to hurt me. I am used to being hurt . . . that way." She hesitated for a long time, inhaling air in gulps as she tried to calm down.

Herman sat still and waited. "I won't hurt you," he said in a low voice.

She took another deep breath. He could see she was considering if he could be trusted. "The German officer I worked for . . . he . . . he took advantage . . . I never knew when . . ." She pulled air into her throat with a wavering sob. "I didn't want to die . . . or be beaten." She looked up at him and continued, defiant now, her voice firm. "What choice did I have?"

"None. You had no choice. Your survival depended on it." Herman tried to keep his deep emotion under control so she would see only his calm. "I'll never hurt you. I promise," he said, his voice steady. "I'll touch you only when you say it is okay." After a moment, he plunged ahead. "I hope you will want me to hold your hand one day."

She lifted her gaze to his face, her eyes brimmed with tears. "I hope . . . I want not to be afraid anymore. I want to have a normal life again." Her hands had been tightly clasped in front of her heaving chest, but now she let out a deep sighing breath and allowed her hands to fall open. "I want to trust again . . . but I need time."

"Of course." He did not reach out to her again but looked into her eyes and felt her gaze warm to him. She had strength and resilience, besides her beauty. "I'll be back," he said. "I'll keep coming back."

Later, as he and Frank drove toward headquarters in the gathering dusk, Herman felt suffused with the antici- pation of pleasure. He was completely charmed by this vul- nerable and desirable Russian and wanted to speak about her. "Her name is Gisela. Such a beautiful name. Like the beautiful peasant girl in the ballet. Giselle. Gisela. She was taken from her school and forced to be secretary to a Nazi lieutenant during the war. Of course, it was terrible for her. We know what those beasts did." Herman rubbed his hands down his thighs to calm himself. What had happened to her made him angry, but he didn't want to share his strong feelings with his driver. "But whatever else happened to her, she also learned flawless German. You should have seen her smile when she asked if I would teach her some English words. For that smile, I would gladly teach her anything."

Frank was unusually quiet. Finally Herman couldn't wait any longer. "What about you? Did you find the Polish lady?"

"A tall, lean Texan always catches the girl. If not a Pole, then a Czech." Frank's eyes sparkled with the fun of keeping Herman in suspense as he spoke in his slow, southwestern way. "Eva, the redheaded laundress, has decided to risk going back to her village near Krakow. She leaves in a few days. But she introduced me to her friend."

Frank paused at this point to light a cigarette on a straight stretch of road where the jeep could steer itself. For several long minutes, he drove with one hand casually on the wheel. He puffed smoke and smiled a Cheshire cat grin. Herman, impatient to hear more, prodded him. "Come on, Sergeant. I order you to cut the crap. What about the friend?"

"Ah, Jana, you mean. She says her name means *Geschenk Gottes* in German. I think that's how she said it."

"Gift from God," Herman translated.

"Perfect." Frank laughed out loud. "She is just that. A beauty. Dark hair curling around her ears. It's short because it was shaved in camp. She learned to make boots, she said, though she was a teacher before the war. Like Eva, she doesn't know much English. But, as I said . . ." Frank let that thought hang in the air. After a few minutes, he added, "I figured out how to tell her I'd be back next week. *'Ich . . . bin . . . nächste Woche.'* Is that right?" For the first time Frank seemed a little uncertain.

Now, it was Herman's turn to laugh. "Well, you said 'I am next week' but she'll probably figure it out."

Several times a week, Herman and Frank visited the camp at Bad Aibling. As soon as their jeep pulled up through the gate, the silent word went out. By the time they reached the commissary building, Gisela would be on the steps rubbing her hands on her kitchen apron.

As Herman walked inside, his gaze locked onto Gisela's eyes, a deep blue that reminded him of the Pacific Ocean. Soon she allowed him to brush her hand with his as they walked to the canteen bar. Frank would sit in the parked jeep for only a few minutes, then casually get out and wander over to the laundry area where he usually could find several girls who smiled at him as they pinned up wet sheets.

Gossip in the camp, fueled by boredom and frustration, could be especially harsh for the young women, like Gisela, who had suffered under the sexual demands of their German captors. Herman worked hard to keep his desire in check as he gained her trust, especially if other residents were around.

When he arrived, she would bring him a cup of coffee, already sweetened the way he liked it. If she had time, they would sit together and talk at the canteen bar, their voices low. Otherwise he stood by her as she stocked shelves, helped customers, washed dishes, or chopped onions for the evening stew. They talked of little things and flirted with their eyes but never touched. People always came in or out, and it was important to be careful. He found it more difficult every day to resist his impulse to embrace her, to kiss her lips, or to touch her firm bottom as he stood next to her. Gradually, her eyes began to let him know she was ready for his touch.

One afternoon, Herman leaned close as they stocked a shelf with soap powder. "Sweetheart, I wish we could be alone for just a minute. I long to kiss you."

Gisela blushed and brushed him away. "Shhh. Someone will hear."

The next time Herman visited, Gisela reminded him that he had promised to teach her some English. Almost immediately, she apologized for having to leave and said she must go into the storeroom and count supplies. She motioned with her head and whispered near his ear. "Go out back. There is a delivery door to the storeroom."

He waited only a few minutes, then loudly said goodbye to the other workers who looked up briefly from their chores. He left by the front door, slipped around to the back of the building, and tapped gently with his knuckles on the delivery entrance. The wide sliding door edged open a crack, and Gisela peeped out and swiftly pulled him in. "Do you want to help me with the counting?" Her smile promised more. "Or will you teach me some English?"

In the quiet, dim storeroom, surrounded by crates of eggs and turnips and sacks of flour, Gisela was a willing student.

"Gisela, sweetheart. *Geliebte. Pass gut auf und ich werde Dir Englisch lehren.* Pay attention now and I will teach you

English," Herman whispered in her ear.

She giggled and brushed her hair back from her neck. "*Es kitzelt.*"

"It tickles." He ran his finger lightly over her ear. "Now listen. This is your hand." He gently kissed the back of her hand. "Hand," he whispered again. "*Hand ist auf Englisch und Deutsch identisch.*"

Gisela looked up, her eyes moist with promise. "Hand."

Herman turned her hand palm up and kissed the workworn surface. "Palm. The palm of your hand. *Handfläche.*" And he kissed it again.

She took his hand and placed his palm against her cheek. "*Was ist das auf Englisch?*"

"Cheek." He moved his hand to her forehead, his fingers caressing her soft skin as they moved down across her eyes, over her nose and mouth, and to her chin. "Face," he whispered. Gently he kissed each eye. "Eyes." He traced her lips with his finger. "Lips."

She smiled and pursed her lips into a tempting pout. "*Und was ist das? Ein Kuss?*"

Herman laughed. "Kiss. In German *Kuss* and in English kiss. *Ich werd'es Dir zeigen.* I'll show you an American kiss." And he covered her lips with his own.

He felt like a starving man who had been presented with a banquet. Every kiss was as intoxicating as a sip of wine on an empty stomach. Desire kindled between them, and the minutes in the storeroom flew away. Herman looked at his watch with regret. "*Ich muss gehen. Ich werde bald wieder da sein.* I must go, but I'll be back."

# CHAPTER 30

# TEARS OF CHANGE

FRANK SEEMED TO BE DELIGHTED with a different girl each time they visited the camp and true to his word, each one was tall. But Herman had found his dream in Gisela. As she came to trust him, their relationship evolved into an affair of intimacy and affection. He was enchanted by her ability to be a shy companion one minute and a flirtatious lover the next.

By midsummer the non-fraternization rules disintegrated, and as a captain and part of Patton's denazification team, Herman was able to get passes that allowed the girls to leave Bad Aibling. This offered them the chance to spend a long Sunday away from the close quarters and gossip of the camp. Herman commandeered picnic supplies from headquarters and Frank brought blankets, American chocolate, and his girl of the moment. Gisela was delighted with any change of scene, and once outside the camp gate, she became effervescent and playful. The Bavarian countryside was open for them to explore, the back roads and wooded hillsides hid countless secluded spots to linger after a picnic lunch.

One afternoon in early September, they traveled almost to the foot of the Alps and found a meadow near a stream and a stand of old trees. Herman had managed to bring an entire cold roast chicken, sliced fresh tomatoes, chilled white wine, and a melon that they put in the stream to cool. This abundance was a rare treat for Gisela and Frank's current girl, Edna. They tore the juicy meat off the bones with their fingers and laughed at their hands which glistened with chicken fat.

Gisela wiggled her greasy fingers in front of Herman's face. "You said Americans eat chicken with their fingers, didn't you? I am an American now." She laughed. "So uncivilized to not use fork and knife. But I like it. I think it makes the meat taste better." She licked her lips in satisfaction and playfully smeared Herman's chin with chicken fat before she collapsed in giggles.

As the mood quieted, Frank wiped Edna's hands with his pocket handkerchief and pulled her to stand up. "We're off for a walk," he said with a grin. "We'll bring back the melon . . . in a while." Hand in hand the two headed, not toward the creek, but toward the nearby trees and the cool of shade and brambles.

Herman and Gisela sprawled on the rough army blankets. He covered her neck with kisses and caressed her softly mounded breasts. A cooling mountain breeze made her nipples stand up against the soft fabric of her blouse and Herman could feel his passion rising. He ran his hand up her leg and under her skirt, the warmth of her thigh promising him more. After her fit of giggles earlier, Gisela seemed to have relaxed into a soft daydream. Herman gazed at her as she lay on her back. He felt the tickle of her fingers as her hand traveled up his arm, across his chest, and finally rested on his cheek. Her body was pliant to his touch and a smile illuminated her face. She looked up at him and traced his jaw line with her finger. "You are good to me," she said in her newly learned English. "I think to love you very much."

Herman pulled her closer. He kissed her softly and gently probed her parted lips with his tongue. His feelings for her were strong. But was it lust or love? He wasn't sure. If he did love her, what would that mean to his dreams? Was he ready to be a married man? He was aware of the animosity ready to explode between Russia and the other allies. Would she jump at the chance to get to the United States? Was she strong enough to brave the difficult adjustment she would have as a Russian in America? The kiss gave him time to think about what he wanted to say.

"Gisela, sweetheart, I love you too." Even as he said these words, his doubts bubbled and wavered near the surface. Were his feelings strong enough to go the next step? He wanted to make her happy, and going to America was the ultimate dream for most of the girls at the camp. He plunged ahead. "Will you go to America with me?"

She put her fingers against his lips. "Stop."

He could barely hear her soft whisper.

"I must speak. My English is not good and you do not understand. I say, I think to love you is easy. But I cannot love . . . not now." Her eyes held an infinite sadness. "You are dear to me. You helped me forget to be afraid. But, I can give my heart to no man—not yet. First, I must find my mother and little sister." Tears stood at the edges of her eyes and one rolled down her cheek. "I know they are still alive, and I will find them."

Herman knew about her mother and sister. They had talked of them before. How hopeless it was, Herman thought, for her to wait in Bad Aibling, each day ending in disappointment when no news arrived of these two lost women. They had been separated three years before, sent in different directions by the war and the conquering Germans. He reached up and wiped the tear from her cheek. "I will help you find your mother and sister. You can all come to America and start a new life. When you can love me enough, I will make you my wife."

"No, Herman. I will not want to go to America. Ukraine is my country. Yes, Russia, too. But Ukraine is my heart."

Herman sat up straight and shook his head in confusion. "You don't mean that. *Ukraine ist kaputt. Der Krieg hat es zerrissen.*" He pulled her up in front of him and said again in English this time. "It is finished. It is torn apart by war."

"*Mein Land ist auseinandergerissen,*" she said, "*aber es ist nicht kaput.* Not finished." She looked serious now. "Ukraine. It will need me. Young people with . . ." She hesitated and finally finished in German, "*mit Stärke, das Land wieder aufzubauen.*" She sat up straight, holding her head proudly as she spoke.

"Young people with strength to build the country again," he translated for her.

"Yes." Gisela's deep feeling showed in her eyes. "Herman, I will stay your girl. I will love you now. But no America for me."

He looked at her longingly and was surprised to feel a sense of relief under the longing. Perhaps this was best. Deep inside, he knew he did not want to take a European girl back to America. He wanted a totally American life when he returned. He realized what he secretly wished for was an American wife—an American dream like his brother had in California. He touched Gisela's chin and pulled her toward him to kiss her lips again. He sat back and looked at her honestly for the first time. His feelings for her were a combination of desire, affection, and friendship but not love. "I promise you, I will do what I can to find news of your mother and your sister," he said. "And for now we will be together."

She smiled and kissed him gently. Her hand lingered on the back of his neck, and her low whisper sent shivers down his spine. "Yes. Now. Only now. That is enough." Her hand slid like warm liquid down to touch him where his hardness still waited and her tongue flicked around his ear. He moved his hand slowly up her thigh again and forgot about the future. It was now, only now, that held him.

WHILE HERMAN WAS LOST IN his romance, he hardly noticed that in Patton's world things were going badly. The general didn't know when to keep quiet. At one press conference, he spouted his opinion that Nazis were no more important in Germany than Republicans or Democrats in the United States. He spoke out against strict and rapid denazification and said that the military government "would get better results if it employed more former members of the Nazi Party in administrative jobs and as skilled workmen." The American press picked up every rumor and printed all of Patton's political blunders.

Soon enough, it became impossible to ignore Patton's verbal indiscretions and Herman watched helplessly as the fighting general openly voiced his unpopular belief that war with Russia was inevitable in the near future. General Eisenhower was fed up. In the first week of October, he removed Patton from his command and assigned him to a paper army whose only task, already half-complete, was to research and compile a history of World War II.

The removal of his hero filled Herman with anger and sadness. He had become a man under Patton and he felt as if he were losing his father all over again. The farewell ceremony for the general was held in the huge gymnasium at the Flint Barracks. Outside, a cold rain poured down, and icy wind whipped around the eaves. George Patton faced his staff with an expression so sad he did not seem to be the same man they had worked under for more than a year.

"All good things must come to an end," he said. His voice broke as he continued. "The best thing that has ever come to me is the honor and privilege of having commanded Third Army. Good-bye and God bless you."

Under the new commander, policy and Herman's responsibilities rapidly changed. Patton's replacement, Lieutenant General Truscott, strongly supported vigorous denazification, and he immediately got down to business. Suddenly Herman seemed to be working around the clock, going with his new superior to meeting after meeting with local officials. As translator, he needed to echo the strict and commanding speech of Truscott and still get cooperation from the locals who were used to having a free rein. It was a delicate task.

Besides his usual work, checking the truth in completed *Fragebogen*, Herman now also was directed to investigate Germans accused of petty crimes and violations, everything from black-market sales to possession of stolen Jewish goods, from hoarding food to forging ration coupons.

The new situation left little time to see Gisela, and their bucolic picnics came to a halt. She clung to him when he was able to visit, but their romance was now usually limited to stolen minutes in the storeroom. Between kisses, they whispered about the upcoming winter. It would be a time of hardship and hunger throughout Germany. Gisella feared that the displaced refugees still in the camps would get only scraps. Perhaps it was time for her to think of returning to the east.

With the war over both in Europe and the Pacific, thousands of American GIs were getting their discharge papers and going home. First one friend and then another left for the States, and Herman's thoughts turned to what he would do if he left the army.

On the evening of December 9, tragic news arrived at headquarters. General George Patton had been seriously injured in a traffic accident and taken to the new Seventh Army hospital in Heidelberg. Herman felt shock and despair as he listened to the dispatch. Patton had broken his neck and was completely paralyzed. Herman's feelings madly gyrated between hope and despair as the reports came in. Finally, on the evening of December 21, 1945, the sad announcement was made—Patton, the hero of the Battle of the Bulge and the taking of much of Germany, was dead.

It was the final straw. Herman made his choice. He would leave the army. He no longer felt proud of what he was doing. He needed to find something more fulfilling than to dig into the petty wartime activities of little men. He added up his days of service and requested home leave.

Before he left Germany, there were two things he wanted to do to finish on a high note of humanity. He had promised to try to find news of Gisela's mother and sister, but there had been little opportunity. Now he renewed his efforts and again contacted his friend Julian, recently assigned to General Eisenhower's headquarters. Surely there was some kind of central information agency that coordinated efforts to find missing persons. Julian, eager to help this time, put his best efforts into the search, and within two weeks, he found Gisela's mother, still in Germany, but in the Russian zone. There was no word of the sister, but there was hope she was alive somewhere in Russia. The mother had received word less than a year ago that the young girl traveled with a band of resistance fighters as they moved toward

Russian territory. Herman was able to arrange transport for Gisela to the camp near Potsdam, where she would be reunited with her mother.

On the icy January morning Gisela was scheduled to leave, Herman made his last trip to Bad Aibling. Together they stood in front of the commissary, no longer caring who saw them. Gisela clung to him, their kisses by turns passionate and tender. Herman could sense her joy and anticipation behind the sadness of the farewell. After he had loaded her luggage onto the transport bus, he embraced her one last time and stroked her hair. "I will always remember you, my little Ukrainian."

"My American." Her smile, usually so sunny, was filled with sadness. "I will not forget." She turned and mounted the stairs into the bus. His last glimpse of her was as she peered through the window and waved good-bye. He watched as she breathed warm air on the inside of the glass and drew a heart with her fingertip. Moist drops of condensate dripped like tears down the foggy window as the bus pulled away.

# CHAPTER 31

# THE BOOK

THE DAYS BEFORE HIS RETURN to America rapidly evaporated. Herman's thoughts continually returned to the man who had helped him at Regensburg.

Over the last months, the SS officer had written him several letters and asked him to visit the camp at Auerbach where he and his SS comrades remained. Herman had not written back. His feelings about Richard Schulze were conflicted. Why did he respect this German—even feel a kinship with him? How would he continue doing his assigned job if he visited a man who had been Hitler's aide, the type of Nazi that his work required him to weed out and expose? But soon no excuse would be needed, and he could do what he had wanted to all along. Within days Herman would no longer work for General Truscott or be involved with denazification. Then he would have two days to get his affairs in order and his bags packed before heading home. He could manage a brief visit and it would not cause a problem. But he needed to act fast. Herman sent a note to Schulze saying he would come to the camp at Auerbach before leaving for America.

Bundled in his woolen greatcoat against the frigid January air, Herman drove toward Auerbach. He hoped it was not a mistake to reconnect with the SS prisoner. The clouds of the previous day had lifted. In the distance the Alps glistened white against the blue sky. Once he had passed the sentries and entered the camp, he saw the unmistakable figure of Schulze standing on a rise, silhouetted by the pale winter sunlight. He felt a surge of compassion for the man who waited so patiently among the stark prison buildings.

Herman climbed out of the jeep and walked over to the towering German. He extended his hand to the man. "Let's not salute but shake hands as friends." The firm clasp of Richard Schulze's hand felt natural in his. "I leave for America soon," he said, "and I wanted to see you before I left."

The German officer clasped Herman by the shoulder like a comrade. "I have waited so long for this opportunity to show you around. We have done miracles here. I am satisfied with all our work and the improvements we have accomplished. I think you will approve." He stood straight and tall and beamed with pride. "This way please, Captain Lang." He strode off and Herman walked beside him on the ice crusted streets.

"You would not believe the mud and dirt we moved to make these roads. We broke up mountains of rock for pavement and all by hand with picks and shovels!" Richard shook his head as if in discouragement, but Herman could see he was grinning at the same time. "In fact we destroyed close to three hundred shovel handles in the process. All the picks went dull with the work." He chuckled. "And we did it all on thin, green porridge. Well, maybe a sausage or two, but the primary fuel was split pea soup."

Herman was impressed by the man's positive attitude.

"Now we're building an athletic field." Schulze pointed to an open area covered in drifts of snow, except for one muddy square surrounded by a rope barrier. "See, we already have a rudimentary boxing ring set up. But it's too cold to use it." He laughed again. "Captain Lang, you would be so proud of what we have done. We even have cultural activities." He pointed to a recently painted fence. "Look, we do art. See there, a hand-painted sign telling everyone to keep the camp clean. We are trying to improve ourselves. Now we study English, and in the spring, if we are still here, we'll offer a class in horticulture and dig a plot to grow vegetables."

Herman enjoyed the tour. He felt the pull of friendship with the German. They had so much in common—a sense of humor, a drive to get things done. He sensed in Schulze an unsinkable joy for life that matched his own. It was easy to forget that the tall man wearing unadorned khaki had once been part of Hitler's inner circle.

"Come," his guide was saying as he led Herman into a whitewashed building. "I want you to hear our choral group."

Inside the building, a group of men waited. Herman was surprised to see so many familiar faces from Regensburg, all still together and kept in camp. He knew that because they had been SS they would not be allowed to return home any time soon. Yet, as he entered the room, they cheered and yelled out "Welcome! Welcome, Captain Lang!"

Richard stood in front of the group and turned to Herman. "We have a special presentation for you." He pulled over a straight-backed, wooden chair and motioned toward it with an elegant sweep of his hand. "Please, sit and be comfortable."

It was embarrassing to be treated like royalty by these battle-tried veterans of the Wehrmacht, but Herman settled into the chair and waited. The men jostled each other as they formed into two rows, the taller men in back. Finally, they stood perfectly still. Richard stepped forward, faced the group, and raised his arms like a conductor. When he snapped his fingers and lowered his arms, the men burst into song, their enthusiastic voices bellowing out a creative ditty. The first words took Herman by surprise. "Welcome to our angel, Herman Lang."

When the song finished, they all bowed from the waist, then stood smiling at Herman. He clapped in appreciation. "Wonderful. You sound like a regular chorus of tenors and baritones ready for a Wagner opera. What are you all still hanging around here for? You should call the Vienna Opera House!"

Richard Schulze rapped on a tabletop for attention. "We wanted so much to express our appreciation for what you did for us back in Regensburg. We had expected hate and violence. And who among us would have blamed you?" Several of the men nodded their heads and grinned. Schulze continued. "But, your treatment of the prisoners there was generous and fair. You allowed us to be part of the solution, and we thank you for that respect." He swept his long arms around to indicate the entire camp. "And, you set us on the path of camp improvement. We continue to this day to follow your inspiration. We have been waiting for months, hoping you would have time to visit. We have made something to honor you, and we wanted to give it to you in person."

From the front of the group one of the men stepped forward. He held a painted wooden box carefully in both hands. With a grin, he thrust it toward Herman.

"Please accept this token of our appreciation," Schulze said, his most solemn tone accompanied by a smile. "We all had a hand in creating this gift, but especially our resident artist." He motioned toward the short, gray-haired man who had presented the box. Suddenly Herman remembered what he had read about this man in the Regensburg files. He had been a renowned newspaper cartoonist before the war, his drawings illustrating approved Nazi dogma. The artist lifted his cap, bowed, and stepped back to be with his friends.

Herman stroked the lid of the box. It was polished smooth and hand painted with an American eagle. Carefully he lifted the lid. Inside lay a hand-bound book covered in tooled leather. The pages inside, each drawn and colored, then laboriously hand-lettered by the cartoonist, told the story of Herman's role at Regensburg and how Schulze and the other prisoners helped. The later pages illustrated the men as they worked to improve the new SS camp at

Auerbach. Herman was depicted as a guardian angel who hovered over them, inspiring their efforts. It was a beautiful book. He knew he would treasure it and appreciate the men who created it for him. The page he liked the best was the one with the drawing of himself taking Schulze off for that first interrogation. The artist had captured the great difference in the two men's heights, but the drawing also revealed Herman's good nature and the worry Schulze must have felt on that fateful day when their relationship had begun.

Herman felt his throat tighten with pride as he walked, shook each man's hand, and thanked them for the gift. He was glad he had made this visit. He knew that though he and Schulze had been on different sides during the war, they were friends now. Even as their worlds separated again, he would make an effort to keep in touch.

He was sorry he had to leave so soon. Schulze accompanied him down the rutted and icy camp roadway to the waiting jeep. The German was quiet as they walked side by side, matching the stride of his long legs to his companion's shorter pace. When they reached the jeep, he put out his hand to Herman. "*Danke*, my friend," he said in a soft voice.

Herman felt a catch in his throat as he answered. "*Danke*. For the book. And for helping me to find again some goodness in Germany."

"Would you live here again? Or have we poisoned the homeland for generations?"

Herman looked up at this man who had been a Nazi but who also had saved the lives of the young men under his leadership. Both concern and guilt were evident in the German's sad eyes. "The hate will pass," Herman said. "Though it could take a generation or more. Men like you must do what they can."

"And men like you also."

"But I can't stay in Germany," Herman said. "There is too much I would need to forget. The world needs to remember the horrors of this war. For some—those who have lost everyone they loved—forgiveness will be difficult, maybe impossible, but eventually we all must move on." He placed his hand on Schulze's arm. "Let's hope Germany can raise a new generation that will be free of the madness of the last twelve years."

Herman saluted and climbed into his jeep. "I am an American now," he said. "I can't wait to begin my American life. But we will stay in touch. I believe that America and Germany will be friends again one day."

He started the jeep and drove out the gate into his future.

# THE TRUE STORY OF HERMAN'S AMERICAN LIFE

THE FIRST THING HERMAN DID when he returned stateside was to visit his mother who was then living in California and whom he hadn't seen since 1939. However, he remained in the United States for only about four months. During that time, he contacted Colonel Allen and General Koch, his superior officers at Lucky Forward, for referrals and help in finding work.

By early May 1946, he was back in Germany, this time as an officer in the army reserves at the War Crimes Trials at Nuremberg. There he was assigned as a research analyst to the office of Chief Counsel, Justice Robert Jackson. This job required that he travel all over Germany and into Czechoslovakia, collecting evidence and testimony for the trial. One of the men he convinced to come forward and testify was his friend Richard Schulze who had firsthand knowledge of Hitler and his inner circle. In the course of his work, Herman interviewed such top Nazis as Herman Goering and Albert Speer.

In the ruined city of Nuremberg, the American staff of the War Crimes Trials was billeted at the Grand Hotel in the heart of the city. The restaurant at the hotel served American food made from airlifted ingredients, and the bar had a dance floor where a band played until midnight. The press corps came frequently to The Grand, and it was there that Herman first met the young newspaper reporter Walter Cronkite, who loved to sit at the piano and play popular sing-along tunes, as well as Edward R. Murrow, known as "The Voice of Europe." It was in Nuremberg that Herman met his future wife, Marge, who was working as a secretary in the office of the Chief Justice.

After the trials were over and the convicted men had been hanged, Herman was transferred to the Special Project Division whose job it was to figure out what to do with the many minor Nazis still in custody. Some had served as witnesses, some were wanted for war crimes in other countries, and some were turned over to the German authorities, but most simply needed to go through the denazification process so they could get a job. Herman's uncle, cousin Max's father, a judge before the war, was now a minister in the city government. Herman made many arrangements through his uncle to facilitate the processing of witnesses and small-time prisoners who seemed to have been simply caught up in the craziness of the times.

Herman and Marge were married in Germany on March 7, 1947. Later that spring they returned to the United States to begin their life together. When Herman searched for a career, he noticed the American public was fascinated with a new type of entertainment—television. He studied television technology in night school and discovered he enjoyed working with the large TV cameras. His first job was as a cameraman for a local New York television station covering the Yankees 1950 baseball season, but within a year he was working for the emerging network, CBS. One of Herman's first assignments for CBS was filming Albert Einstein on his eightieth birthday. For the next forty-one years, his job allowed him to meet hundreds of celebrities.

In the beginning, Herman worked in the Manhattan studios where live programs were filmed. Everything had to be right the first time as mistakes couldn't be corrected by editing—whatever happened, the viewer saw. Herman filmed daily soap operas, news shows, and weekly variety and comedy shows, and worked with such stars as Jackie Gleason, Garry Moore, Ed Sullivan, Bob Hope, and his favorite, Edward R. Murrow. It was filming Murrow's *Person to Person* show that allowed him to spend a Thanksgiving with President Eisenhower and his family and later visit the penthouse of a new, young starlet, Jane Fonda.

Herman became talented at panning in with his powerful zoom to catch telling moments at special events. During his career, he worked magic with his camera at every Thanksgiving Day Macy's Parade in Manhattan, all the political conventions, both Republican and Democratic, every inaugural parade in Washington, DC, and at least ten space shuttle launches at Cape Canaveral, as well as the at-sea retrievals. He was assigned important sporting events where the director often positioned him as high up as possible because of his talent with the zoom. Herman filmed the

Cotton Bowls, Orange Bowls, and Super Bowls from the very top of the stadium or from inside the circling Goodyear Blimp. At the Masters Golf tournaments, he perched atop a two-story high, mobile crane. He loved sports of all kinds but considered baseball boring to film because "when you get the camera on the batter and he hits the ball, you have to follow it. But then you don't see the runners."

Herman met and filmed every US president from Dwight Eisenhower to George Bush Sr. He worked on the White House tour project with Jackie Kennedy in January of 1962, and on the day John F. Kennedy was shot, Herman was the man holding the camera on Walter Cronkite as this famous journalist struggled to tell the nation of the beloved president's death. Only days later, Herman was stationed on Independence Avenue in Washington, DC, filming Kennedy's funeral.

When asked what show he liked to work on the most, his answer was always the same. "My favorite is the Miss Universe Pageant. It sure beats football!"

Over the years, Herman was awarded six Emmys for his camera work and was featured in several magazine and newspaper articles. His experiences working with General Patton and at Nuremberg were always mentioned as the highlights of his early years, but Herman himself was more interested in his years at CBS meeting famous stars and filming major political events and US presidents.

In 1996, at the age of seventy-six, Herman retired to spend some quiet years with his wife. He filled his days with reading, stamp collecting, working with stained glass, and gardening. Herman died quietly on February 10, 2006.

# TIME LINE OF ACTUAL EVENTS

## 1920

APRIL 15    Herman is born in Meiningen, Germany

## 1933

JANUARY 30    Hitler appointed Chancellor of Germany

APRIL 1    First nationwide Nazi Boycott of Jewish businesses

## 1935

JULY 20    Death of father, Hugo Lang, by heart attack

AUGUST    Herman sent to live in Suhl and attend business school

SEPTEMBER 15    German Reichstag passes the Nuremberg Laws

## 1938

NOVEMBER 10    Kristallnacht; Herman flees to Meiningen

DECEMBER 1    First Kindertransport train from Germany to England

## 1939

FEBRUARY 6    Herman's German passport is issued

MARCH 3    Herman arrives in Britain

END OF AUGUST    Clara arrives in London

| | |
|---|---|
| SEPTEMBER 1 | Germany invades Poland |
| SEPTEMBER 3 | England and France declare war on Germany |
| NOVEMBER 18 | Herman sails to New York on the *Husima Maru* |
| DECEMBER 2 | Herman arrives in New York and travels to Chicago |
| LATE DECEMBER | Herman visits his brother in Laguna Beach, California |

## 1940

| | |
|---|---|
| JANUARY 6 | Herman begins working at The Town House Hotel. |
| MAY 10 | Germany invades Holland, Luxemburg, Belgium, and France |
| MAY 27 TO JUNE 4 | Dunkirk evacuation |
| JUNE 22 | France surrenders to Germany |
| SEPTEMBER 7 | First major German bombing of London |
| | The Blitz lasts until the spring of 1941 |
| SEPTEMBER 10 | San Ysidro (Tijuana) incident |
| SEPTEMBER 16 | Draft Law passed |
| OCTOBER 16 | Registration Day for first draft |
| OCTOBER 29 | First lottery of the pulling of selective service numbers |

## 1941

| | |
|---|---|
| MARCH 24 | Herman buys 1935 Ford Coupe for $381.15 |

| | |
|---|---|
| APRIL | Herman turns 21 and must register for the draft |
| | Germany invades Greece and Yugoslavia |
| MAY | President Roosevelt declares "national emergency" |
| JULY | Term of enlistment for draftees is extended to 18 months |
| | Herman receives word from draft board of his 1A status |
| LATE OCTOBER | Herman reports for duty to US Army |
| | Stationed at Camp Roberts, CA, for basic training |
| DECEMBER 7 | Pearl Harbor bombed |
| DECEMBER 8 | United States declares war on Japan |
| DECEMBER 11 | Germany declares war on the United States |
| | All terms of enlistment are extended until end of war |

## 1942

| | |
|---|---|
| | Herman stationed at Fort Lewis, WA |

## 1943

| | |
|---|---|
| MARCH 12 | Herman becomes US citizen |
| APRIL | Herman has reached rank of staff sergeant |

| | |
|---|---|
| APRIL (CONT.) | Herman tries to get in Army Air Corps |
| | Herman writes letter to President Roosevelt |
| | Herman attends Desert Training in the Mojave Desert, CA |
| SUMMER | Herman is at Military Intelligence Center, Fort Ritchie, MD |
| FALL | Herman's mother, Clara, arrives in United States |

## 1944

| | |
|---|---|
| WINTER | Herman attends Officer Candidate School at Fort Benning, GA |
| MARCH 28 | Herman graduates Officer School as a second lieutenant |
| MAY | Herman arrives in England |
| JUNE 6 | D-Day landings by Allied forces in Normandy, France |
| JULY 9 | Herman is attached to Patton's Third Army |
| | Herman arrives in Normandy, France |
| | Herman works in section G2, IPW team |
| NOVEMBER | Third Army takes Metz |
| DECEMBER | Battle of the Bulge |

## 1945

| | |
|---|---|
| MARCH | The Third Army crosses the Rhine River |
| APRIL 12 | President Roosevelt dies |
| APRIL 27 | Dachau Concentration Camp liberated by American forces |
| APRIL 30 | Hitler commits suicide in Berlin |
| MAY 7 | Germany signs surrender |
| MAY 8 | VE day; the war is over in Europe |
| | Herman organizes Prisoner of War Enclosure, Regensburg |
| JUNE 22 | Herman is awarded a commendation for work with POWs |
| | Herman works as interpreter in Bad Tölz with Patton |
| AUGUST 6 | Atom bomb dropped on Hiroshima, Japan |
| SEPTEMBER 2 | Japanese sign surrender; the war in the Pacific is over |
| OCTOBER 5 | Patton leaves the Third Army |
| DECEMBER 22 | Patton dies from injuries sustained in a traffic accident |

## 1946

| | |
|---|---|
| JANUARY | Herman applies for leave and travels home to the United States |
| FEBRUARY 2 | Herman applies for separation from the army |

| | |
|---|---|
| APRIL 7 | Herman's separation becomes official |
| MAY | Herman gets job with the Office of the Chief Counsel for War Crimes and returns to Nuremberg, Germany |
| OCTOBER | Herman meets Marjorie Bannister |

## 1947

| | |
|---|---|
| MARCH 8 | Herman marries Marjorie Bannister in Fürth, Germany |
| SUMMER | End of Herman's work with the Nuremberg Trials |

## 1951

Herman begins working for CBS

## 1991

Herman begins telling his story to his niece

## 2006

| | |
|---|---|
| FEBRUARY 10 | Herman dies in his sleep of heart failure |

# HISTORICAL PEOPLE
# FROM HERMAN'S LIFE
# 1944–1947

COLONEL ROBERT S. ALLEN (b. 1900–d. 1981)
Chief of Combat Intelligence and Executive Officer of G2 in the Third Army during World War II. Both before and after the war, he was a well-known newspaper journalist in Washington, DC.

WALTER CRONKITE (b. 1916–d. 2009)
A well-known American television journalist, he began as a newspaper reporter for the United Press during World War II. He covered battles in North Africa and Europe, then after the war covered the Nuremberg Trials. In 1950, he joined CBS and began his television news career.

GENERAL DWIGHT D. EISENHOWER (b. 1890–d. 1969)
Eisenhower was Supreme Commander of the Allied Forces in Europe during World War II. In 1949, he became Supreme Commander of NATO. From 1953 to 1961, for two terms, he was the 34th President of the United States.

## GENERAL HOBART R. GAY (b. 1895–d. 1983)

A friend of George Patton, he served as the general's Chief of Staff from February 1944 until Patton's death. Gay was in the car at the time of the accident that killed Patton. He served in Europe until 1947 and later in Korea.

## HERMANN GOERING (b. 1893–d. 1945)

A leading member of the Nazi Party and the commander of the German Luftwaffe. He was found guilty of crimes against humanity at the Nuremberg Trials and sentenced to be hanged. He committed suicide in his cell just hours before the sentence was to be carried out.

## JUSTICE ROBERT JACKSON (b. 1892–d. 1954)

US Attorney General from 1940 to 1941 and an Associate Justice of the US Supreme Court from 1941 to 1954. In 1945, President Truman appointed him to be Chief US Prosecutor at the Nuremberg Trials.

## GENERAL OSCAR W. KOCH (b.1897–d. 1970)

Head of intelligence section of Patton's Third Army during World War II. In 1946, after the war, he established the first peacetime Combat Army Intelligence School in the United States.

## EDWARD R. MURROW (b. 1908–d. 1965)

An American radio and television journalist who became well-known because of his radio news broadcasts from London during World War II. He began his career in 1935 with CBS. After the war, he created two famous TV shows, *See It Now* in 1950 and a celebrity interview show, *Person to Person*, in 1953.

## GENERAL GEORGE S. PATTON (b. 1885–d. 1945)

Commanding General of the US Third Army in the European Theater in World War II from January 1944 to October 1945. Nickname given to Patton by the press—"Old Blood and Guts." Nickname given to Patton by his staff—"Georgie." Patton was known for his aggressive battle techniques but also for his verbal indiscretions and lack of political correctness. Patton quote: "Lead me, follow me, or get the hell out of my way."

## RICHARD SCHULZE (b. 1914–d. 1988)

Waffen-SS officer who served as adjutant to Adolf Hitler and later as the last commander of the SS Officer Candidate School in Bad Tölz, Bavaria. After the war, he changed his name to Richard Schulze-Kossens.

## ALBERT SPEER (b. 1905–d. 1981)

Hitler's chief architect. In 1942, he was appointed Reichminister for armaments and war production. He was one of the main defendants at the Nuremberg Trials where he was sentenced to twenty years in Spandau prison. Speer was the only Nazi leader to publicly repent his crimes. After his release, he wrote a successful book based on his Nazi years, *Inside the Third Reich*.

# COMMENTS FROM A RITCHIE BOY

*Immigrant Soldier* started out as a meticulously researched biography of German-Jewish refugee Herman Lang, who escaped from his homeland just before the Nazis sealed the borders of the Third Reich. He traveled first in England, then in the United States, where he was drafted into the US army. It is to Kathryn Slattery's credit that she managed the transformation from nonfiction to fiction without losing any of the story's inner truth. What her hero accomplished and endured actually occurred or certainly might have happened. I say this from the perspective of someone whose life paralleled that of her protagonist, a personage whose real-life model she came to know in his later years as a dear friend and beloved uncle.

As a contemporary of Lang, a soldier who moved up the ranks from private to captain, it is easy for me to affirm that his life, however extraordinary, followed the dramatic path described in the following pages. He escaped from Germany through the connivance of a Nazi police officer—as a reluctant payback for a past kindness by Lang's family. I have known that such exceptions did happen. After a brief stay in England, he took safe passage on, of all things, a Japanese ship. It should be remembered that Japan had already entered into an alliance with Germany as early as 1936 through the so-called Komintern Pact. Yes, with some chance connections, such a voyage could occur. He rose from the position of a busboy at a Hollywood night club to a decorated daredevil World War II officer in US Military Intelligence. I believe Lang's story only proves once more the validity of Tom Brokaw's label "The Greatest Generation" for the men and women who came of age in the 1940s.

What Lang achieved has been chronicled in part by the accounts about a wartime phenomenon nicknamed "The Ritchie Boys," a group of soldiers of which I was one. Mainly recently arrived refugees conversant in the language, custom, and culture of the German enemy, we were assembled together with experts on the other enemy countries, particularly Japan and Italy. Our ranks were further swelled by native-born Americans equally as knowledgeable as we foreign-born specialists. There was even an African-American officer who was in charge of our recreation hall. We did not know at the time who he was, though we learned he was proficient in German language and culture, skills acquired at the Eastman School of Music. He turned out to be no less a personage than William Warfield, arguably the greatest baritone of his generation. In later years, I was able to be reunited with him after the war when he gave a concert in Detroit.

This conglomerate group arrived for intensive training at Camp Ritchie, Maryland, after having completed basic instructions at other camps. Our approximately two-month "curriculum" included the best techniques for interrogating prisoners of war, assessing captured German documents for tactical and strategic importance, reading aerial maps, and drafting propaganda, leaflets, and radio scripts.

Captain Lang's career is a demonstration of an adept student who, upon arriving in Europe, put his learning to effective use. He extracted information, sometimes by ingenious methods, from the most hard-boiled Nazis.

Many of us also found our own method of sharpening the skills acquired at Camp Ritchie into finely honed tools to fit situations encountered in the field. For example, Captain Ed Dabringhaus, who had escaped from Germany together with his father, pretended that his father had been killed in 1933 during the purge of labor leaders. That put a sense of outrage into his interrogations. Then again, there was my method. During some of the toughest types of questioning, the identification of strategically important targets for our air force, I disguised myself as a Soviet commissar intent on sending recalcitrant prisoners into Soviet captivity. Most German prisoners feared nothing more than being captured by the Russians.

Certain assignments handed us by higher headquarters involved considerable danger. Occasionally, a Ritchie Boy would go on patrol to capture prisoners when the flow of POWs had dried up. Captain Walter Midener, for example, received a Silver Star for bringing about the mass surrender of a German unit. Sergeant Sy Lewin was charged with inducing Germans to surrender. He approached the German front lines with a sound truck and, using a microphone, appealed directly to the enemy to capitulate. His sound truck was blown up several times. Sergeant Tom Angress jumped behind German lines during our initial paratroop attack just hours prior to D-Day without ever having jumped before.

Our efforts did not go unappreciated. We received personal and unit citations during the war, decorations afterward, and as a capstone, we were told recently by a leading intelligence military historian that 65% of crucial tactical and strategic information was provided to higher and lower headquarters by the Ritchie Boys. For many of us, it was also an accolade that a documentary film made about us by a German filmmaker, received several prizes here and abroad and was nominated for an Oscar. It is fair to say that the success of the Ritchie Boys saved American and even enemy lives.

*Guy Stern, Distinguished Professor Emeritus.*
*German and Slavic Department, Wayne State University*

*Director, Zekelman International Institute of the Righteous*
*Holocaust Memorial Center*
*Zekelman Family Campus*
*Farmington Hills, MI*

# GLOSSARY

ALLIES—The 26 nations that collectively fought against the Axis in World War II, but most especially, the United States, France, the United Kingdom, and Soviet Russia.

ANSCHLUSS—The occupation and annexation of Austria by Nazi Germany on March 12, 1938. It was one of the first major steps by Hitler to create a Greater German Reich. The German speaking Republic of Austria ceased to exist as a fully independent state from this time until late 1945.

ARYAN—Originally a language grouping referring to Indo-European tongues. In Nazi doctrine, the word Aryan came to mean a non-Jewish Caucasian, especially a person of Nordic stock. Jews and Gypsies were labeled as non-Aryans.

BITTE—The German word for "please."

BLITZKRIEG—German word that means literally "as fast as lightning." Since the late 1930s, it has come to mean "lightning war" or any strategic attack carried out in a devastatingly rapid way with a combination of tanks, bombing, artillery, and airborne troops. Now it is used to mean any military operation carried out with surprise, speed, and concentration.

BROWN SHIRTS—Nickname given to the Storm Troopers of the SA, a paramilitary, street army that was a major strength behind the early Nazi Party. After 1934, they lost power to the SS.

CARBINE—A firearm similar to a rifle. However, it is usually shorter in length and somewhat less powerful. It tends to be easier to handle in close-quarter combat than the longer rifle.

C.O.—Commanding Officer.

COM Z—Communications Zone. During World War II in the ETO, Com Z was commanded by Lieutenant General John C. H. Lee. This section was in charge of equipment, as well as supply distribution and delivery.

D-DAY—June 6, 1944, the day of the invasion of Western Europe by the Allies in World War II.

DISPLACED PERSONS (DPs)—Jews and others who did not wish, for one reason or another, to return after the war to their original homelands. It included peoples who had been ejected from, or fled, their homes, such as people of German origin living in Poland who fled the advancing Russians. They were placed in DP camps until new homes could be found for them.

DOG TAGS—Metal identification tags worn around the neck by United States soldiers. When Herman got his first dog tags in October of 1941, they would have had the following information: name, military serial number, blood type, tetanus immunization, name and address of next of kin, religion. Later in the spring of 1944, when he became an officer, the new tags would no longer include the information about next of kin.

ETO—European Theater of Operations.

FRAGEBOGEN—Questionnaire used by the military government to help determine the previous Nazi affiliations or sympathies of German citizens. The long form asked everything from family background to church and political affiliations, from education and training, to jobs and public offices held. There was even a question which asked applicants to list all travels outside Germany, including military service, the purpose of that travel, and if they spoke any foreign languages.

FÜHRER—Adolf Hitler was "Der Führer" of Nazi Germany. This translates as the leader or dictator.

G2—Intelligence Section of the US Army. G2 Intelligence at Lucky Forward, Patton's mobile headquarters, was made up of several teams and the commanding officers, Colonel Oscar Koch and Colonel Robert Allen.

GEMÜTLICH—German word that means warm, friendly, and pleasant.

GENEVA CONVENTIONS—A group of three treaties created over a period of sixty-five years, starting in 1864. The rules of the 1929 Geneva Convention defined what a prisoner of war was and established the treatment of prisoners from the moment they were captured until they were returned to their native countries during prisoner exchanges or at the end of the war.

GESTAPO—Shortened term for the German Secret State Police (Geheime Staatspolizei). The Gestapo were political police with powers to imprison without trial.

HEDGEROWS OF NORMANDY—This countryside was a patchwork of thousands of small fields enclosed by almost impenetrable hedges. The hedges, besides being a tangle of brambles, vines, and trees, grew atop earthen mounds several feet thick and three or four feet tall. These "hedgerows" offered perfect defenses for the German soldiers who used each small field as if it were a fort.

HITLERJUGEND (German Hitler Youth)—Nazi youth organization for boys 14 to 18. Founded in 1922, membership was mandatory after 1939. There was a similar institution for girls called the Bund Deutscher Mädel, or BDM.

HOWITZER—A type of field artillery or cannon. A howitzer is different from a standard cannon because of its ability to fire at high angles into the air and deliver plunging fire, thus raining exploding shells down on the enemy from above.

HÜRTGEN FOREST—A small, 50-square-mile forest located on the border between Germany and Belgium. A long and bloody World War II battle in Hürtgen Forest lasted three months during the cold winter of 1944/45.

INFANTRY—Military units that fight on foot using machine guns, rifles, mortars, and hand grenades as weapons.

IPW—Interrogators of Prisoners of War. They worked in teams, usually consisting of five or six men per team, including at least one officer, sometimes two.

JERRYS—Slang term for German soldiers. Also, in a more derogatory way, Germans were often called "Krauts."

KINDERTRANSPORT—Following the November 10, 1938 pogrom in Germany, the British government responded to what was happening to the Jews in the Third Reich by permitting an unspecified number of children under the age of 17 to enter the United Kingdom on temporary travel documents, with the intention that they would be reunited with their parents when things returned to normal.

KRISTALLNACHT (Night of Broken Glass)—A violent, planned pogrom that occurred in Germany, Austria, and parts of Czechoslovakia on the night and morning of November 9–10, 1938. This pretty name was intended to make light of the extent of the pogrom, but it was a name that would stick and become a symbol of the start of the Holocaust.

LODEN-GREEN—A deep olive or gray-brown green color typical of traditional Bavarian, Tyrolean, and Austrian garments. The fabric is derived from the coarse, lanolin-rich wool of mountain sheep. To produce Loden fabric, strong yarns are woven loosely into cloth, which undergoes a lengthy process of shrinking, eventually acquiring the texture of felt and becoming quite dense. It is then brushed with a fuller's teasel, and the nap is clipped, a process which is repeated a number of times until the fabric provides good warmth for the weight and is relatively supple, windproof, and extremely durable.

LUFTWAFFE—The German Air Force headed by Hermann Goering.

MP—Military Police. They were nicknamed "Snowdrops" because they wore white helmets, gloves, and belts.

MARKS—Before the advent of the European Union, the official currency of Germany was the Deutche Mark, and under Hitler's government currency was known as the

Reichsmark. However, it was always simply referred to as "marks" for short.

MISCHLING—A German word that means "half-breed." The term was originally applied to animals and later to children that resulted from unions of white colonists with black natives in Germany's African colonies. The Nuremberg Laws of 1935 used this term when it created two new racial categories: half-Jews, called "Jewish Mischling first degree," had two Jewish grandparents; and quarter-Jews, called "Jewish Mischling second degree," had only one Jewish grandparent.

NUREMBERG LAWS—Between 1933 and 1939, over 1,400 specifically anti-Jewish laws were passed in Germany. The Nuremberg Laws were those Nazi laws passed in September 1935, which took German citizenship away from Jews, defined them racially, and set up rules for their interaction with non-Jews.

PANZER DIVISION—An armored division of the German Army, consisting mainly of tanks and organized for making rapid attacks.

POGROM—An organized massacre or violent persecution, especially of Jews.

POW—Prisoner of War.

RATIONS—A fixed allowance of food for the military, especially during times of hardship. Two types of military rations were used during World War II:

C-RATIONS—For tactical situations, rather than active assault. These rations (about 4,000 calories) consisted of canned meals such as stew or hash and were more bulky to carry. C-rations were not widely available until the second half of World War II.

K-RATIONS—A lightweight ration (3,000 calories) to be used during combat. Three meals, each packaged separately, consisted of canned meat or cheese, beverage powder, dry fruit or biscuits, and chocolate or hard candy. Toilet paper, a disposable can opener, cigarettes, and a wooden spoon were also included.

RED BALL EXPRESS—A system of trucks that carried supplies from the beachheads in Normandy to the forward divisions. The trucks were operated around the clock by mainly black service troops.

SA—Abbreviation for Sturmabteilung (assault division). The SA members were also known as Storm Troopers or Brown Shirts. A paramilitary organization in the Nazi Party, they played a key role in Hitler's rise to power.

SS—German for Schutzstaffel, the elite corps formed in 1925 as Hitler's personal guard. They came to be the controlling agency of all German police. The SS was the major organization for the persecution and murder of the Jews, including running the concentration camps.

SS JUNKERSCHULE, BAD TÖLZ—The officer training school of the Waffen-SS. Operated between 1937 and 1945, it was somewhat equivalent to Britain's Sandhurst and America's West Point. Instruction consisted mainly of athletics, military strategy and field exercises, and Nazi ideology.

SOLDBUCH—Paybook and identification document carried by every German soldier.

THIRD REICH—Term given by Hitler to his regime (1933–1945).

TOJO (Hideki Tojo)—A general in the Imperial Japanese Army and Prime Minister of Japan during most of World War II. He was directly responsible for the attack on Pearl Harbor, which led to war between Japan and the United States.

U-BOAT (*U-boot* in German)—Abbreviation of *Unterseeboot*. It was the common name for military submarines operated by Germany, particularly during World War I and World War II. Their primary targets were merchant convoys.

USO—United Service Organization. A private, nonprofit organization, it was established in 1941 and is still going strong. Their mission is to provide morale, welfare, and recreational services to the men and women of the American military.

WAFFEN-SS—Military arm of the SS, organized as an elite force for combat.

WAR CRIMES TRIALS AT NUREMBERG—Trials of twenty-two top Nazi war criminals by an international tribunal of United States, British, French, and Soviet judges. The trials took place in Nuremberg, Germany, between November 1945 and October 1946.

WEHRMACHT—The Unified Armed Forces of Germany from 1935 to the end of World War II. It consisted of the army, navy, and air force.

YIDDISH—A language based on several High German dialects, it also incorporates elements of Hebrew, Aramaic, Slavic, and Romance languages. The development of Yiddish began around 1250 AD and reached its apex in the 1700s. It is written with Hebrew letters and was once spoken by millions of Jews of different nationalities around the globe. By the early twentieth century, it was in common usage mainly in the Jewish settlements of Eastern Europe.

# ACKNOWLEDGMENTS

Throughout the many years I have been preparing for and writing Herman's story, my friends and family have given me continued encouragement and support. Most especially, for the more than ten years it took me to complete the manuscript in its several versions, the four women of my writer's critique group have steadfastly given me the input I needed to keep going. I thank you all—Donna Becker, Donna Feeney, Denise Yaru, and the sadly missed Ruth Sultzbach. I also want to thank my dedicated and helpful "beta-readers" for their suggestions and corrections. These include Sam Kriegman, Lesley Danziger, Anita Halton, Robert Courdy, Deana Pink, Jeannette Pease, Jim Girdlestone, Marion Coste, and Janet Long. To my tireless editor, Lorraine Fico-White, for her support, suggestions, and more than a year of work, I extend my unmitigated gratitude.

This book could not have been written without the assistance of many people who did not know me—people who gave hours of their time to an unknown writer with a story to tell. Two of these special people stand out—without them the story would have lacked depth and authenticity.

During my visit to The National Archives in College Park, MD, Paul B. Brown, a research specialist in the Modern Military Records section of the Textural Archives Services Division, kept me from becoming lost in a maze. From the beginning, he showed a special interest in my project, and his knowledge of the time frame I was working with helped lead me to much important information. In addition to Mr. Brown and the rest of the staff at the National Archives, I would like to acknowledge the professional and courteous help of the research staff of the United States Army Military History Institute in Carlisle, PA.

As I worked to flesh out the background for Herman's story, I searched every possible lead from the National Archives to the internet. It was "The Richie Boys" website connected to the 2004 documentary of the same name that led me to Gerd Grombacher. In hours of interviews and countless e-mails, GG gave me his time, his memories, and his insight. I am proud to have been able to know him during his last year.

As a result of my efforts to contact others who served with Herman Lang or who also attended the intelligence training center in Maryland, I have become a part of a wider network of surviving Ritchie Boys and their descendants. Many of these gentlemen have shared their stories with me, and I am grateful to all of them who answered my questions, either by e-mail or in person. I especially want to thank Guy Stern and Ralph Hockley (Ritchie Boys) for their time reading my manuscript and checking for inaccuracies.

I will be forever grateful for three men who have been important in my life and who, all three, helped and encouraged me through the years I spent working on Herman's story. My love and special thanks to Tom Slattery, German Crespo, and Robert Courdy.

# AUTHOR'S NOTES

This book, though it closely follows a true story, is a work of fiction. The novel was based, first of all, on hours and hours of conversation with my uncle, Herman Lang, between the years 1991 and 2006. All these interviews were recorded and transcribed. He loved telling humorous stories from his life and chuckled at his memories. He shared with me his many albums of photos and news clippings. But when it came to details, Herman's memory often failed. In order to bring time and place details to the story, I usually had to look elsewhere. This led me down a long path of research. I traveled to London to interview my aunt, Edith, and to Chicago to talk with Herman's cousin, Leonora. Through e-mail, telephone, and personal interviews, I also was able to talk to other Ritchie Boys who lived through similar experiences.

The events in this book, as they pertain to Herman's life, are totally based on his memories. In the process of writing the novel, I have often needed to extract a short comment from Herman's interviews and create from that a dramatic scene with conversation. I have also used the memories of other Ritchie Boys and historical research to inspire details. Because the historical background and how it affects Herman's life is so important to this story, I have endeavored to make all historical data, whether it is the small details or the larger events, accurate and true.

Herman's friends, associates, and family are drawn from his memory or my own personal knowledge. A few characters are composite characters, some based on other Ritchie Boys, and some based on Herman's friends and relatives. Other characters are entirely fabricated by me. When necessary, I have changed names slightly to protect the privacy of my sources. Historic personalities, such as General George Patton, Colonel Robert S. Allen, and the German, Richard Schulze, are in the book because their association with Herman actually occurred. These men are portrayed as accurately as I know how.

With the help of my sources, I created a novel as accurate to Herman's experiences and to the historical facts as possible. However, using my imagination, many details, dramatic scenes, and dialogue were added or embellished. Any errors or inaccuracies are entirely my own.

# READING GROUP GUIDE FOR
*Immigrant Soldier, The Story of a Ritchie Boy*

1. How did you experience *Immigrant Soldier?* Were you engaged immediately or did it take a while to "get into it?" What about the novel contributed to your ability to be interested in the story?

2. *Immigrant Soldier* is one man's story. The plot moves Herman along from one stage of his life to another and has been described as "a coming-of-age story, an immigrant tale, and a World War II adventure." Which of these stories was most interesting to you? Why?

3. What are Herman's motivations and goals? How do they change? How do his choices and actions help or hinder his success? Do you think he achieves his goals in the end?

4. How does Herman change as he moves from one stage of his life to another? In the first chapter, he is only nineteen years old and later, in two backstory chapters, his childhood is described. What kind of teenager is Herman in the beginning? How did his childhood influence his emerging character? What type of man does he become by the end of the novel?

5. During the course of *Immigrant Soldier*, Herman has many close relationships that are important to various stages of his experience. Which of the supporting characters did you find most interesting? Most likeable? Least likeable? How did they influence Herman's development?

6. Describe the dynamics between Herman and his older brother, Friedel (Fred). How did their relationship change from boyhood to adulthood?

7. Four women were especially important in Herman's life – Clara (his mother), Molly, Aunt Nelda, and Gisela. How did each of these women influence Herman or change his perspective?

8. Is *Immigrant Soldier* a plot-oriented book or character-driven book? If plot-driven, what action interests you the most? Is the plot predictable or does it have unexpected complications? If character-driven, are Herman's goals and actions believable and justified?

9. Which parts of the novel or which of Herman's actions did you find disturbing or emotionally difficult to read? Why might the author have included these episodes in the novel?

10. Most of *Immigrant Soldier* is told from a single point of view – Herman's. Almost all scenes have Herman present and tell only what he would see and hear. Where

did the author describe a scene which Herman does not witness? Did the change in point of view bother you? Would you have liked there to be more scenes that showed something Herman did not take part in?

11. What main ideas – themes—does *Immigrant Soldier* explore? How are these ideas reinforced? Where does the author use symbolism or foreshadowing to add to the significance of the main ideas? Which passages do you find particularly insightful or profound? Which passages seem to illustrate the novel's theme?

12. *Immigrant Soldier* is closely based on a true story. Describe how this may or may not have increased your interest in reading it and/or distracted you. Identify passages you know are true and those you think are the author's creation.

13. What did you learn from *Immigrant Soldier* to add to your understanding and previous knowledge of WWII and the Holocaust?

14. The plot of *Immigrant Soldier* stretches over eight years. Did you find the ending justified and satisfying? Why or why not? If not, how would you change it?